Donation (LGI)

(Occupational Therapy)

20/5/05

D1588518

Healing dramas and clinical plots
The narrative structure of experience

There is a growing interest in "therapeutic narratives" and the relation between narrative and healing. Cheryl Mattingly's ethnography of the practice of occupational therapy in a North American hospital investigates the complex interconnections between narrative and experience in clinical work. Viewing the world of disability as a socially constructed experience, it presents fascinatingly detailed case studies of clinical interactions between occupational therapists and patients, many of them severely injured and disabled, and illustrates the diverse ways in which an ordinary clinical interchange is transformed into a dramatic experience governed by a narrative plot. Drawing from a wide range of sources, including anthropological studies of narrative and ritual, literary theory, phenomenology and hermeneutics, this book develops a narrative theory of social action and experience. While most contemporary theories of narrative presume that narratives impose an artificial coherence upon lived experience, Mattingly argues for a revision of the classic mimetic position. If narrative offers a correspondence to lived experience, she contends, the dominant formal feature which connects the two is not narrative coherence but narrative drama. Moving and sophisticated, this book is an innovative contribution to the study of modern institutions and to anthropological theory.

CHERYL MATTINGLY is an Associate Professor of Anthropology and Occupational Therapy at the University of Southern California. She is the author (with Maureen Fleming) of *Clinical reasoning: forms of inquiry in a therapeutic practice* (1994).

Healing dramas
and clinical plots

The narrative structure of experience

Cheryl Mattingly

CAMBRIDGE
UNIVERSITY PRESS

PUBLISHED BY THE PRESS SYNDICATE OF THE UNIVERSITY OF CAMBRIDGE
The Pitt Building, Trumpington Street, Cambridge CB2 1RP, United Kingdom

CAMBRIDGE UNIVERSITY PRESS
The Edinburgh Building, Cambridge, CB2 2RU, United Kingdom   http://
www.cup.cam.ac.uk
40 West 20th Street, New York, NY 10011–4311, USA   http://www.cup.org
10 Stamford Road, Oakleigh, Melbourne 3166, Australia

First published 1998
Transferred to digital printing 2001

Printed in Great Britain by Biddles Short Run Books, King's Lynn

Typeset in Plantin 10/12pt   [CE]

A catalogue record for this book is available from the British Library

Library of Congress Cataloguing in Publication data

ISBN 0 521 63004 5 hardback
ISBN 0 521 63994 8 paperback

Contents

Preface

This book gave me trouble. For one thing, there was the difficulty of voice. How much should I reveal of my own prejudices, my own quite individual experiences of the people I studied? I chose to write from a fairly personal perspective, especially in the first chapter and again in the third one which begins the ethnography proper. Or, more accurately, I waffled. I wrote and rewrote. Some versions were highly revealing and confessional. I especially confessed a conversion which life among occupational therapists forced upon me. In doing so, I faced the contemporary anthropologist's dilemma. I didn't want to hide in my writing or pretend to an objectivity which masked the realness of my encounters. But I didn't want to write a book about me either. I had some theories about narrative I wanted to give a central place in my account. However, when I edited myself out entirely, I confronted a different sort of problem. The verisimilitude went too. As a reader, how could you tell where you were? The solution, provided by the venerable realist in the genre of ethnography (painting pictures from a "God's eye" perspective) didn't appeal to me. If I was going to give a concrete account of the ethnographic scene, I was going to put a real narrator (me) in the scene as well. "The new ideal," Suleiman writes about the introduction of the "I" into literary criticism, "is founded on the premise that since all writing is done by some-body for some-body, it is not merely permitted, but downright valuable, to remember who you are as you write" (1994: 2). In writing this ethnography, I have tried to remember who I am, and even who I once was when I first encountered occupational therapists. Ultimately, my solution has been to flit in and out of the pages of this text. Sometimes, when it seems to matter, I make an entrance. Sometimes, when I think I'll only be getting in the way, I hold back and offer a third-person portrait of life in the clinic.

I hope I have solved the writing problem in a way that works. But entering the scene at all raises yet another difficulty. How are occupational therapists going to feel when they read of my ambivalence toward them, especially at the beginning of my research? But if I don't describe this, how will I be able to tell anyone how I began to sense their strength, a kind of female force I had never reckoned with before I came to study them? Occupational therapists are mostly women and the fact is that, growing up, I didn't like women all that well. They didn't have much power, as far as I could see. And most of them seemed to do awfully boring things: housework, for instance. I was probably one of the last generations to suffer through all-girls "home economics" classes where not only did you have to learn how to cook, you even had to learn how to sew. I was abysmal at it all and I wished with my whole adolescent heart that I had been born a boy. Or that girls could avoid all that homemaking stuff and read books or go on adventures all day long. Meeting up with the occupational therapists was a little like returning to that home-economics class filled with good cooks and girls who could sew a straight zipper effortlessly. I was intimidated, lonely, and (in my heart) a little superior. Wasn't I an anthropologist, after all? Didn't I belong to a profession in which you got to read books and go on adventures for a living?

My meeting with the occupational therapists was a very good thing. I found out what, as an anthropologist, I should have known all along, that cooking and clothes and other homemaking concerns are central threads in the "webs of significance" we call culture. Just because these therapists were buying turkeys at the Stop and Shop instead of herding yaks in the Himalayas didn't obviate this essential truth. And therapists were stranger than I thought. The longer I stayed with them, the trickier it became to make broad claims. Yet, this book abounds in generalizations because, in the end, I have some general things I want to say. This, perhaps, is what will give them most pause when they read this book. Where do these grand statements come from? they may ask. Don't I know them better than this? In many ways this is a book about practical action and practical reasoning. Theory about action is necessarily crude compared to the nuances of particular actions themselves. Theory is meant to be general, to rise (at least some distance) above any specific context which it tries to explain or interpret. But practical actions, and the considerations which prompt them, are grounded in concrete situations, situations which have never presented themselves in quite this way before. So when I say that occupational therapists think this and do that, I am missing a lot about the particularities, contradictions, and oddities that spring up when you look at what any given therapist does or thinks or feels on any given occasion. But, this is the least of it.

My concern to create theory about therapeutic practice is complicated by my concern to remember who I am as I write. Theory-making and confessing become impossibly intermingled. Perhaps theorizing always carries this danger; it's just that in these contemporary times we are trying to admit it a bit more often than we once did. Still, I am left with the worry that the very people I have written about will sometimes feel betrayed by my words. I could have edited my prejudices more carefully. Initially, I saw therapists the way I remembered my midwest cousins – as extremely normal. Of course, once I got closer, these first impressions were something of an embarrassment; an awkward attempt to sum up an entire profession in tidy little statements, a need to get a grasp of the cultural whole. Later I had to ask myself, if they were so full of common sense, so practical, why was there so much whimsy among them? Bartenders by night, secret landscape painters, former actresses, obsessed rock climbers, classical pianists who also loved botany? In the end, I left these first impressions in the final versions of the text.

I gave drafts of this manuscript to two of my therapist friends to read. They have tried to say it politely, but they are puzzled by my writing. I don't sound familiar to them, especially not in the portions of this book when I travel back to the time when therapists were strangers to me, when I made sense of them by trying out different generalizations, including some fairly dismissive ones. One of these friends put it as nicely as she could. "You are kind of judgmental here aren't you?" she noted. "This is very different than the other things you have written about us." "Maybe some people won't like this when they read it," I suggested anxiously. "No," she replied, "I'm not sure they will." This is no small issue. I have made two kinds of enduring friends since college. One kind are anthropologists or closely related academics, mostly those I got to know in graduate school. The other are occupational therapists. Perhaps some of these friends, people who trust me, are going to feel slighted by my characterizations of them or the people they treat.

The ideas in this book gave me trouble as well. For a long time I was afraid of them. When I was in graduate school, and even as an undergraduate literature major, I longed for a way to think about the art in accidental stories, in practical stories. The stories people told in their lives and especially in their work, just as a part of getting along and getting things done. I loved literature and I even had a certain fondness for folklore and myth, but these were not the stories I wanted to spend my life studying. They were far too grand, far too culturally demarcated as special texts or performances. The stories linguists and some folklorists explored were more to my liking, having in them a certain everyday careless quality. Some linguists even concerned themselves with the aesthetics of their stories. Jacobson and Labov come instantly to mind. But still, it wasn't the grammatical or even the conversational properties of stories which I especially cared about. I was more fascinated by what people were doing with stories, how their stories guided their actions, how stories were about something and that something was of tremendous interest in people's lives.

In the late seventies, when I started graduate school at MIT, there existed a strange sort of program, the Division of Study and Research in Education, which attracted a collection of linguists, philosophers, cognitive psychologists, psychiatrists, artificial intelligence people, and assorted other intellectual mavericks. Jeanne Bamberger and Donald Schön ran a seminar there, the "Metaphor Seminar," which met every Friday morning, year in and year out. The way we studied metaphor was very much the way I wanted to study stories, as something to think with. Although there existed an impressive theoretical literature examining the conceptual properties of metaphorical thought, there was little yet written about narrative thought. Artificial intelligence researchers and cognitive psychologists were beginning to write about scripts but their idea of scripts was very far from my idea of a story. And I knew I was not only interested in stories in a cognitive sense, as a way of reasoning, but also in some way I couldn't quite articulate yet, stories as a way to imagine possible lives, to feel emotions, to give "form to feeling," as Suzanne Langer would say. I was forced to go on my own intellectual quest, reading from here and there while trying to piece together a set of ideas that could help me examine everyday stories in a way that suited me.

Things have changed considerably. The mid-eighties mark the beginning of what has turned into an avalanche of studies on narrative, studies which address many of the questions that have fascinated me for a long time. Anthropologists have been an important part of an exploration of narrative as a vehicle for shaping thought, practice, the emotions, the self. In 1986, when I began to study occupational therapists, I joined an on-going seminar at Harvard in medical and psychological anthropology, headed by Arthur Kleinman, Byron Good, and Mary-Jo DelVecchio Good and funded by the National Institute of Health. Several members of this Harvard group were interested in narrative and were beginning to write about narrative as part of a "meaning-centered" approach to medical and psychological anthropology. I found an intellectual home in these discussions. Still I was unnerved by what I wanted to write about narrative in clinical practice. As I followed occupational therapists in a single hospital, I began to see that what I really wanted to say about narrative had little to do with anyone's storytelling and more to do with a way to understand the structure of clinical practice. I was interested in the role of narrative in the creation

of experience, taking that term in the strong sense used by such
hermeneuticists as Dilthey and Gadamer. Or, drawing from the different
language offered by Kenneth Burke, I wanted to talk about the
"dramatism" in clinical practice.

But could I really be audacious enough to claim that stories could be
made without being told? Was that even a sensible statement? Did I
mean this in some essentialist way? As in, life just *is* a narrative? Or did I
mean it in a metaphorical way? As in, narrative offers a useful model for
examining action and experience? These are the questions that plagued
me and that, in some ways, plague me still. One doesn't want to be
essentialist in this day and age but on the other hand, a metaphorical
route seems rather spineless. As though one were saying, let's just
pretend, for the sake of intellectual play, that life is *like* a narrative.

One irony in my own struggle over these conceptual matters is that
narrative is now everywhere on the intellectual scene. Hence, it may
seem no more than common sense to say that narrative underlies all our
thought and action, the very nature of our selfness. While I have worried
about trying to claim too much, others may wonder what all the fuss is
about. I suppose I think narrative is still worth a fuss. Narratives do
indeed play a powerful part in our thoughts and actions and in our
constructions of our selves. But how does this happen? And does this
mean everything is narrative? Is there anything not narrative? Are some
actions more narrative than others? Are some narrative forms and
genres more appropriate as models for understanding actions or
thoughts or selves? All these questions are still worth asking, it seems to
me. I ask some of them here.

Acknowledgments

Since this book was so long in the making, my thanks must extend back to graduate school days at Massachusetts Institute of Technology. Donald Schön helped me to think about the complex relations between theory and practice and the now defunct Division of Study and Research in Education provided tremendous stimulation from its cadre of philosophers, linguists and cognitive and developmental psychologists. James Howe and Jean Jackson, also at MIT, helped me to think through my emerging ideas of narrative as they related to my ethnographic material.

The medical anthropology group at Harvard, under Arthur Kleinman, offered a whole new direction to my thinking as I began to connect narrative to the phenomenology of illness and the practice of healing. My work with the Danish Culture and Medicine Group, under the direction of Uffe Jensen at the Department of Philosophy at the University of Aarhus, has led me to explore critical perspectives on clinical practice.

Mary-Jo DelVecchio Good and Byron Good have been strong supporters of this book from the first. I cannot thank them enough, both for their encouragement and their prodding which moved me to completion of this long project. Mary-Jo DelVecchio Good, Michael Carrithers, and Deborah Gordon gave me extremely useful editorial suggestions which led me to pare down a much longer manuscript to the present incarnation. I want to gratefully acknowledge the many other readers of this manuscript, in its various versions, who gave me some excellent advice along the way, especially Uffe Jensen, Ole Dreier, Arthur Kleinman, Linda Garro, Linda Hunt, Mary Lawlor, Eric Jacobson, Glenn Bidwell, and Paul Brodwin. Toward the end of this writing, talks with Uffe Jensen deepened my understanding of narrative and self-identity and a series of discussions with Jerome Bruner about narrative in social action helped me clarify my arguments about therapeutic plots and the creation of desire.

In the last but not least category, I wish to thank Maureen Fleming,

Nedra Gillette, Ellen Cohn, and a number of other occupational therapists in the Boston Clinical Reasoning Study who helped me to enter the world of practice and see it from an "insider's" perspective. Maureen Fleming taught me many new things about clinical reasoning and Mary Lawlor, a later collaborator, has taught me much about the social world of therapeutic practice. The occupational therapists whose therapeutic practice I studied in Boston, Chicago and Los Angeles have made me welcome. They talked to me, let me watch them work and videotape them. Several have invited me into their lives and now they are friends. I don't know how to express sufficient gratitude for this openness. Bill Roubal gave steadfast moral support and encouragement during the final year of writing and listened on many a night walk as I talked out my ideas. To him I owe a special thanks. I also want to thank Eva Anger who was a wonderfully patient typist and careful manuscript reader.

Gary Kielhofner at the University of Illinois, Chicago and Florence Clark at the University of Southern California were generous in providing departmental support. Finally, I want to gratefully acknowledge the research grants which supported the collection and analysis of ethnographic material that comprise this book as well as the evolving development of its conceptual framework. Grant support was provided by the American Occupational Therapy Foundation, the American Occupational Therapy Association, the US Department of Education, and Maternal and Child Health. Earlier versions of some portions of this book were given as presentations at the American Anthropology Meetings, published in the *American Journal of Occupational Therapy*, *Social Science and Medicine* and *Clinical Reasoning: Forms of Inquiry in a Therapeutic Practice*, co-authored with Maureen Fleming.

Attention to human suffering means attention to stories, for the ill and their healers have many stories to tell. Serious illness takes people from ordinary to extraordinary. Trying to understand those with severe illness may be rather like, as Sacks says, making "house calls at the far borders of human experience" (Sacks 1995: xx). The stories of the very sick and disabled comprise a "literature of extreme situations" (Broyard 1992: 41) The need to narrate the strange experience of illness is part of the very human need to be understood by others, to be in communication even if from the margins. This book considers the relation between narrative and that essential human experience – devastating, life-altering illness. Illness, especially chronic illness or severe disability, reveals much about how a culture conceives life in time, being as a kind of becoming marked by transitions, transformations and the inexorable progress toward death. There is more than one kind of death possible, of course. Serious disability may allow you to live for years and years, for an entire span of life, and yet force a death of self and the painful recreation of some new self. Narrative plays a variety of roles in this grim terrain.

Narrative constitutes a mode of thought and representation especially suited to considering life in time, shifting temporal shapes, and the human path of becoming where death is never far away. If narrative is based, as Jerome Bruner (1986, 1996) notices, on a "breach" of the commonplace, then profound physical and mental suffering constitutes one breach that seems to demand a narrative shape. It is one liminal place within the human condition that calls for sense-making and this often takes narrative form.

Speaking of the need for narrative among the very sick, the literary critic Anatole Broyard, dying of cancer, writes: "My initial experience of illness was as a series of disconnected shocks, and my first instinct was to try to bring it under control by turning it into a narrative. Always in emergencies we invent narratives" (1992: 19). If the ill, and their healers

1

as well, turn to narrative in emergency, trying to wrest control of overpowering experience, how does narrative allow such powerful configuring? What is it about narrative which makes it so natural, even inevitable, as a form with which to come to grips with life-altering illness? What is the relation between narrative and experience which aligns them so closely that it is difficult to talk about the one without speaking of the other?

I came to these questions gradually, and my answers grew more complex as I watched occupational therapists treat patients. For two years, beginning in 1986, I conducted an ethnographic study of occupational therapists in a large (900-bed) teaching hospital in Boston. I have stayed close to occupational therapists since my first encounter with them. My initial research led to subsequent studies in other sites where I observed therapists working in special education classrooms, inner city pediatric clinics, acute and rehabilitation hospitals, and chronic care facilities. I also came to give presentations and teach graduate courses to seasoned occupational therapists where I heard stories of their work. Occasionally, therapists wrote down the stories they told and gave them to me as case stories. Some of these appear in this book. The main protagonist in my research has been the occupational therapist and she is likewise the central character in the analyses of clinical interactions offered here.[1] While the data which comprise this book are drawn primarily from the initial ethnographic study in Boston, some examples, and certainly the level of analysis, reflect my nine years of close acquaintance with this professional world.

My studies of occupational therapy have led me to reconsider the relationship between narrative and experience. I have gradually shifted from seeing stories as (merely) after-the-fact accounts of experience, or cultural scripts which provide general guidelines for interpreting particular experiences, or oral performances which create as well as comment upon prior experiences – though these are all reasonable and useful ways to understand narrative's relation to experience. Narrative, I will argue in this book, not only functions as a form of talk; it also serves as an aesthetic and moral form underlying clinical action. That is, therapists and patients not only tell stories, sometimes they create story-like structures through their interactions. Furthermore, this effort at story-making, which I will refer to as *therapeutic emplotment*, is integral to the healing power of this practice. Thus, this book considers the narrative structure of action and experience.

From reference to perlocution to emplotment: a personal tale

My own interest in stories and their role in professional practice emerged long before my acquaintance with occupational therapists. Over the years I have examined a variety of practices and wondered about the nature of thinking which led people to become expert at doing something. I have considered practical wisdom in the broad Aristotelian sense not only as technical knowledge about the means to achieve ends, but as a wisdom concerning moral questions about which ends were worth pursuing (Aristotle 1985). In different language, I have been interested in how people not only solved problems but how they set them (Schön 1983, 1987; Mattingly 1991a). From earlier studies of other professional groups, I realized that problem-setting often occurred through storytelling (Mattingly 1991b). Professionals were particularly likely to tell stories when they needed to make sense of difficult relationships with actors whose behavior directly effected their own work – managers, clients and the like.

In examining the place of storytelling as part of a problem-solving process, I considered stories in the ordinary way, as something people told about things that had happened to them and others – events largely propelled (and experienced) by human actors. In this investigation of practical stories, I was initially concerned with reference, with how narrative referred to a world beyond it. As an aesthetic form, how did it shape the way people perceived practical problems? This referential function took a more complex turn when I went to the World Bank in 1983, for I began to recognize that storytelling involved far more than retrospective glances at past events.[2] I spent three years studying project officers, those front line Bank professionals who assist in putting together and supervising international development loans. I listened to their stories and watched them at work in the central Washington office and in the "field." I witnessed the process by which project officers in the Bank's urban division helped design and recommend urban development projects for third world cities. These project officers were variously trained as economists, financial analysts, architects and engineers. As part of their craft, they learned to become storytellers as well. As I observed them in action and listened to stories about their activities, I gradually began to notice that there was a more complicated, interesting and interwoven relation between telling stories and making practical decisions than I had initially realized.

When I first accompanied a mission team, this one supervising several urban projects in Calcutta, I noticed the very active, constructivist way project officers used storytelling. A major part of the team's task, as they met at night to share notes from their individual daily rounds to various urban ministries, was to try to construct a collectively shared story about what was going on and, within that story, what their role as interventionists should be. This was an actor-centered discourse in which events were described in a (more or less) chronological fashion and their unfolding was linked primarily to the actions of human agents. The project officer who ran the mission acted as chief storyteller, gathering story bits and story versions from each team member in turn. Although the team members were technical specialists in various sectors, in water and sewerage, in city finances, in transportation, housing and the like, the team spent little time trying to understand the technical problems a development project was facing. Rather they focused on constructing a story about why responsible actors in the field – the heads of various city departments responsible for certain pieces of the urban project – were not taking the proper responsibility to deal with these technical problems.

Project officers concerned with a host of technical difficulties described problems not as technical hold-ups but as obstacles created by problematic intentions of the responsible actors – "irresponsibility" or "lack of discipline" as they often said. They offered narrative accounts, constructing stories which linked what was happening to prior actions of various key political or business leaders. These were narrative explanations in the strong sense that the key causal factors cited in the stories concerned the reasoning of central actors.[3] For instance, project officers would explain the sewage problems in the new housing site not primarily by the poor soil or inferior cement which might have been immediate causes but by the motivations of actors that allowed houses to be built on poor soil or allowed inferior cement to be purchased.

Narrative explanations were often trickier and harder to come by than technical ones. Technical problems were often easily understood. Reasons *why* these particular problems had developed in the first place or why they were not being solved – and what the team should be doing to try to get them solved – were much more opaque. These became the focus of storytelling efforts. The team would try to understand why the responsible government agency had allowed a housing project to be allocated worthless land that couldn't be properly drained, or why they had bought bad cement for the same price they could have purchased good cement – what private contractor was overcharging or who was in on the "syphoning" of government funds. Sometimes they would invite their own "native informants" to the hotel for after work drinks in order to check their interpretations.

I began to see that these World Bank project officers, who had the job of intervening in situations they did not have the time to understand very well, were constantly trying to construct stories to get some fix on what was going on, especially who was to blame, so that they could figure out what they ought to do and especially what they ought to say in their reports to the Bank management on the project's progress. I recognized that stories were not just told after experience but were constructed while people were still very much in the midst of action. This active storytelling played a critical role in team strategizing about how to turn project implementation in more desirable directions. Thus, I began to examine narrative as an aesthetic form with rhetorical powers, one which could become a persuasive tool for convincing others to see the world in a certain way.

The immense perlocutionary force of narrative (to borrow a term from Austin 1962) became apparent particularly in oral negotiations between Bank project teams and country officials. The dominant form of argument to country officials was narrative. The mission team, and local officials as well, told stories about what the problems were, how the project had evolved to address those problems, what the roadblocks were to carrying out those projects, and therefore what needed to be addressed to solve the roadblocks, all as part of a narrative. Both groups tried to impose a particular history in their storytelling and argue for what ought to follow as a natural, even an inevitable, next step, given what had gone before.

When World Bank project officers sat in the evening drinking scotch in Calcutta's Grand Hotel and pondering why roads were not built or poor quality cement was so expensive, the stories they told were social and political in nature and in intent. They were engaged in a complex social activity in which their own personal experiences talking things over with the Minister of Finance or the local building inspector played an enormous role. They were telling very personal stories about very social events which would have extensive political consequences. These personal stories were then woven into a collective story to be later used in arguments to country officials who were presented with an oral history which opened along the lines of "Ten years ago, when this project was first conceived . . ."

Like the World Bank project officers I studied, occupational therapists tell stories to their clients and cohorts as part of their everyday efforts to get things done. Stories have many purposes in their work lives. They tell stories of clinical experiences, their own or others, to entertain, to gossip, to confess, to argue, to reveal who they are. Often they tell stories, especially about work experiences which are puzzling, powerful or disturbing, in order to render those experiences more sensible. Storytelling offers one way to make sense of what has happened and this makes stories essential to practice. Therapists seem to require a recounting of past events in order to situate their current work. It is as though they consult a kind of time map, discovering where they can go, and where they currently stand, only by glancing back at where they have already traveled. Such storytelling, of course, is a highly rhetorical and social sense-making activity. Not only do occupational therapists tell stories to personally orient themselves in their work, they also tell stories to clients and colleagues in attempts to persuade relevant others to see themselves as actors in particular kinds of therapeutic plots. Storytelling thus becomes a significant action used to "further" the direction they wish therapy to take.

I might have written an ethnographic account of storytelling among the occupational therapists, for it plays a potent role in shaping their work. And, in fact, the clinical examples in this book are filled with stories told by therapists and patients. However, I want to address the even more subtle role narrative plays in their clinical practice by examining clinical action itself as an "untold" story. The heart of this book concerns a difficult claim that we can think of (at least some) therapeutic interactions as narratively structured. Clinical interactions sometimes take the shape of emergent stories, "proto-narratives," in Ricoeur's terms. Ricoeur (1984, 1985, 1987) contends that action is in quest of a narrative. Whether or not this holds generally true, it has been very compelling in my research that most occupational therapists want therapy to be experienced by their patients as significant. They are in quest of dramatic plots that will transform the painfulness, irrelevance or sheer tedium of therapeutic activities into important events, ones that figure for the patient as critical episodes in their healing experience. Therapists want, as they often say, "something to happen" in therapy, by which they often mean something memorable, something they and their patients can recall later, can recognize as a milestone, even a transformative moment, along a path from illness to rehabilitation.

The narrative turn in anthropological studies of illness and healing

In examining the place of narrative in clinical work, I join a conversation which has grown rapidly in the past several years. Medical anthropologists, sociolinguists, psychologists, and a host of other students of healing practices have become increasingly fascinated with what we can learn about the beliefs, perceptions, actions and experiences of healers, the ill and their families by attending to narrative. This attention has produced a fertile and broad range of research.

Stories are not new to anthropology, of course. They have always mattered to anthropologists as a form of data about experiences of illness and practices of healing, though the fact that information from informants so often comes in narrative packages has very often gone unremarked. In addition to the analysis of myths, folktales, proverbs and the like, anthropologists have long been interested in stories of personal experience in the form of life histories (Radin 1983 [1926]; Peacock and Holland 1993; Crapanzano 1977a, 1984; Frank 1996; Langness and Frank 1981).

Anthropologists have relied upon stories to examine such things as folk explanations of illness, curing rituals, practical strategies for seeking health care and for caring for ill family members, and interactions between healers and patients. Stories have played a part in these studies because anthropologists have routinely relied upon informant accounts either as a means of access to events they could not witness or as a way to learn something about their interlocutor's experiences and beliefs about illness. In eliciting informant accounts, many times what they have heard were stories.

The recent narrative turn is, in this respect, recent mostly in noticing that stories are what anthropologists are very often getting. While some anthropologists still draw upon stories in a casual way (as the incidental form in which the data comes), the trend is toward a stricter view. Contemporary treatment of illness and healing narratives is marked by increasingly self-conscious strategies for eliciting and analyzing stories. Part of this self-consciousness involves coming to grips with what is meant by a story. There are many ways to define a story and many approaches to considering the relation between story and experience. Particularly for those working within linguistic and semiotic paradigms, defining narrative and sorting out what is to count as narrative and non-narrative discourse is a central task. Within some traditions, especially those influenced by structuralist literary theory, "narrative" and "story" refer to distinct phenomena. From a quite different position, some performance-minded anthropologists object to spending much time defining narrative *per se* simply because they deem it misleading. The issue is not what a story is, as some kind of text, but what a storytelling episode is – and does – as some kind of social act.

In my own analysis, I presume that stories concern action and experience. To put the matter simply, *stories are about someone trying to do something, and what happens to her and to others as a result.* My definition is clearly rooted in a Western (even specifically Aristotelian) literary tradition, captures the structuralist focus on form, the traditional mimetic focus on narrative as representation of event where "event" is composed of both action and experience (Aristotle 1970). I emphasize the "eventness" of stories, their portrayal of human actions and the placing of these actions within a plot which has beginning, middle and end. This has been the ground for most universalizing descriptions of narrative. However, it is just as important that narrative recounts both actions and experiences, that is, how events act on protagonists and what meaning this carries for them. By attending to human actions and human experiences, narrative investigates human character. A narrative reveals character as both illuminated and constructed through events (Ricoeur 1992; Polkinghorne 1991; Carr 1986; Burrell and Hauerwas 1977; Murdoch 1972). But a narrative is not definable only in terms of its content. It is also marked by a style of presentation, by its highly connotative language. Thus, narrative is characterized by form in a second sense, by an evocative and seductive prose which is directly related to one of its primary functions – its rhetorical power to persuade. The successful story makes the audience care about the events and experiences it recounts. And in recounting "what happens," it also casts events in a particular light.

To summarize, three features of narrative form make it especially appropriate for addressing illness and healing experiences. One, *narratives are event-centered*. They concern action, more specifically human action, even more specifically, human interaction. They concern social doings. Two, *narratives are experience-centered*. They do not merely describe what someone does in the world but what the world does to that someone. They allow us to infer something about what it feels like to be in that story world. Narratives also recount those events that happen unwilled, unpredicted, and often unwished for by the actors, even if those very actors set the events in motion in the first place. Narratives, one could say, are about the unintended consequences of action (Arendt 1958). Three, *narratives do not merely refer to past experience but create experiences for their audience*. Narratives mean to be provocative. They request a different response from the audience than denotative prose. Narrative offers meaning through evocation, image, the mystery of the unsaid. It persuades by seducing the listener into the world it portrays, unfolding events in a suspense-laden time in which one wonders what will happen next.

Becoming self-conscious about narrative raises questions previously neglected in medical anthropology. Are some ways of defining narrative better than others? Do we need to define a story in culturally specific ways? The notion of narrative may ring suspiciously of an ethnocentric universalism, without sufficient attention to the cultural differences which render both terms of the equation, "story" and "experience," open to cultural variation. The very notion that narrative is iconic, which is part of a traditional Western view, is challenged by studies of dramatic forms in cultures where narrative or dramatic structure is significantly different (Becker 1979).[4]

There is also the problem of connecting stories to *personal* experience. Current analysis of narratives, especially within medical anthropology, focuses increasingly on personal stories of individual experience rather than collective stories, such as folktales or myths. Even when anthropologists are concerned to analyze culturally shared knowledge, they are likely to work with personal tales rather than cultural myths (Farmer 1994; Garro 1992, 1994). What is the epistemological status of the personal story told to illuminate someone's personal experience, an account that not only concerns observable actions or culturally shared beliefs but private emotions and ruminations?

Finally, there is a question of analytic strategy. Which of the many traditions of narrative analysis are most useful for anthropological purposes? In attending to the narrativity of their data, or setting out to elicit narratives, anthropologists have depended upon a number of theoretical frameworks and research traditions. Interpretive lenses may be strictly cognitive or extremely phenomenological; sense-making may be focused on face-to-face interactions, on cultural activities of entire social groups, or on the interface between personal experience and cultural models of thought and action. Narrative theory has been imported from other disciplines (sociology, linguistics, psychology, literary theory, philosophy) as well as other sub-fields within anthropology. Some of the most interesting work on illness and healing narratives published in anthropological journals has been carried out by scholars who are not medical anthropologists. Despite wide variations in method, subject matter and analytic frame, narrative-centered renderings of illness share some common threads.

Broadly speaking, what draws these studies together is a focus on the meaning-making aspects of illness and healing. They tend to fall into what has come to be known as an interpretive or meaning-centered paradigm of medical anthropology (Kleinman 1980, 1988; Kleinman, Eisenberg and Good 1978; B. Good 1994; M. J. Good 1995). Scholars interested in narrative have, by and large, emphasized activities through which healers, patients, and their kin construct and negotiate interpretations of their experiences and use those interpretive frames to guide future actions. Often, though not always, there is an interest in the dramas which surround illness, in the temporal contexts in which illness occurs, and in illness and healing as dynamic processes in which meaning is not a given but something actors struggle to discover.

This turn to narrative has meant greater analytic attention to the particular case, in all its particularity. The study of context, which anthropologists have always cared about, is reframed from an idealized version of social activities in general (kula ceremonies among the Trobrianders), or a life history (the typical Tikopian man), to detailed examination of particular events and lives. Individual experience is quite often the subject of analysis. Generally, a micro-ethnographic approach has been used, one which concentrates on the analysis of face-to-face interactions or close readings of texts culled from interviews. Illness has very often emerged as something experienced, represented, negotiated by individuals. Even when illness has been placed within large-scale structures, the economies and policies of nations, narrative-based studies have tended to bring the analyst's focus close to individual actions and experiences. Because personal narratives offer symbolic and metaphorical readings of personal experience and action, these aspects of cultural life play a large role in narrative-centered studies of illness and healing.

Recent emphasis on narrative in medical anthropology reflects a broader trend in how social practices are conceived (Carrithers 1992). Geertz (1980) has suggested there is a cross-disciplinary shift from mechanistic to dramatistic metaphors currently refiguring social analyses. This refiguring has no doubt played a role in drawing attention to narrative in clinical practices, for a narrative approach to interpreting medicine in Western contexts (with its underlying mechanistic metaphors) suggests a concern to reframe not only anthropological theory but the self-understanding of clinical practices (M. J. Good 1995; Hunter 1991; Mattingly 1991b). Here, anthropologists have been joined (or been inspired) by clinicians themselves who have attended to the narrative qualities of their work (Coles 1989; Sacks 1987, 1995; Luria 1972; Brody 1987; Kleinman 1988). Psychology, psychiatry and psychoanalysis, particularly, have been in the vanguard in considering the narrative aspects of their work. Some have gone beyond looking at narrative as a sort of "raw material" offered up by the patient and begun to reconceptualize therapeutic practice and healing in narrative terms – as a "root metaphor" for psychology as a whole (Sarbin 1986; Gergen and Gergen 1986), or for particular branches of psychology such as family systems theory (Zimmerman and Dickerson 1994), psychoanalysis (Schafer 1981; Wyatt 1986), clinical psychology (Polkinghorne 1991), and cognitive and developmental psychology (J. Bruner 1986, 1990a, 1991, 1996).

Narrative studies that have most influenced medical anthropology fall into four main analytic genres: (a) discourse analysis; (b) life history studies; (c) cognitive studies; (d) aesthetic or literary studies. These categories are quite fluid, for there are cross-fertilizations which have produced, for instance, cognitive approaches to life histories (Agar 1980; Linde 1986) and these have been used, in turn, by anthropologists studying illness as a reconstruction of self-identity (Cain 1991). Furthermore, anthropologists have felt quite free to move eclectically among these traditions, combining in bricoleur-like fashion ideas and methods from here and there as these have been deemed useful in analyzing their stories.[5] In the face of much analytic inventiveness, contemporary narrative traditions do not represent stable, mutually exclusive or well bounded systems of thought. Nevertheless, they have emerged from various home disciplines which often define narrative in distinct ways.

Stories as speech acts

Labov's linguistic studies of narrative (Labov 1972, 1981; Labov and Fanshel 1977; Labov and Waletzky 1967), Austin's (1962) work on speech acts, and the ethnomethodological tradition of discourse analysis (Cicourel 1983) have inspired the study of narrative as *speech act*, as an element of conversation between healers and patients. Here, sociologists have certainly taken the lead (Mishler 1984; Riessman 1990, 1993) but they have had a wide reading among anthropologists. Within this analytic tradition, narrative is defined, first and foremost, as a linguistic unit, one of several, used for the "recapitulation of past experience" (Labov 1981: 225). As a unit of discourse, narrative can be distinguished from jokes, plans, explanations, and other sorts of conversational structures (Linde 1986: 186). In Labov's seminal work, narrative is defined as consisting of at least two past tense event clauses where the order of the clauses represents the order of events (Labov and Waletzky 1967). The Labovian tradition emphasizes the role of grammatical sequencing in both defining the narrative unit and in its connection to experience. The linguistic feature of narrative which allows it to relate past experience is a "rule of narrative sequencing . . . which allows the listener to infer the reported temporal order of past events from the temporal sequence of clauses in the report of those events" (Labov 1981: 225).

This linguistic definition is given an interactive twist by those who emphasize the reciprocal role of teller and receiver in the creation of the story. A narrative becomes then, not simply a discourse unit which is "about" a past event but a speech act which is co-constructed in a relationship (Rittenberg and Simons 1985; Paget 1988; Riessman 1990; Mishler 1984). As such, it is an "accomplishment" produced by a variety of actors and shaped through social conventions which govern how stories are to be told and taken up by the audience (Atkinson 1990: 5).

Narrative studies of patient/doctor communication have addressed power through examination of a subordinate (patient) voice which is in contest with a prevailing and powerful medical voice. Analysis of interchanges between doctors and their patients often show patient narratives as neglected or reorganized through the doctor's "medicalizing" discussion. In this vein, they are part of a broader investigation of doctor/patient communication which has a long tradition in discourse analysis (Fisher and Todd 1983; Labov and Fanshel 1977). "Doctor talk" often emerges as a kind of anti-narrative speech act, a "literary rhetoric" (Anspach 1988) which gains its perlocutionary power precisely through a set of discursive moves which suppress personal narrative, such as adoption of the passive voice and consequent elimination of agency.

Illness stories as life histories

Life histories do not comprise a single approach to narratives, offering instead a "confusing welter of different approaches" (Peacock and Holland 1993: 367). Though the life history is the oldest and best-known use of personal narrative in anthropology (Langness and Frank 1981), paradoxically the narrativity of the life history is often ignored. It is not uncommon for anthropologists to treat the life history as a transparent medium for the investigation of something else. This neglect of the story as text or as oral performance has been critiqued by a number of anthropologists (Crapanzano 1980; Peacock and Holland 1993; Agar 1980).

More recently, some anthropologists have attended to narrative as form and examined the relation of narrative content to plot structure (Ginsburg 1987). Growing interest in biography and autobiography (Monks and Frankenberg 1995; Garro 1992) have also provoked greater attention to the relation between narrative form and narrative content in life histories. Some have emphasized the performative aspect of life histories, connecting narrative content to the process by which the life history is constructed. Narrative becomes a social performance created as part of a developing relationship between informant and ethnographer (Ortiz 1985). Crapanzano (1980) speaks of the interview situation as one of "mutual transference" where the process of narrative promotes a definition of the listener as well as the teller.

Anthropologists have tended to draw upon life history methods to locate the meaning of an illness or disability within the framework of a whole life, rather than, say, a clinical conversation or an analysis of multiple discourses within medical talk. Life history approaches have been particularly valuable in looking at how a chronic or congenital condition shapes a person's sense of identity and selfhood (Obeyesekare 1981; Frank 1984, 1986; Kaufman 1988; Monks and Frankenberg 1995; Cain 1991). Life histories offer a processual rather than a static view of cultural life (Peacock and Holland 1993) which has proved useful in tracing illness experience as an on-going history. Life histories tend to emphasize the need for persons to find coherence and continuity in their lives (Linde 1993), and telling a life story becomes one device by which persons try to interpret disruptive illnesses in life context (Becker 1994; Kaufman 1988).

Stories as cultural scripts

Within a cognitive frame, stories have been examined as strategies for organizing personal experiences into culturally intelligible scripts. These, in turn, provide models for action (Quinn and Holland 1987). Stories can encode cultural models about what is normal by providing examples of violations of proper behavior. Since the stuff of narratives is the abnormal, the improper, and other departures from the norm, stories offer rich vehicles for passing along cultural knowledge about such matters as how to identify the appropriate social role as caregiver for an ill family member (Price 1987), how to survive on the streets as a drug addict (Agar 1980), or how to adopt the proper cultural identity associated with a particular diagnostic condition (Cain 1991). Life histories may be treated from a cognitive perspective in studies which examine the explanatory systems individuals draw upon to attribute causes to past actions and offer a guide to future ones (e.g. Agar 1980; Linde 1987).

Stories can communicate cultural knowledge about the cause of an illness (Early 1982, 1988; Price 1987). More inclusively, they can provide the prime material in which an illness is represented at a societal level. This is illustrated most graphically in situations where a new illness such as AIDS comes on the cultural scene, introducing a culturally unfamiliar crisis which calls for sense-making (Farmer 1994) or where a disease such as diabetes or TMJ rises to the forefront of social consciousness and seems to demand new explanations (Garro

1994). Stories can provide a means for allowing individual actors to make sense of and "come to terms with" difficult or unfamiliar experiences of illness by fitting personal experience into "pre-existent cultural models" (Matthews et al. 1994: 789). Cognitive anthropologists have examined stories as places in which individuals are able to both give expression to an experience which is intensely personal and at the same time (or, as part of the same process) give a culturally informed meaning to their experience (Garro 1992, 1994; Holland and Kipnis 1994).

Stories as aesthetic expressions

The poetic force of narrative has often been noted. Anthropologists have helped illuminate how every society deploys poetic devices to dramatize and underscore core cultural beliefs (through rituals and myths) and help its members make sense of their lives. The relation between poetic discourse and philosophy (or cosmology) is a very basic one, by no means specific to Western cultures.

Narrative's well-known propensity to offer an emotionally charged, symbolically provocative rendering of experience has been routinely linked to its power to illuminate personal experiences of illness and healing. Telling stories of one's life may allow the ill or the disabled, who are so often voiceless, to "give voice" to their personal experience (Frank 1996). Healers too, may be able to give a different kind of voice to their practice when they describe their work in narrative terms rather than the flattened prose of biomedical discourse (Sacks 1984, 1995; Coles 1989; Mattingly forthcoming).

Sometimes the aesthetic force of narrative has been linked to its healing powers. Healers may draw upon narrative to encourage powerful reframings of illness that actively change the sufferer's perception of his own body and personal experience. In studies of healing rituals, narratives (often cultural myths) are treated as one among a range of multi-media poetic forms that give ritual its perlocutionary power (Tambiah 1985; Leach 1976). Narratives become one medium through which the healer tries to connect a person's individual experience to an ideal or preferred narrative, and healing itself is equated with the rhetorical task of persuading the patient to see her experience in a certain way (Turner 1992). Stories which are located in ritual actions may take on special therapeutic powers; indeed, certain kinds of stories may have their special place as an integral part of a healing ritual. These "magical stories" are analyzed as part of a more complex ritual event in which they are but one of several mechanisms used to induce healing (Bilu and Witzum 1993). Some of the most interesting current investigations draw upon classic studies of myth and ritual, reworking these in light of contemporary healing practices. Such reworking is especially interesting when categories developed from the study of "exotic" practices are returned to Western contexts. "In psychotherapy," Kirmayer writes, "metaphors get linked together to form more or less coherent narratives . . . in healing rituals, the underlying myth can be described as an extended metaphor" (1993: 175).

Despite clear recognition of the aesthetic properties of narrative, and some growing attention to literary theory and hermeneutic philosophy in the analysis of illness and healing (B. Good 1994; M. J. Good 1995; Jackson 1994; Mattingly 1991b, 1994), there has been far less use of literary frameworks than might be expected, as Byron Good (1994) points out. Writers drawing upon linguistic and cognitive traditions of narrative analysis are often cognizant of its aesthetic form but artistic qualities are generally subordinated in favor of other concerns. Studies of illness and healing which do attend to narratives as poetic devices have tended to turn to semiotically informed anthropological models, such as those that have been used to analyze myths (Leach 1976; Lévi-Strauss 1962, 1963), models of ritual performance (Laderman and Roseman 1996; Kapferer 1983), or combinations of performative and semiotic frames (Tambiah 1985). One can also see a growing interest in examining ritual as theater (Turner 1986a; Kendall 1996).

My own analysis of therapeutic emplotment draws largely from literary criticism and hermeneutics. The hermeneutic tradition in philosophy has historically informed dramatic and aesthetic notions of social action in anthropology, including Turner's concept of social dramas and Geertz's notions of action as text. It has also influenced some strains of literary theory, particularly reader response theory (Iser 1974, 1978). The hermeneutic tradition since Dilthey (1989) has explored the aesthetic structure of action and the phenomenology of aesthetic experience. The work of Ingarden (1967), Gadamer (1975, 1979), and Ricoeur (1984, 1985, 1987) gives the fullest contemporary expression to this line of thinking. The voices of these hermeneutic philosophers will be heard in later chapters, but not always in any explicit way. My reading of them has infiltrated my own perspective such that the interpretations I make of my ethnographic data, in fact the very way I initially experienced the clinical world I represent here, are doubtless colored by their work.

Literary theory does not offer a single approach to the study of narrative. Instead, it offers diverse, even widely opposing perspectives on what a narrative is and how it is to be analyzed. On one end, a semiotically inspired "narratology" has attempted to identify a minimal universal form which could properly be considered narrative. The quest for universal form has especially influenced semiotic traditions of narrative analysis, best exemplified by the French structuralists (Barthes 1974, 1975a, b). Following the Russian formalists like Propp (1968) who studied fairytales, narratologists have been energetic advocates and explorers in the search for fundamental narrative form.

On the other end, performative traditions have resisted designating narrative in formal terms, stressing narrative as a social act highly sensitive to context, something constructed "between" text and reader (or teller and audience). When pressed to give some formal definition of narrative, they have taken a much looser approach. Herrnstein-Smith, for example, declares tendentiously that narrative is simply "someone saying something to someone else" (1980: 228). The capacity of a narrative to structure and guide the experiences of the audience is most thoroughly discussed in the literary tradition known as reader response theory (Suleiman and Crossman 1980; Olsen 1978), a heterogeneous movement that has sparked "readings" informed by paradigms as disparate as a deconstructive semiotics (Barthes 1974, 1975b) and the phenomenology of aesthetic experience (Iser 1974, 1978).

One might reasonably ask, why address the prosaic storytelling of ordinary people or their real life dramas by turning to theory dedicated to the study of the imaginary, even the fantastical? What does Western literary theory have to offer when its exemplars range from sailors wooed by sirens to Connecticut Yankees who find themselves in King Arthur's Court? What have these exotic creatures and their implausible adventures to do with the excruciatingly real travails of the very ill and their healers? Anthropological studies provide one kind of cross-cultural answer. The exaggeration, play, and love of the fantastic so often found in ritual, myth and folktale across a wide variety of cultures is evidently particularly suited to our human need to understand and cope with the very real things that happen to us. Obviously, the fictional seems to be very useful for getting at what really matters, or how we really feel, about things that actually happen.

In turning to Western societies, Aristotle provides another kind of answer. The poetic narrative offers knowledge about the human condition not available from history, he claims, because poetry offers an imitation of real life that condenses it, weeding through the irrelevancies that muddy ordinary perception and experience (Aristotle 1970). (This thesis is discussed in more detail in chapter 2.) The literary narrative, as Roland Barthes says somewhere, "admits no noise." Literature turns a philosophical eye on human experience, depicting what is *at stake* in a range of human situations that confront us all, though these situations play themselves out in innumerable particular ways. Most significant for my purposes, Western literature very often emphasizes life's moral ambiguities (Nussbaum 1990; Kundera 1993). It does so by drama-tizing the gap between a protagonist's expectations and the events that transpire, by keeping the reader breathlessly suspended as she wonders what will happen next (and therefore experiencing not-knowing in an emotionally charged and entertaining way). Modern and postmodern novels are especially notable for their "what if life were like this" experiments in which it is often difficult to tell right from wrong. In some periods of Western literature, these aesthetic tactics have been used to seduce the reader into embracing a morally certain way of life. Ambiguity is merely a short-lived experience which reinforces a firmly held social code. But, in modern and postmodern times, times "after virtue," as Alisdair MacIntyre (1981) would say, literature has explored and questioned any certain cultural view. Such questioning turns out to be a key feature of the therapeutic plots which comprise this book.

About, very different kind of defense of the literary emerged for me from my experience with occupational therapists. As a researcher, I found that my longstanding interest in literary theory and hermeneutics was instrumental in providing conceptual tools for excavating the everyday aesthetics of their practice. But I presumed that therapists were not going to find much from the likes of Aristotle's *Poetics*, Barthes' *S/Z* or Burke's *A Grammar of Motives* that spoke to their own clinical experience. What I had not bargained for was that my way of looking at things would become so interesting to those I studied, and especially, that what I brought from my love of the literary and philosophical would prove to be of such practical import.

About a year and a half into the first ethnographic study of occupa-tional therapists I conducted in Boston, the therapists I had been interviewing and observing for so long were getting quite anxious to know what I was making of their work. I had put off saying much for as long as possible, worried a bit about "contamination" of findings but even more nervous that they would think me needlessly esoteric and presumptuous for seeing their work in fanciful ways. However, at some point I was cornered and agreed to talk to them about what I was seeing in their practice. One day I met with a group of the seven or eight therapists whom I had followed most extensively. I (quite bravely, I thought) determined to talk about my new and still rather ill-formed ideas about therapeutic emplotment and even to say something about what I drew from literary theorists to develop this notion. The example I first gave them was my analysis of a session I had observed with one of them where the therapist treats a young man with a severe head injury. The entire treatment session consists of about a twenty-minute walk through the corridors of the hospital in a wheelchair. Few words are spoken. (This case is presented in chapter 4.) I wanted to offer a very ordinary moment of practice because I hoped they might see that even the most mundane moments can have their poetry and that poetry may be the most important thing a session offers. I wanted them to see this but I also felt foolish because I knew this literary language was very far from the "factual" and "objective" discourse by which they routinely described their own work to colleagues and clients.

As I told my version of this spartan session, the therapist I was describing looked at me quizzically, not quite sure whether to be disturbed or flattered, seeing herself held up in a very peculiar light. But she was intrigued. The other therapists in the room were not only interested, they helped me to think out the implications of my ideas by offering other examples of their work that exemplified how stories were created in practice. To my great surprise, they were captivated by my odd portraits of them and they began to see their work illuminated in a way it had not been before (Mattingly, Fleming and Gillette, 1997). Their excitement gave me courage. I began to present my analysis to larger groups of occupational therapists at local and national meetings. I'm sure a substantial number regarded me as irrelevant or even dangerous, trafficking as I was in the non-scientific. But many others were so interested and enthusiastic that I even agreed that the first publications of this research would be written to them rather than to an academic audience (Mattingly 1991a, b, c, Mattingly and Fleming 1994). The book which Maureen Fleming and I wrote is now a standard textbook in many graduate and undergraduate courses in occupational therapy. Several of the practice's theory-makers have taken up the idea of therapy as narrative emplotment in their own studies (Clark 1993; Helfrich, Kielhofner and Mattingly 1994; Mallinson, Kielhofner and Mattingly 1996). Of course, my research occurred at a fortunate time. Many scholars were turning to narrative to examine illness and healing and this work was beginning to emerge in print; this surely made my interpretations more palatable.

Still I continue to be amazed at how practical this literary line of inquiry has turned out to be. In the Western world, we have for a long time accepted the overwhelming distance between high culture (with its Aristotles and Shakespeares) and everyday life. Anthropologists particularly worry that as we take a literary turn in our analytic approaches we sacrifice having anything to say to the "man or woman on the street." Perhaps we have been mistaken.

Narrative, actions and experience

This book is, on the one hand, an ethnography of occupational therapy which attends specifically to narrative as a structure of that practice. But it is also intended as a more general meditation on some central anthropological and philosophical questions about the relation between narrative, action, and experience as these play out in the world of clinical activity. The basic argument of this book, elaborated in the context of occupational therapy, is that narratives are not just about experiences. Experiences are, in a sense, about narratives. That is, narratives are not primarily after-the-fact imitations of the experiences they recount. Rather, the intimate connection between story and experience results from the structure of action itself. Many kinds of social actions (including many therapeutic interactions) are organized and shaped by actors so that they take on narrative form. Thus narrative and experience are bound in a homologous relationship, not merely a referential one. There are quite practical reasons for this need to create narratives out of actions. The pragmatics involved will be explored in later chapters as I analyze clinical interchanges between occupational therapists and their clients.

I am not alone in looking at how narratives shape action. Cognitive anthropology offers the notion of narrative scripts that guide action and discourse. Some discourse studies consider simultaneously "narrative event" (content), "event of narration" (performance), and broader cultural contexts which influence and are influenced by this storytelling. The approach which probably comes closest to mine does not start from a consideration of narrative at all but from the study of ritual. Studies of ritual performance, particularly those influenced by Victor Turner's notion of ritual as social drama and as theater, also tend to emphasize the aesthetic elements of social action and take some of their inspiration from hermeneutics. Further discussion of this relationship is offered in the concluding chapter.

By and large, however, I part company with major traditions of narrative analysis in considering action as narrative and in the way I look at the relation between stories and actions. Generally, anthropologists who study narrative, even those interested in the role of stories in the life of a social group, have considered the relation between story and experience through an exclusive treatment of stories, either as texts or as performances. On the whole, folklorists, linguists and anthropologists who study story performance and focus on the cultural context in which stories are told do not also study the very specific practices which are being described in stories. Conversely, those who study a group's practices, even when they have an interest in how the group narrativizes their practices, rarely examine the structure of the stories told and the structure of the practical experiences to which those stories refer. Yet this is an immensely fruitful exploration, not only as a way of studying a group's storytelling practices but as a way of examining how members of a social group understand and direct their primary social activities. Renato Rosaldo is quite right when he concludes an essay on Ilongot hunting stories by suggesting a connection between the act of story-telling and the active shaping of lived experience. "The stories these Ilongot men tell about themselves both reflect what actually happened and define the kinds of experience they seek out on future hunts. Indeed, their very postures while hunting resemble those used in story-telling, and in this respect the story informs the experience of hunting at least as much as the reverse" (1986: 134). Like the Ilongot hunters, the stories occupational therapists tell define the kinds of experience they seek – and, I would add, try to shape.

In attending to therapeutic emplotment, I attend to action and experience both as personal and as something socially constructed. I emphasize the metaphoric and phenomenological side of health care, examining clinical interventions as transactions between the world(s) of biomedicine and the life worlds of patients. The notion of therapeutic emplotment offers one way to examine the social construction (and reconstruction) of illness and healing as a fluid, shifting process influenced not only by large structural conditions and cultural meanings but also by the exigencies of the concrete situation. Equally important, a narrative analysis of clinical interaction helps to uncover the moral dimensions of clinical practice. A central difficulty with clinical renderings of patient sufferings is that in their abstractness, the world of the patient is left out (Frank 1996). This world is above all a practical and moral one in which patients have life projects and everyday concerns, things "at stake" (Wikan 1990, 1991). What comes to be "at stake" for any individual depends, in part, on the "local moral world" the patient inhabits. Illness, from this point of view, creates a "resistance" which hinders or prevents the sufferer from carrying out plans and projects (Kleinman and Kleinman 1991, 1994, 1996).

Occupational therapists often implicitly recognize and inevitably negotiate the moral. Clinical encounters carry a moral resonance rarely brought into explicit focus because such a focus does not conform to the cannon of "appropriate" clinical talk or the explicit, sanctioned struc-ture of clinical action. A narrative analysis offers a way to examine clinical life as a series of existential negotiations between clinicians and patients, ones which concern the meaning of illness, the place of therapy within an unfolding illness story, and the meaning of a life which must be remade in the face of serious illness.

In medical anthropology we have quite rightly noticed the profoundness of severe injury or disease which does not merely damage a body but a whole life. We have documented the miscommunications which so often characterize patients' discussions with doctors and other healers of Western medicine. We have also criticized the culture of biomedicine for being insufficiently mindful of personal, familial, institutional and cultural factors that influence how a disabling condition is experienced and handled by the person who is ill. We have been less attentive to how the illness experience is addressed in clinical practice, especially among lower-status health professionals who spend sustained time with patients. A hospital world operates in two time spaces. One is the time paradigmatically expressed by the doctor – fast and efficient. Doctors move quickly in the hospital wards. Their time is expensive. They cannot afford to linger too long in any one spot. The other is the time of the lesser health professional: therapists, aides, sometimes nurses. Things move more slowly here. These professionals may spend an hour or more a day with a patient, and some of this may be quite informal. On the spinal cord unit I observed, for instance, the nurse's station served as a sort of hospitality center and one could always find patients in their electric wheelchairs who had stopped by for a visit.

I do not want to extol the virtues of hospital life, nor minimize the powerlessness of patients. The clinic is, in many respects, a cruel place, not well equipped to deal with tragedy. Yet it is an oversimplification to suppose that only anthropologists and the ill care about the phenomenological side of disease and disability. The first times I observed therapists with their patients, I sometimes had to leave the room because I had not yet acclimatized to the level of suffering I witnessed. It was not only the patients themselves who moved me, with the intensity, the sadness, of their interactions with therapists. I watched these therapists move in close, touch distorted bodies, bend to hear inaudible words. Therapists were not always sensitive and sometimes the tasks they set patients were thoughtlessly foolish or degrading. They often appeared unaware themselves of the profound human problems they were addressing. When they reduced their practice to helping someone feed himself, viewed as a kind of low-level technical task, they neglected the immense implications of their work and their patients' struggles, the level of shame and despair which accompanies loss of the simple skills of everyday life. But when therapists recognized the subterranean phenomenological waters beneath a humdrum task like relearning to dress oneself, their practice was directed more to the illness experience than to the disease.

There was more generosity than I was prepared for. I saw small kindnesses rather than life-saving interventions. These went almost unnoticed by the therapists themselves. Generosity and small attentions are not the stuff of the medical chart. Even when something more dramatic occurs (trying to help a despairing person find a reason to stay alive), there is no place to formally record these actions. They are undocumented exchanges, not part of the official purview of the occupational therapist. Therapists personally valued their own kindness and their imaginative capacity to link their interventions to the lives of their patients, but because there is almost no language within biomedical discourse for recognizing and examining exchanges which address the illness experience and because this is not a "reimbursable" part of treatment, the phenomenological aspects of treatment are quite neglected, carried out almost furtively. These attentions to the illness experience constitute an "underground practice" in occupational therapy and doubtless many other health professions (Mattingly and Fleming 1994). Taking careful note of the narrative structure of clinical interventions reveals "hidden values" within biomedical practice which run counter to the dominant metaphor of body as machine that holds such persuasive force in Western medicine (Kirmayer 1988; Gordon 1988). Put differently, it reveals how some health professionals, some of the time, recognize a physiological body which is inextricable from the imagined and lived body, the body which carries a person through social space and time.

What follows

Before considering the narrative structure of clinical interactions, I want to deepen the problem. The peculiar idea that stories structure experiences requires careful attention for there is nothing simple about the notion that we "live out stories." What story comes to mean as an organization of action is different than what it means as retrospective talk. It is also different from the imposition of pregiven narratives upon the action scene. Chapter 2 centers on the debate within anthropology concerning the relation between story and experience. This debate, which concerns the problem of narrative reference and the status of "experience" as a prelinguistic category, has been taken up most explicitly within anthropology by its "postmodernists" but has been discussed most thoroughly outside anthropology within modern and postmodern literary theory. Against the prevalent positions within anthropology and literary theory that abandon any referential relation between story and experience, I argue that one can reasonably speak of a correspondence between the structure of narrative discourse and structures of action and experience. This is not because narrative, in some simple way, copies action, but because there is a homology between the structure of narrative and the structure of action.

Chapter 3 introduces the ethnographic scene within which the arguments about the relation between story and experience offered in the introductory chapters is now concretely examined. This chapter, and the following three, consider the narrative structure of therapeutic practice through examinations of clinical interactions between occupational therapists and patients. In the third chapter I take a detailed look at a single interaction between a therapist and two spinal cord patients; I argue that there are multiple ways this ordinary interchange is given narrative structure by its participants. Chapter 4, "Therapeutic Plots," asks the question: If therapists and patients seem to need to create stories out of clinical time, why is this so? This chapter considers the nature of this therapeutic practice, how "healing" is understood, and why the structure of the practice gives therapists (and patients) practical reasons for turning clinical time into narrative time.

The fifth chapter looks at therapeutic time as a "short story" within the longer life story of a patient. It addresses the need for therapists and patients to find some way of making therapeutic work a meaningful short story within a person's life. In considering the relation of therapy to the patient's sense of self, I place my argument within anthropological discussions of self and personhood, particularly those discussions that have used narrative as a way of conceiving how selves are socially constructed. I also introduce Lyotard's "little narrative" and Bakhtin's "dialogical narrative" to extend my notion of the therapeutic plot as it connects to a life plot.

At a minimal level, all clinical interactions may be said to have a narrative structure. However, some clinical moments are more narrative than others. Chapter 6 examines those features of clinical practice which subvert or threaten the formation of therapeutic narratives in clinical time. I also address a rather different problem: the threatening plot. If there can be too little narrative in clinical work, there can also be too much, or too much of the wrong sort. In previous chapters, the narratives constructed appear to be beneficent, integral to healing within this practice. But not all stories are good ones. Some therapeutic plots are dangerous. I examine some of these threatening narratives and where their danger lies.

The concluding chapter argues for the need to examine narrative within studies of illness and healing in a way which connects narrative more closely with social action and experience. I compare the notion of therapeutic emplotment with other traditions that explicitly address the relation between narrative and social action, particularly performative approaches to ritual healing which consider ritual events as social dramas.

2   The mimetic question

Who could deny the power or need for narratives in understanding, interpreting and communicating experience, or the "call of stories" (Coles 1989) when trying to make sense of the extraordinary and the disorienting? But there are radically different positions which explain why narrative has this power. One, a realist or mimetic stance, assumes that at some deep level there is a natural correspondence between life as lived and life as narrated. The naive version of this is that narrative simply represents experience. A second position, far more pervasive among contemporary scholars of narrative, is anti-mimetic, presuming that narrative derives its power by transforming and distorting life as lived. And further, that experience requires the transformation and distortion that narrative imposes in order to be meaningful. An important variation of this anti-mimetic stance is the performative position which contends that the significant relation between narrative and experience is not referential but emerges in the experience of the narrative as performed. The meaning is located in the event itself, the "creation of presence" (Schieffelin 1996: 59).

I offer a third position which rejects both naive realism and the variety of anti-mimetic positions now predominant. The third alternative, already suggested in Chapter 1, will be briefly outlined here and gradually developed throughout the remaining chapters of this book in the context of ethnographic material.

The realist position: narrative as imitation of action and experience

The irresistible urge to catch hold of experience by putting it in narrative form and the further urge to believe one has captured something true belongs to what is often termed the "realist" position. It belongs to the commonsense view that, when we have an experience and we want to tell others about it, we tell a story. We draw upon narrative to recreate the experience, to reproduce events that occurred in an "experience-near" way (Wikan 1991; Badone 1991). We also tell stories to say something about who we are. For everyday stories refer back to their narrator as well. "Very simply, we human beings seem to have a basic need to be understood by others" and offering one's life story to another is a way to do this (Ortiz 1985: 107).

However basic this need, when considering the relationship between story and experience a number of difficulties appear and any easy sense of "naturalness" is quickly dispelled. One obvious difficulty concerns the validity of narratives which purport to be accounts of things that actually happened. Anthropologists have long been suspicious of the stories they have heard from their informants. Life history approaches have always drawn fire for their problematic epistemelogical status. The difficulty posed in verifying personal accounts of past events has led to a pervasive mistrust of their scientific worth. Boas felt that narrators were probably going to lie and exaggerate (Peacock and Holland 1993: 367). A story, after all, is a rhetorical structure which is meant to persuade, to provide a perspective on what happened as part of telling what happened. Informants are prone to distort their stories because they fashion them with a particular audience in mind, shaping versions according to the public face they wish to present (Hazen 1995).

One response to these difficulties has been an attempt both to "check the facts" against informant accounts wherever possible and to separate "bare facts" from the "narrator's perspective" (Rittenberg and Simons 1985), relying here on the linguist's distinction between the "event structure" of the narrative (which is directed to "reporting the facts") and the "evaluative structure" in which the narrator gives a clear personal interpretation of the meaning of events (Linde 1986).

Some have argued that the issue of accuracy and validity is not always important because the real issue is not so much an "objective" account of events that happened but a record of how those events were interpreted and experienced by the actors. Peacock and Holland usefully distinguish two different realist positions. One, which they term a "factual approach" treats narratives as data about observable events which need to be checked for accuracy. A second, "subjectivist" approach equates narrative with personal experience. Narrative is a "window on the psyche" (Peacock and Holland 1993: 369). The life history approach, at least for some of its proponents, has been tied to an investigation of subjective experience, the inner life of the other. Radin sought from his informants an "inside view of their culture" as they described it and felt the only legitimate method for access to this inside view was through the life history (Dwyer 1979). From this "subjectivist" perspective, the primary value of narrative is precisely its capacity to offer an "inside view." This, more than any "factual" content, is what matters. Thus, one can "bracket . . . the question of relation to some postulated real world" (Linde 1987: 351). Psychoanalytic discussions follow along similar lines, and a distinction has been made between factually accurate "historical truth" and the speaker's interpretive perceptions of events' "narrative truth" (Spence 1982). "The report of eyewitnesses and contemporaries, in other words, is a narrative and not historical truth" (Wyatt 1986: 197).

But this argument poses new problems. Even those attempting to "bracket" the issue of factual veracity are troubled by how clearly narratives can portray an informant's personal experience. Anthropologists have always worried about trying to represent the internal world of subjective experience. One may be able to report and analyze public events and institutions by eliciting their culturally shared meanings, but how can one get at private and personal meanings? How, after all, can one know other minds? The "other minds" problem is exacerbated when considering stories told by those who are culturally distant.

The problem here, of course, is not a simple one of deceitfulness but a thornier issue of how to represent something like experience faithfully. If one thinks at all about the relation between stories and experiences (especially personal stories about life experiences) an ambiguity immediately arises. We may begin quite simply with the idea that stories are something told about experiences. First we have an experience, we live through something, something happens to us, and then – if we choose – we tell a story about it. Somebody may ask us, "So tell me what happened?" or "What was the experience like?" and we will likely tell a story.

So far it is all quite straightforward. But what about the fact that when we tell what happened our story is shaped to fit the interests of the audience or to persuade our listener to adopt a certain perspective? Such shaping is unavoidable. We know this very well for as listeners to the story, we may consider the story a simple representation of the experience, a transparent mirror, but we are just as likely to recognize that story as one possible version of the events and know that other stories could be told. When the storyteller is done, for instance, we may ask "So what was the other person's story?" In so asking, we raise the question of in what sense that story is "about" the experience. We cannot even rest with the notion that "each participant has his story" for the same narrator could well tell his story any number of ways, depending on inclination and audience. This means a story is not even a clear mirror of a person's own particular experience of some set of events. The Roshomon problem is compounded. If a story is not a clear mirror, what kind of mirror is it? How does the structure of the story relate to the structure of the experience as lived through by its participants?

Beyond naive realism: a return to Aristotle

Among many anthropologists, especially postmodernists, any mimetic position is equated with what is variously termed "naive realism," "empiricism," or "positivism." The key argument here is that there is an analytic necessity to distinguish past events and discourse about them. The distinction is such that any correspondence theory of language must be discounted. "Only a naive positivist would believe that expressions are equivalent to reality; and we recognize in everyday life the gap between experience and its symbolic manifestation in expression" (E. Bruner 1986: 6). Aristotle is generally credited with providing Western literary theory with its representational position. However, the mimetic position he articulated is, in fact, far more subtle than the "naive realists" anthropologists have criticized. It is worth attending directly to Aristotle's arguments because, in Western literary theory, the discussion of the relationship between narrative and experience begins with him.

Narratives, Aristotle argues, are "imitative processes" (1970: 15) and what they imitate are "men in action" (1970: 17). Notably, "action" is an inclusive term here which also includes feelings and experiences. Through imitation, narratives mirror the world of action and experience. Aristotle sees the urge toward poetic art as rooted in a natural human capacity to imitate, a capacity so basic it distinguishes humans from other animals. Imitation provides humans their primary vehicle for learning about how to live. However, poetic imitation (the drama) is not a simple copy of events, for actual events are necessarily particular and chancy but poetic imitation concerns kinds, universals.

Aristotle thus contrasts narratives which are sheer imitation of action (histories) from poetic narratives which have a plot. Plot is that structuring device which gives poetic narrative its capacity to deal in universals by placing actions within a coherent whole with a beginning, middle, and end. Plot gives the outline which allows us to comprehend – and take pleasure in – a succession of incidents in a single, unified figure. "The most beautiful pigments smeared on at random," he writes by way of analogy, "will not give as much pleasure as a black-and-white outline picture" (1970: 26).

The well plotted narrative is "firmly compacted" such that if any component event "is shifted to another place, or removed, the whole is loosened up and dislocated" (Aristotle 1970: 32). Through this artful structuring, no incident happens by mere random chance; rather each leads inexorably (though in the best plots, unexpectedly) to the conclusion. The emplotted unity Aristotle speaks of is ordered teleologically, as a movement toward an ending. But Aristotle thinks that life as lived does not guarantee any such clearly marked unity, is unlikely to cleanly reveal relationships among events and their contribution to a final "single result." Actual events, as they fall out, do not lend themselves in their natural order to the workings of a plot. Relations among events in life in any particular case are likely to be merely chancy, unrevealing of any deeper (moral) laws about probable or necessary relations.

Hence Aristotle contrasts life as lived which is liable to trivial succession, one thing just happening to follow on another, to life as emplotted, structured by a compacted movement with a clear beginning, middle, and end and with each episode in its proper place. Histories lack plots, as Aristotle sees it, precisely because they are governed by a correspondence to action, constrained to follow the facts. The historian is bound by what actually happens, not by the demands to create a single unified action as structured by a plot. Since the historian is required to report all that happens as it happens within some given time period, he cannot shape the succession of events in such a way that they are clearly "pointed toward the same goal" (Aristotle 1970).

Already in Aristotle, then, despite an emphasis on narrative as imitation, an opposition is set up between life as lived, the life of real time, and the artificial unity given to life through the structuring device of plot. By declaring the philosophical seriousness of poetry as compared to history, Aristotle is claiming that this artifice allows us to contemplate the deeper truths of the nature of action and experience. The key opposition for Aristotle, Ricoeur (1984) points out, is "one thing after another and one thing because of another." One thing after another is merely successive but one thing because of the other is causal (Ricoeur 1984: 41).

Aristotle gave formal definition to a broadly held classical view of the relation between story and experience, one in which poetic narrative imitates action and experience through clarification and condensation, revealing causal connections between motive, deed, and consequence which also allows a moral reading of events. The purpose of a narrative is not simply to tell what happened but to provide a moral perspective on past events. Hannah Arendt (1958), gives a central place to storytelling as a vehicle for articulating and reinforcing the Greek *polis*, a community of individuals in which heroic action figured as the prime exemplar of good citizenship. Stories preserved ephemeral heroic moments, allowing them to function as object lessons for the community. The Greeks believed that the story outlived the act itself only if it was told well. It was not enough merely to report something. The bard "straightened the story" – set it right (Arendt 1958). Truth, in the deepest sense, was not best accessed through the most literal recounting. The confusion and ambiguity which characterizes events-as-lived had to be distilled into a harmony, a whole, from which the particular meanings of the actions could be understood.

The Greeks also recognized the need for temporal remove from the lived event in order to get at the deeper meaning of lived experience. Arendt argues the necessity for a certain distance in time if the meaning of actions is to become apparent. Actions, as she contends, are really only beginnings. Their meaning only emerges as they play themselves out in the "web of human relations" which they necessarily enter. A narrative reveals the meaning of actions because the sequences of occurrences and sufferings that certain actions bring about are played out in it. This meaning is not available to the actor in the midst of action for he cannot yet know what consequences will follow from what he does. A narrative, in this sense, is a kind of summing-up. It is only by looking back that the real meaning of the initial actions can be understood (Arendt 1958).

Even the ancient representational view of narrative, then, presumes that a well-told narrative, at least a poetically well-told one, "straightens" events in order to bring out a deeper meaning. This view also presumes that a gaze directed backward from the position of spectator offers more truth than is available to the actor. The anti-mimetic view currently powerful in narrative theory can be seen as an intensified focus on how stories are "straightened" and an accompanying disinterest or disbelief that life as lived bears much resemblance to the narratives we tell about it. The difference in position is not between a simple copy theory versus a more sophisticated literary model of narrative but between a belief that the "straightening" actually reveals a deeper truth about the nature and form of lived experience (uncovers "universal truths" Aristotle would say) and a contemporary deeply ironic view that narratives have little to tell us about the form and feeling of our lives.

Narrative as transformation and distortion of experience

In anthropology, doubts about the "authenticity" of narrative have been most starkly and thoroughly raised in examinations of the ethnographer as narrator of fieldwork experience. The anthropological rejection of the mimetic position is related to the rise of narrator reflexivity in which writers "call attention to the fictionality of their work" (Fischer 1986: 232). The fundamental argument here is that any story which purports to be about prior actions and experiences inevitably distorts those experiences. Thus, the notion that narrative portrays human action is an "error of realism" (Reddy 1992).

Contemporary anthropological doubts about narrative's referential capacity carry a complex message. Postmodern sceptics could hardly be further from Boas in questioning the authenticity of personal stories about life experiences. Whereas Boas saw the unreliability with personal narratives as an argument to collect one's data in other ways, postmodern anthropologists see these obvious epistemological difficulties as something which gives narrative its appeal. Personal narratives are lauded precisely because they call their own authority into question and reveal the difficulty of grasping the Other. Personal narratives also point to the difficulty in moving from a single informant's account of events to a generalized description of what a collectivity does, thinks, or feels (Dwyer 1977, 1979).

Anthropologists speak of the ethnographic text as a "story" (even when not organized in formal narrative fashion) to emphasize its "fictionality." Ethnographies are "neither recreations nor simple translations of other moments" (S. Roseman 1991: 521). Traditional or "realist" ethnographies, which may tell no stories in the usual sense, come under fire for disguising their underlying narrative structure. The ethnographic text, writes Atkinson, is based on an underlying narrative form which "portrays the world as a series of patterned and comprehensible events (occasions, actions) by virtue of its narrative ordering. Time, causality and agency may all be conveyed at an implicit level in narrative form" (Atkinson 1990: 105).

The main argument here is that no ethnography can be understood as an authentic imitation of the "native's" version of a cultural world. The ethnographer inevitably skews things because there is a fundamental ontological distinction, an unbridgeable gap, between the two central acts of anthropology: text-making and fieldwork experience (Clifford and Marcus 1986; Marcus and Cushman 1982; Marcus and Fischer 1986; Tedlock 1983; Tyler 1987). The translation of experience into text "necessarily involve(s) the transformation of experience into fictional 'productions'" (Roseman 1991: 505).

Distortions introduced by text-making are partly due to the rhetorical nature of the task. Narratives are intended as authoritative statements, making an argument about what happened as part of describing what happened (Geertz 1988; Pratt 1986, Roseman 1991). Taussig asks provocatively, "Can't we say that to give an example, to instantiate, to be concrete, are all examples of the magic of mimesis wherein the replication, the copy, acquires the power of the represented?" (1993: 16). Events selected, their chronological ordering, and how they are described, contribute to a particular interpretation of events. We are persuaded as we are "lifted out of ourselves into [the] images narratively painted" (Taussig 1993: 16). Narrative, in other words, has no "bare facts." And of course, ethnographies offer a double distortion since in many senses they are stories of other people's stories.

What is experience (such that stories cannot imitate it)?

From a postmodern perspective, personal narratives about personal experiences merely make vivid the problems faced by any ethnographic accounts – their inevitably fictional status. The fictionality of narrative is often linked to its capacity to order experience. Humans are deeply concerned with order, coherence, continuity. Even a sense of self rests on these qualities (Ewing 1990, 1991; Linde 1993; Kirmayer 1992) for "we cannot live without searching for stories to give coherence to our lives" (Kirmayer 1993: 180). But many anthropologists also argue that this deep human concern does not coincide with our experience of life; rather it is something we "do to" or "impose upon" lived experience. Anthropologists have contrasted narrative with life-as-lived, defining narrative as that which "distorts" experience and, in so doing, renders it orderly. Narrative has been embued with tremendous power, in this ability to capture experience by taming it.

If narrative offers all this to experience, what characterizes non-narrated or pre-narrated experience? What sort of ontological status does it have? The overwhelming answer is that it is an amorphous beast, if it can reasonably be said to exist at all. Experience lacks coherence (Wyatt 1986; Badone 1991; Linde 1993; Myerhoff 1986). Experience, especially experience of the self, is fragmented and continuity is an "illusion" (Sahlins 1985).

If experience is fractured and formless, it is also fleeting, ungraspable. Experience is often said to be ineffable, impossible to capture through any discursive measure. Many of our experiences are "inchoate;" one cannot get at their "essence" (E. Bruner 1986; Clifford 1983, 1986). Furthermore, one person's experience is inaccessible to others, belonging to an invisible inner domain of thoughts and feeling. Anthropologists commonly draw a distinction between a knowable terrain of observable, public actions and a mysterious inner plane of interpretation (Abrahams 1986; Geertz 1973). "A life as lived is what actually

happens. A life as experienced consists of the images, feelings, senti-
ments, desires, thoughts, and meanings known to the person whose life it
is" (E. Bruner 1984: 6). Experience is fragile, easily influenced, and this,
too, makes it elusive. When anthropologists try to understand human
experience "they contribute to human experience, distort its variety, and
thus make it all the more difficult to grasp" (Dwyer 1979: 205).

More dramatic is the claim that there is no such thing as experience, at
least not as a phenomenon in its own right. If there is no such thing, what
gives us this phenomenological "illusion?" One answer is – narrative
itself. There is no reality without narrative (White 1980, 1987). Because
we have stories, we believe we are having experiences. Experience is, at
best, derivative of prior discourse, an enactment of pre-given stories.
Rather than action preceding stories, stories precede and help us to make
action coherent. As actors, we are governed by stories. This view is
shared by scholars ranging from performative, structuralist, and cognitive
traditions. As Bauman (1977, 1986) puts it, "Events are not the external
raw materials out of which narratives are constructed, but rather the
reverse: Events are abstractions from narrative. It is the structures of
signification in narrative that give coherence to events in our understanding . . ." (1986: 5). We need not be aware, of course, of the
culturally created stories which govern our experiences and actions. Lévi-
Strauss makes the extreme case when he declares that "myths operate in
men's minds without their being aware of the fact" (1962: 12).

This strong position has been given a prominent, if controversial,
place within psychoanalysis (Spence 1982; Rosenwald and Ockberg
1992; Schafer 1981; Wyatt 1986). Experience, at least past experience,
is declared a fictitious category. "The past cannot be said to be. Instead
we should say rather the past is made whenever it is reconstructed"
(Wyatt 1986: 196). Many literary theorists concur. Past experience is
not preserved as a coherent whole, as something "organized, integrated,
and apprehended as a specific 'set of events'" unless imbued with these
qualities through the social "act of narration" (Herrnstein-Smith
1980: 229).

The most thorough and well-articulated renunciation of any mimetic
view of narrative comes from narrative theorists themselves, particularly
literary theorists. Modern and postmodern narrative theorists, for the
most part, see it as both naive and false to treat narrative as a direct or
natural expression of action and experience. Many anthropologists,
especially those with a postmodern bent, have adopted this skepticism.
Here, the question is not whether stories are true or not but a deeper
question of correspondence between narrative as form and the form of
action and experience.

Contemporary literary theory generally holds that narratives are a dramatic transformation of lived experience because there is a difference between our life in time as we actually live it and the way time is structured in narrative. Narrative theorists do not just deny a simple empiricism, a notion that stories somehow directly describe events apart from interpretation (a view also contrary to those writing about illness experience); they even deny any direct relation between experience as felt and interpreted by an individual and the story that individual might tell about his experience. They doubt that the structure of experience and the structure of narrative have much to do with one another. Narrative, in this view, is a mythical imposition of coherence on what is otherwise formless experience.

More specifically, the structure of beginning, middle, and end is one we find in narrative and lack in life. The distinction between lived time (experience) and narrative time is critical to contemporary conceptions of plot, point of view, and style. These fundamental literary concepts are defined in part by their role in transforming and distorting life-as-lived. There are three key objections to the view that narratives represent experience. One is that lived experience is formless, or at least plotless. A second is that a narrative requires a narrator, that is, an authoritative point of view which surveys the whole action landscape from beginning to end and recounts the story events in a particular way (one which ultimately gives the story its meanings and morals) from this privileged perspective. A third objection comes in the form of a disdain of the whole issue, a declaration that past experience is simply not what narratives are about. To what do narratives refer? One answer is that narrative meaning is largely intertextual; the primary reference is not an extralinguistic realm of lived experience but a world of other texts. A second answer is that reference is quite beside the point. Narrative meaning is in the performance itself.

1   Life-as-lived lacks plot

The dominant position in contemporary literary theory is that the structure of experience is distinct from the structure of narrative and particularly that experience lacks the unifying structure which plot gives to literary narrative. This argument is buried deep within the language of literary theory, guiding the important distinction between "story" and "narrative." "Story" refers to the sequence of events which the narrative is "about." Narrative, by contrast, refers to the actual discourse that recounts the events. In this demarcation, "story" is a simple chronological structure which can be reconstructed from the narrative discourse. And, of course, narrative discourse is nearly always out-of-(linear)-order; drama depends upon such devices as withholdings of crucial events, foreshadowings, and backward glances. This convention of narratology which separates story and discourse reinforces story-telling as a kind of artifice or distortion of what is more basically a simple next-next sequence (Culler 1979, 1981). Jonathan Culler sums up the major traditions of narrative study represented in the American, French, Russian, German, Dutch, and Israeli schools by saying "there is a considerable variety among these traditions, but if these theorists agree on anything it is this: that the theory of narrative requires a distinction between what I shall call 'story' – a sequence of actions or events, conceived as independent of their manifestation in discourse – and what I shall call 'discourse,' the discursive presentation of events" (1981: 169–170). Story and discourse are defined precisely by their difference.

Structuralist and poststructuralist accounts depend upon an essential ontological assumption about the nature of lived experience designated as "story." What can be said about this prior state of events? The "story," "fabula," or "histoire" as it is variously called? It is treated as a *chronology*, a simple arrow in time. The primary logic which relates one event to the next is temporal. As evidence for this prior chronological "content" narrative theorists offer the fact that we can know the same "story," although we will not necessarily have heard the same narrative text (Bal 1985: 5). That is, we can recognize the story as the same across different textual versions, even when these differ considerably. We can find ourselves telling the "same" story, each a different rendering, even a "new discourse." We may say, no matter how varied the version, we also claim to be revisiting the "same experience." It is this feature of storytelling which prompts narrative theorists to treat the prior events (the experience) as an "invariant chronological core" and the actual story-as-told (discourse) as a "modification or effacement of the order of events" (Culler 1981: 171). Above all, then, discourse is about a distortion of time, prolonging a few precious moments, skimming a month at a time, entire years, intimating the ending in the beginning, blithely shifting scenes and times and sequences in order to further the plot.

Within the Anglo-American tradition, the separation of lived time and narrative time can be seen even prior to the influence of the Russian formalists and French structuralists who have so shaped modern narrative study. E. M. Forster, writing his highly influential *Aspects of The Novel* in 1927 distinguishes "story" and "plot" and in so doing distinguishes narrative time and lived time. He relies on a disparity between sequential time and emplotted time to analyze the nature of plot. In an Aristotelian move, he opposes sequence and plot. The story (mere sequence) "runs like a backbone – or may I say tapeworm, for its beginning and end are arbitrary" (1927: 27). In being mere sequence, the story "narrates the life in time" (1927: 29). The more complex organization is given by the plot. Forster visualizes plot as "a sort of higher level official" concerned that everything which happens is marshaled in such a way that it "contributes to the plot." Through such marshaling, events are transformed from a relation of mere sequence, the monotonous structure of time, to a relation based on causality. Forster defines plot as against story, causal relations as against sequential relations. And most of all, plot as against time.

This separation of experience and narrative is not confined to literary accounts of narrative concerned primarily with the imaginary. It has also been strongly taken up in the philosophy of history which concerns itself with "real events" (White 1972, 1973, 1980). Hayden White, following the structuralists, argues that stories are a certain kind of artful illusion in which "events seem to tell themselves" (1987: 3). But real events, White notes, do not in fact "tell themselves" at all. This makes the possibility of narrating stories about real events a puzzle. A historical narrative is created out of the "chaotic form of 'historical records'" and is a kind of wishful "fantasy" that real life actually had the coherence and order which governs the meaning of the historical narrative *written story* (White 1987: 4). This is not merely a formal difference; the historian's plot gives events their moral significance. A history is a cultural form which imposes a structure of moral meaning on the bare chronicle of events. Unlike Aristotle, who believed only poetic narratives could make a moral claim on their listeners, White argues that history too, when told as a story (as distinct from the annals of medieval times which were sheer chronology) is a poetic structure around which particular events can be charged with moral significance and which provides culture with certain moral lessons. Even "true stories" from this point of view are fictions because they pretend to a coherence and integrity missing in life (Herrnstein-Smith 1978).

Literary theorists especially object to the notion that experience is "closed off" the way time is in a narrative. Narrative theorists have not only argued that different narrators will tell different narratives about the "same" set of events but that narratives simply are not representative of experience at all. Louis Mink, for instance, argues that the bounded character of narrated events is an artifice derived from the telling of the narrative itself, not from the events it relates (1987). Seymour Chatman is even more emphatic that endings belong only to narrative events, not to life. The notions of "beginning," "middle," and "end" apply to story-events as imitated, rather than to real actions themselves, simply because such terms are meaningless in the real world (1978: 47). These critics believe that what allows narrative to help us "make sense" of our experience is precisely this structure of beginning, middle, and end but that such sense-making, whether the content is purportedly "true" or not, is an "explanatory fiction." We have a need for endings, Frank Kermode tells us, but these are myths, fictional patterns imposed on historical time. Narratives give us various fictions of the end, though "the end is like infinity plus one and imaginary numbers in mathematics, something we know does not exist but which helps us to make sense of and to move in the world" (Kermode 1966: 37).

Literary theorists influenced by structuralist (including deconstructive) and poststructuralist traditions make an even stronger case for the separation of narrative from lived experience. Their claim is that narrative is not in any important sense concerned with time at all while lived experience is. In dividing narratives along a diachronic axis and a synchronic axis and favoring the latter as providing the deep (i.e. "real") meaning of the narrative, they dismiss time (and experience) altogether. Roland Barthes (1975a) closely follows Lévi-Strauss in declaring that in narrative, chronological succession is "absorbed" into an atemporal configuration. And Vladimir Propp (1968), the Russian folklorist who so influenced the French formalist perspective, uses a mathematical metaphor in his analysis of folktales, treating the various elements of the tale as "functions" which can be restructured temporally in any number of ways to produce different meanings.

2   Lived experience lacks an authoritative point of view

When narrative theorists describe narrative as something told rather than lived, they especially have in mind the role of the narrator. Narratives, as told, rely on a disparity among points of view. At the simplest level, narrative incorporates three different perspectives: the characters, the audience, and the narrator. Among these, the narrator has the authoritative voice (Scholes and Kellogg 1966). This narrator may be represented as a main character from a later perspective, as in the first person story. Or, she may be represented as a witness who took no real part in the action. Or, she may be the teller of someone else's tale, as in third person narrative. In a written text, the narrator is distinguished from the author, or, more accurately, the "implied author" (Booth 1974; Chatman 1978) that is, the "scribe" who is implied by the text which has been created, the one the reader must infer from the text itself. Many written texts offer multiple perspectives embodied in an implied author, a narrator, and each of the characters. In oral tales, narrator and author are merged but the narrator's perspective is distinct from any character in the story.

Unlike the characters and (possibly) the audience, the narrator knows the ending. From his retrospective perspective, he is able to select the relevant events and reveal their causal relations because he knows how events unfolded to bring about the particular ending which, narratively speaking, gives meaning to those events. Stories, as Ricoeur says, are read backwards. Narratives are teleological structures. They are ordered around an ending and it is the ending which has a fundamental role in shaping the meaning of the narrated events (Olafson 1979; Ricoeur 1984). The narrator begins at the end in his organization of the story though he is likely to tell it, more or less, from the beginning, creating Barthes' "chronological illusion." Events may just seem to naturally unfold in a narrative as though they "told themselves" as White (1987) has noted, but this is pure deception. The story's structure exists because the narrator knows where to start, knows what to include and exclude, knows how to weight and evaluate and connect the events he recounts, all because he knows where he will stop.

The characters act from their limited perspective, unable to read the eventual meaning that their actions and experiences will take on. The narrator or implied author, who knows what happens, tells the story teasingly, suspensefully hiding and revealing the meaning of actions by giving the audience clues and foreshadowings of what is to come. Even a familiar audience who know the ending as well as the narrator may, if caught up again by the story, adopt a certain breathless questioning. Following a story involves a continual "and what then? and what then?" puzzling, as Ricoeur (1976, 1978) points out. In this puzzlement, the audience share with the characters a stance of openness toward the future which stretches before them unknown and still potentially shapeable.

The narrator is, in an important sense, outside the story, even in a first person account (Chatman 1978). Narrative drama is heightened through disparity between the narrator's point of view and that of any character. Narratives are built on a difference of understanding. Even the morally certain tale, the one where there is a definite "truth" to be known, is "ineluctably ironical" because there always exists an inequality of knowledge (Scholes and Kellogg 1966: 240). Because the narrator and, therefore (to a controlled extent) the audience, always has a superior understanding of unfolding events, stories remind us of the ignorance of the actor. Any narrative contains a tacit reminder of the fallibility of action and perception, the potential fruitlessness of earnest gestures. Since narratives are always about surprises, this heightens their ironic character. Narrator and audience are positioned to anticipate unexpected passes which are completely beyond the awareness of the characters. The hearer of a tale, unlike the actor in the midst of things, is made keenly aware of the miscalculations of action.

The gap between lived experience and storytelling is further widened because to "know" something in these two different situations is to know in a very different way. The cognitive act of remembering is different than that of apprehending in the moment. While even direct apprehension is, of course, not so direct, requiring much conceptualizing and imagining, remembering is distinguished in literary theory (and in philosophy) from directly experiencing because it is a purely conceptual act (Chatman 1978) – an act of imagination. If imagination is defined, following Sartre and others, as making present what is absent (Kearney 1988; Arendt 1971) it is clear that remembering relies completely on this imaginative capacity. While the characters in the story are perceiving the story-world, apprehending and responding (in part) to what is in front of them, the narrator who is no longer (or never was) in the story-world sees that world in a very different sense. The narrator is imagining this world rather than perceiving it. So, too, of course, is the audience.

This is an informed imagination. The narrator makes present what is absent in an authoritative way. Narrators acquire authority through a number of different literary devices, depending upon the genre. For instance, in the traditional epic, the narrator's authority comes from tradition. In history (beginning with the classical Greek histories), the narrator gains authority as an investigator, a kind of detective of truth who goes out and amasses the evidence. "He examines the past with an eye toward separating out actuality from myth" (Scholes and Kellogg 1966: 242). A quite different source of authority is the "eye-witness." This is the authority accruing to the first person tale.[1]

In the world of fictional narrative, narrators often not only know the future (how things turned out after all) but also what is in the minds of various characters. In first person narratives which now figure prominently in medical anthropology and are central to my own study, narrators do not have the same sure access into the inner recesses of other characters as they do in most fictional, mythical, or historical works. However, even in personal accounts, a backward glance is often guided by a much surer understanding of other actors than the glance which guided action in the first place. Motives hidden or misinterpreted while in the midst of action are often depicted in the story as they are later uncovered. In fact, discoveries of interpretive mistakes are a key topic of narrative. When occupational therapists told stories, they often noted such errors. "At the time John was so annoyed with me, I thought it was because he was just exhausted," they might say in one of their patient stories, "but later one of the nurses told me that his discharge date had been postponed." These declarations of the actor's fallibility reinforce the view that life-as-lived does not proceed with the clarity afforded the retrospective witness.

3   Representation is beside the point: narrative meaning lies elsewhere

The final broad critique of a mimetic position is not a commentary on experience, *per se*, but on narrative itself. Put simply, the presumption is that referential meaning is irrelevant. Or, that if narrative has a reference, it is not some set of prior experiences and events. This indifference to the referential question is taken up by two very disparate camps – structuralists and performance-centered theorists. The (largely) French structuralist tradition has been the preeminent force in effecting a separation between lived experience and narrative. From structuralist perspectives, the meaning of a narrative is within the text or between texts, intertextual, not some world "out there." Since narrative meaning can only be located within structures of discourse, narrative is more usefully defined as a "way of speaking" than a "form of representation," as Hayden White notes (1987: 2). Meaning becomes an increasingly grammatical affair.

Narratologists, particularly Roland Barthes, have been heavily influenced by Lévi-Strauss' (1962, 1963, 1969) study of myth and by the Saussurian framework Lévi-Strauss employed in his analysis. The attempt to uncover a pure consistent form underlying the multiple versions of narratives was prompted both by Russian formalists and by Lévi-Strauss' innovative study of myths. A major underlying assumption in structuralist studies of narrative is that meaning lies in relations among elements, not in their isolation – or in any direct reference to a world. This is an elaboration of de Saussure's (1959) study of the "sign" applied to larger textual works. Lévi-Strauss helped fuel an interest in applying linguistic theory to larger textual units such as narrative.

Structuralism divides narratives from experience by promoting a focus on textual meaning which can be defined linguistically rather than by reference to cultural and personal experiences existing outside a textual universe. This semiotic concept of meaning creates a way for literary theorists and anthropologists to analyze more complex textual and cultural wholes as systems of connection and especially of contrast

(Leach 1976: 13). Lévi-Strauss' study of myth follows Saussure's semiological assumptions. For Lévi-Strauss, a single myth is a construction of relations among elements. These elements, the "mythemes," are themselves bundles of relations that exist apart from their use in any given myth.

For all practical purposes, time disappears in structuralist accounts. This, more than anything, inseparably divides lived experience from narrative. Within a semiological framework, the true meaning of narrative can only be discovered by separating the narrative into a sequential (time-bound) structure and one governed by deeper, atemporal structures. Time, even time represented intratextually, is a surface mask which must be uncovered if the deep meaning of the story is to emerge. Narrative discourse, properly analyzed, retreats farther and farther from the domain of temporal existence, from historicity. Not only is time in narrative discourse disconnected from any phenomenological life-in-time, it even serves as a kind of surface fluff which must be discarded. This structural lesson is played out in the distinction between the syntagmatic and paradigmatic axes, a division which also originates in Saussure. This dichotomy reinforces the comparative unimportance of the syntagmatic as against the paradigmatic. In narratology the syntagmatic is associated with the chronology of the "story," a simple diachronic structure of movement through time.[2]

Syntagmatic relations are linear, corresponding to the linear feature of discourse and to its temporalness, its diachronic character. Each mytheme in the syntagmatic relation takes its meaning from an opposition to the elements which precede and follow it. Syntagmatic relations are like the melody, Lévi-Strauss tells us. Paradigmatic relations, by contrast, are synchronic, linking mythemes to intertextual sets which include elements outside the particular given myth. Reading a myth (in the structural sense) is like reading an orchestra score. "An orchestra score, to be meaningful, must be read diachronically along one axis – that is, page after page, and from left to right – and synchronically along the other axis, all the notes written vertically making up one gross constituent unit, one bundle of relations" (Lévi-Strauss 1963: 212).

To *tell* the myth, to recognize its storyline, Lévi-Strauss (1963) remarks, we need only recognize the syntagmatic relationship; to *understand* the myth we must read it paradigmatically. Paradigmatic or vertical relations get at the "deeper" (unconscious) layer of meaning by recognizing mythemes and whole myths as part of a single system. These vertical relations form associative groups of elements which look different in their content but actually "carry the same message," Lévi-Strauss argues. Particular narratives are, in this view, merely structural transformations of one another – a reordering of odds and ends in yet another attempt to answer some logical problem. Mythic narratives are the result of cultural bricolage.

Semiological analyses of narrative are careful to disconnect narrative meaning from human experience, at least any particular human's experience. Again, Lévi-Strauss' analysis of myth serves as a paradigm for this analytic assumption. For Lévi-Strauss, of course, the principles of mythological thought, like linguistic rules, are not used at the conscious level, and so have little to do with concrete, felt human experience. Rather meaning is only to be located in the combination of elements which are part of the structural underpinning of the storyline like the grammar which underscores discourse. To adopt Lévi-Strauss' orchestral analogy, for semiologists it is in the harmony rather than in the melody that the heart of the music lies.

This rejection of experience takes on a more radical tone in post-modernism. Narrative, so important in much contemporary anthropology, has been a form (in Western societies at least) concerned with notions disfavored in literature's postmodernism: the self, the experience of time, the need for aesthetic expression of an inner domain of thoughts and feelings. As defined by its major thinkers (especially Lyotard, Kristeva, Calvino, Jameson) and figures of central influence to the movement (Derrida, Lacan, Foucault, Barthes), postmodernism rejects belief in the self, speaking of the "death of the subject."[3] With this has died the "idealist" belief in the project of human imagination and its capacity to shape history (Kearney 1988). The idea that aesthetic expressions give voice to experience is to be discarded because it presumes an inner life which must be given public voice. Contemporary theory has "been committed to the mission of criticizing and discrediting this very hermeneutic model of the inside and the outside" (Jameson 1991: 12). Calvino pronounces that the "notion of man as the subject of history is finished" (in Kearney 1988: 172). Postmodern thinking is resonant with an earlier structuralism in treating human subjectivity and creativity as a romantic illusion (Lacan 1977). Stories speak through me; I do not speak through my stories. Postmodernism speaks a language in some ways reminiscent of Lévi-Straussian structuralism. Synchronicity is favored over a diachronic rendering of human existence. While narratives are essential, they are "discontinuous" and "episodic," fractured rather than unified or progressive. Postmodernists announce the "disappearance" of time itself. Jameson speaks of the weakening of a notion of historicity, a new valorization of surfaces, a "new depthlessness" as he says (1991: 6).

Among performative theorists, the argument is distinctively different.

Experience is indeed important and, in fact, is constitutive of narrative meaning, but this is not the experience to which a narrative refers. What matters instead is the experience and action created by telling the story. What the story "does," to paraphrase Austin. The "formal" properties of the narrative are not internal to the text, or even its intratextual relations, but to the performance itself (Herrnstein-Smith, 1980). In anthropology, interest in performance-centered analyses of narrative as speech act have grown out of earlier work in folklore and the "ethnography of communication." A focus on performance, declares Schieffelin, means a movement away from attention to "structures of representation" and toward attention to "processes of practice" (1996: 59).

Performance-centered approaches offer their own arguments for rejecting any representational view of narrative. They point out the validity problems raised by many others which cast doubt not only on informants but on the ethnographer (as storyteller) herself. But, they also attend to narrative as a performance which makes a certain meta-communicative request of the listener; namely to suspend disbelief (Atkinson 1990: 117).

The basic argument is that what really matters in getting at narrative meaning is the event of narration, because how a story is narrated and how it is understood depends upon who is listening and other relevant features of the context of narration (Bruner 1984; Bruner and Gorfain 1984; Bauman 1977, 1986; Hymes 1972; Myerhoff 1986). Narrative meaning is not something which belongs to the narrator so much as something which is co-constructed in a social interaction (for example, an interview) between speaker and listener (Riessman 1990; Mishler 1984; Atkinson 1990; Fisher and Todd 1983; Crapanzano 1980; Dwyer 1979). It emerges out of a social encounter which may prove to be quite powerful, and mutually seductive, as in some psychoanalytic and ethnographic encounters (Ortiz 1985). "For it is clear," writes one psychoanalytic commentator, "that stories or narrative are somehow jointly produced, and not by the patient alone, as it might appear on first glance; but between patient and therapist through a subtle and elusive interaction of the two" (Wyatt 1986: 195). Thus, storytelling is inevitably "dialogic narration" (Bruner and Gorfain 1984: 73) and what may appear as an autonomous text is better understood as a "social transaction" (Herrnstein-Smith 1980: 232).

The narrative structure of action and experience

Even if performance-minded scholars are right to focus on the contextual features which give a story its particular meaning, or more basically, which control the way a story is created, are they prepared to abandon all notions of referential meaning? Does it matter that storytellers and their audiences often believe the story is *about* something which happened to someone? If the content of the story influences the meaning, we are still left with the problem of reference. Given the distortions of lived experience which narratives (as texts and as performances) introduce, in what sense can we claim that narratives are *about* experience? Is there any sense in which life-in-time is more than sequence? And is there any sense in which we, as actors, adopt the point of view of the narrator, reading our actions backwards from an ending which we somehow know? In what sense (if any) is the structure of actions within a narrative analogous to the structure of actions carried out in the "real world"?

The opposition between narrative and experience registers sensibly only by positing a false notion of what prior events are and how they are structured. If lived experience is treated as more structurally complex than brute chronology – one thing just happening to come after another – then this necessarily lessens and muddies the division between the two. Whatever it is that narrative discourse represents, it is not brute chronology. Literary theorists, historians, sociolinguists, and others whose primary concerns are written and oral texts have not investigated the structure of lived experience and thus the distinctions between life and art rest on far too simple a view of how life-in-time is experienced. In the case of narrative fiction, this may not matter. But if we are speaking of "true" narratives, ones that purport to be about actual experience, then the distinction throws a false light on the nature of experience.

Anthropologists have also been a bit too exuberant in noticing that (field) experience can never be adequately captured in any written discourse. Recognizing this inevitable gap does not necessitate adopting the position that experience itself is a prelinguistic bombardment of the senses or that the only meaning available to the actor is pregiven in cultural scripts and rules. What is needed is a theory of emergent meaning that does the following: (a) recognizes the place of cultural scripts but also the importance of immediate contexts; (b) acknowledges the powerful role of discourse in shaping meaning, but also attends to non-linguistic action; (c) accounts not only for the public meanings shared by a cultural group but offers a means for interpreting private meanings, the "inner landscape" of an individual's motives, desires, beliefs, emotions.

There are, in fact, occasional moments of doubt in the minds of those narrative theorists who so strongly want to separate narrative from experience. On the one hand, there is the modern and postmodern yearning to liberate narrative from its role as imitation of action, events, experience. On the other hand, this release from imitation also seems to spell the end of narrative itself. The ambivalence is eloquently marked by Genette: "It is as if literature had exhausted or overflowed the resources of its representative mode, and wanted to fold back into the indefinite murmur of its own discourse. Perhaps narrative . . . is already for us, a thing of the past, which we must hurry to consider as it retreats, before it has completely disappeared from our horizon" (1982: 143). Abandonment of all referential concerns implies an abandonment of narrative itself. E. M. Forster admits, almost parenthetically, that life is in fact experienced as more than mere sequence. Life is "measured not by minutes or hours, but by intensity, so that when we look at our past it does not stretch back evenly but piles up into a few notable pinnacles, and when we look at the future it seems sometimes a wall, sometimes a cloud, sometimes a sun, but never a chronological chart" (1927: 28).

If our experience of passing time, of its movement, does not stretch along evenly, but piles up, quickens, condenses, opens onto clouds or suns, this suggests a much more complex reading of the shape of life experience, one which brings it closer to a narrative structured by plot. There are also hints of an interest in looking again at the question of reference among a few anthropologists and folklorists who reject naive realism but admit difficulties in completely abandoning the view that life is (at least sometimes) like a story.

I follow Aristotle's insight that narratives and experiences are deeply intertwined but I ascribe a very different cause to this close connection. Aristotle argued that narratives imitate life not in the sense of literally copying it, but through the poetic capacity to turn the noise and incidentalness of everyday life into a compacted causal argument (a plot) in which one thing after another was transformed into one thing because of another. This poetic extraction of events from their immersion in the everyday was an imitation which involved a kind of clearing away of the accidental and contingent to reveal an underlying or deeper "logic" that uncovered life as it truly was. For Aristotle, appearance served as a kind of mask, a camouflage, and narrative provided the poetic means for clearing the path obscured by the sheer multitude and triviality of historical events.

I contend, instead, that narrative imitates experience because experience already has in it the seeds of narrative. Further, the narrative structure of action and experience emerges in large part because actors have a need for narrative. In turning to the world of occupational therapy, I will argue that therapists are continually engaged in deciphering the actions of others. This latter task makes them, in an important sense, readers of unfolding stories not of their own making.

Not only do they have motives which guide their actions, plots of their own, they also are constantly reading the actions of others, particularly their clients, trying to discern what motivates the behavior they can outwardly see. They try to "find the story" which makes sense of what they observe. To understand what someone is doing is to posit a larger story of which any particular action is but an episode. Action is only comprehensible as part of larger narrative contexts as MacIntyre (1980, 1981) has argued. To understand the actions of another, therapists struggle to identify those narrative contexts which render the particular actions they observe in others meaningful.

Furthermore, therapists and their clients have a practical interest in constructing an "untold story" out of discrete episodes. They have a need not only to make sense, as Goffman (1974) says, but to create sense out of situations, and a fundamental way they create sense is by shaping the next-next character of on-going action into a coherent narrative structure with a beginning, middle, and end. The interest in coherence and order is only one motive for attempting to play out a situation in such a way that a narrative (a desirable one, the right kind of one) can be told. Therapists require their actions to be not only intelligible but to get them somewhere. They act because they intend to get something done, to begin something, which they hope will lead us along a desirable route. They suffer because it so often does not. And they act, with what Kermode (1966) calls the "sense of an ending." Because they care about that ending, they try to direct their actions and the actions of relevant others in ways that will bring about the proper ending. They try to make actions cumulative (Olafson 1979). Put narratively, they try to take the episodes of action and structure them into a coherent plot.

A plot gives unity to an otherwise meaningless succession of one thing after another. Quite simply, "emplotment is the operation that draws a configuration out of a simple succession" (Ricoeur 1984: 65). What we call a story is just this rendering and ordering of a succession of events into parts which belong to a larger narrative whole. Particular actions then take their meaning by belonging to, and contributing to, the story as a whole. To have a story at all is to have made a whole out of a succession of actions. This "making a whole" is also making meaning such that we can ask what the point or thought or moral of the story is (White 1980, 1987; Ricoeur 1984). Narratives give meaningful structure to life through time. To borrow from Ricoeur's argument, action can be understood as an as yet untold story. Or, in his provocative phrase, "action is in quest of a narrative" (1984: 74).

Contrary to Aristotle and later literary theorists, history as lived experience is not formless succession. Life is not experienced as one thing after another because actors work to create a story-like quality to their actions. Being an actor at all means trying to make certain things happen, to bring about desirable endings, to search for possibilities that lead in hopeful directions. Even if most of experience is suffering, as Arendt (1958) tells us, because our actions are taken up, reworked, and redirected by the responses of other actors, we still have some success some of the time in working toward endings we care about. And sometimes we are even able to negotiate with other actors so that we can move in directions cooperatively, cumulatively. Formlessness is not so much a description of the structure of everyday life as a depiction of despair. The essence of meaninglessness is when lived experience seems to be driven by no form other than brute sequence. In the following chapters, I elaborate these abstract claims in ethnographic context.

3   The checkers game: clinical actions in quest of a narrative

Upon arriving in the highlands of Burma or the sad tropics of Brazil, one expects to have an adventure. Even if one will be creating vast, indecipherable kinship charts, even then, one can hope for pleasures and dangers of an unimagined variety. But these were not places I was going. It was late summer, 1986, and I was returning to Boston, a city I had known for more than ten years, well loved and very familiar. I was not studying ghost dances in Bali, shamanic healing in Nepal, headhunting in New Guinea, or sexuality in the Trobriand Islands. Rather, I was setting off to study women therapists in a hospital in Boston. Middle class, white, suburban fed. Not women I had ever been interested in. In fact, not women I knew anything about. Occupational therapists. Who were they? For me, this was a job, which was almost the whole point. The strong spark of interest I felt was primarily at the salary (steady income) and the hope that I would be able to carry out an ethnographic study of my own design. There was the odd fact that this profession had the idea of funding an ethnographic study of its clinical reasoning and had sought me out to conduct it. It is not often a group wants to hire an anthropologist to come and study them. I was intrigued.

Once in Boston, my first research task was to find the proper clinical site. I wanted to spend my time in one hospital so that my study of individual therapists and their thinking was contextually placed. I knew perfectly well that no practitioner reasons in a social vacuum or with only the client's needs in mind. Thus, I wanted to understand how the professional and organizational cultures played a part in shaping the way individual therapists, in their treatment of patients, decided what the problem was and what their role was in solving it. My plan was to live and work among a group of staff therapists for two years, observing clinical interactions, interviewing therapists about what they were doing, videotaping sessions, attending staff meetings, going to lunch, getting invited to parties and, in general, inserting myself in any way possible into the lives of my interlocutors. In other words, I had the usual plan to carry out an ethnographic study.

48

My idea for the perfect site included one with a number of experienced therapists, including some with a reputation for excellence in the occupational therapy community. My funders (the American Occupational Therapy Association and the American Occupational Therapy Foundation) also strongly recommended that I study expert therapists. Quite naturally, they wanted any study of clinical thinking to reflect competent rather than inept or novice practice. This suited me as well because I knew that experienced practitioners tended to be less guarded in their responses to interview questions and more comfortable in admitting to thoughts and actions that might be less than canonical, from the standpoint of the professional community.

As I saw it, a perfect site would be a friendly one. I wanted to find a group of therapists who were actually interested in participating, who were themselves intrigued with the idea of investigating their own practice and not, on the whole, terribly defensive about their work. I wanted talkative, open and interesting interlocutors, ones who were not too afraid of the hospital hierarchy, not too worried that if they said the wrong thing it could cost them their jobs. My previous ethnographic research with World Bank professionals had taught me the tremendous difficulty of studying practitioners who felt they were working in a hostile climate. Thus, I was also looking for a hospital environment that did not, by and large, terrorize its staff.

I began my search with virtually no idea of what occupational therapists actually did. My initial presumption (weren't they some sort of vocational counselors?) was quickly dispelled by my efforts to read up on them in occupational therapy journals. This reading did little to clarify things. While I began to have an idea of what they were not, I couldn't quite grasp what they were. Mostly they treated clients with physical disabilities but this treatment was evidently not confined to the physical body. They treated the "whole person," they wrote of themselves. (What could that possibly mean?) They were concerned with helping persons with disabilities adjust to the "real world," with helping people relearn "skills of daily living" (what were these?) so that the disabled could continue, as far as possible, to function in their chosen occupations. Such occupations included, I discovered, not only work but leisure activities. They included, as far as I could tell, anything at all that people do, even things one forgets people do, like turning on a light switch or tying shoes.

My floundering was not helped by my general ignorance of the clinical world. I had never studied a medical profession, never had much liking for hospitals. As I began to explore Boston hospitals, I suddenly found myself spending whole days trying to find my way down endless hospital corridors with the aid of colored lines (red, blue, yellow) painted on the floors. I noticed two things. Like the World Bank where I had just been working, I was always having to sign in and out at the entrance, as instructed by guards. I wondered what their top secrets were, so that they had to keep such track of things. Also, I was surprised by the lack of men. I had been deceived by television shows and folk wisdom into supposing that hospitals were full of doctors; male doctors. Instead, physicians of any gender were in scarce supply; those one did see were always rushing by. Instead, some more ancient scheme prevailed: women of lower status tending the old and sick.

In those early days, there were times when occupational therapists seemed familiar to me, like my female cousins from Akron, Ohio. But then I would lose sight of them again. Whatever else, this was not life in *McCall's* or *Cosmopolitan*. And who were these mysterious people, the very ill? Ostensibly they were from my own culture but they struck me as far more foreign than the Bengali officials I had once interviewed in the airless offices of Calcutta or the Kenyan film crew I had trooped around with, trying to capture life in urban squatter settlements outside Mombasa and Nairobi.

While growing more puzzled, I finally settled on a large teaching hospital as my research site. It served a wide variety of clients, including many from the inner city. For two years, I followed a group of fifteen occupational therapists (all women) as they treated their patients, sometimes videotaping them, sometimes interviewing them about the sessions, more rarely interviewing the patients as well. I spent time in acute neurology, in two out-patient clinics, one for patients with hand injuries, another for very young pediatric patients with disabilities, in a spinal cord unit, in a rehabilitation unit for respiratory patients, and in a psychiatric ward. I sat in on clinical sessions and staff meetings of every sort. I also went to lunch with therapists, "overheard" conversations in hallways, elevators, waiting rooms and cafeterias. I made friends with some therapists, both those whose practice I studied and those who became collaborators in the research. Like many professions (including anthropology), occupational therapy provides a powerful social world, a close-knit community which binds people far beyond their commitments as co-workers. I accumulated, as one does, thousands of pages of field notes as well as transcriptions of interviews and of some of the videotaped sessions. I did not collect or interpret this data alone, but developed a research team consisting of myself and a group of occupational therapists.[1]

My gradual discovery of these therapists and their powers was, in part, the discovery of women in a woman's world. Over 95 per cent of

occupational therapists are female and it was two years before I observed
a male clinician. This world contained all those excruciatingly familiar
female items, baby showers, diet books, sales in Filene's basement, but
other things too, brave female capacities I had never noticed went hand
in hand with the new kitchen tiles. Most of all, it contained dirt, in Mary
Douglas' (1966) sense. The cheerful willingness to live in a polluted
land. More than that, a fierceness to become intimate with those with
"spoiled identities," in Goffman's (1963) important phrase. This fierceness did not always translate into wisdom. These women were not
always Goffman's "wise persons." They had their own ideas about what
a good patient should do, should endure, should dream about for their
future. They could get quite annoyed when their notions were resisted.
Sometimes they talked to patients as if they were very young children,
dismissed them, pushed them away in irritation or incomprehension.
And yet, I could not brush aside these women, or the femaleness of their
concerns with the details of everyday life: making toast, buttoning
buttons, combing hair. The very same items that had so engrossed the
adult women of my childhood – keeping your room clean, keeping your
voice down – this stultifying world of manners and chores was transformed in front of my eyes into a domain of deep significance. It is one
thing to rail against taking a bath as a child; it is quite another thing, as
an adult, to find oneself suddenly forced to be bathed by others.

Therapists are rather an odd lot in the specialized world of the clinic,
for occupational therapists address an almost limitless range of dysfunctional problems which can arise with disability. They define their task as
helping persons regain function, as far as possible, in the major occupations of their life, including work, play and what they call "activities of
daily living," meaning self-care skills.

There is a certain fluidity in this practice from the ridiculous to the
sublime, from the trivial to the essential, as therapists shift from playing
endless games of checkers with spinal cord patients or teaching cardiac
patients to cross-stitch, to engaging patients in intense discussions about
why they shouldn't just give up and die. And, more strangely still, often
the most profound discussions interweave, even appear to depend upon,
the homely "treatment modality" of turning magazine pages with a
mouthstick or taking a trial run maneuver in and out of the hospital gift
shop with the new wheelchair. The most mundane acts, putting socks
on, eating spaghetti with an adaptive fork, easily become invested with
symbolic meanings. I witnessed many a backgammon game in the spinal
cord unit, for instance, in which winning the game by "going home"
came to have multiple meanings.

Fleming (1994) has called occupational therapy a "common sense practice in an uncommon world." Within the non-ordinary world of the clinic, therapists ask patients to engage in a range of humdrum daily activities that characterize commonsense life outside the clinic. They traffic in the habitual, the tacit knowledge of the able-bodied who heedlessly open doors, take showers, and turn on their computers. The haphazard holism of the profession is reflected in the equipment therapists call upon to carry out their treatment. Occupational therapy treatment rooms contain tables with mats and plinths (for relearning sitting balance and other body training), wheelchairs, splints of all sizes and shapes, and a hodgepodge of non-clinical looking paraphernalia which belong to adaptive kitchens and adaptive bathrooms, as well as closets stuffed with games and arts and crafts materials.

Although therapists do not always start out to do so, they very often end up negotiating with patients about what dysfunctional problems therapy will address in terms of the very deepest issues of how a patient's life story will be remade to accommodate a new body. (Will a therapeutic goal be relearning handwriting in order to continue one's law practice? Or, adapting one's golf clubs and relearning golf in order to discontinue one's law practice and retire early to Florida?) Chronic illness and suffering, from a narrative perspective, often generate a narrative loss as well as physical loss as patients restructure lives in new ways to accommodate increasingly disabled bodies. Simply devising an appropriate treatment plan tends to propel the therapist into worrying about how to insert therapy in some meaningful way into a life which is in radical transition.

These women with their weekend gardenia plantings were fierce in their determination to sweep the corners free of dying where they could. Patients would return to their jobs, their wives, their toilets and bathtubs, their woodworking and law practices, their golf and kitchen chores. They were missionaries of common sense and decent morals. Armed with these, they marched into bad situations to see what could be done. My encounter with the occupational therapists plunged me into a world darker than any I had lived in, a world that seasoned therapists traversed easily, full of good practical ideas. The existential and the commonsensical traveled side by side.

This book is not an ode to housekeeping, though it has close ties to that essential phenomenological territory, the habitus. It is not even, at some level, especially about occupational therapy. I take a particular glance into the clinical world in an attempt to understand the places of narrative in healing. I use occupational therapy, the healing practice I know, as a window into issues that are deeply implicated but also go far beyond this profession. The practice of these healers, low-status, nearly invisible in the medical world, reveals much about how narrative shapes the domain of chronic illness and disability, that space where one does not get well though one may no longer be ill.

For all this occupational ordinariness, this business of everyday chores, there runs just beneath the surface of the occupational therapy session a deep narrative search for how a patient's life story should unfold in the face of debilitating illness. In the case that follows, I explore this narrative undercurrent as it evinces itself in a small snippet of interaction between a therapist and two spinal cord patients. The segment, transcribed from a videotape, covers about twenty minutes of a treatment session in which the therapist and patients organize to play a checkers game. This is the most humdrum of sessions. No healing drama, no therapeutic transformation, is anywhere in sight. And yet, watching sessions like these began to give me the idea that there was more happening in this therapeutic work than meets the eye and that this "more" involved the quest for a recovery narrative which therapist and patient could both embrace. I observed this particular session one March afternoon in 1987 a few months into my first ethnographic study. A research assistant videotaped the session.

In introducing this slice of everyday therapeutic practice, I mean to address some of the difficult questions raised in the previous chapter. In what sense can we claim that narratives are *about* action and experience? Is there any sense in which life-in-time is more than sequence? And is there any sense in which we, as actors, adopt the point of view of the narrator, reading our actions backwards from an ending which we somehow know? In what sense (if any) is the structure of actions within a narrative analogous to the structure of actions carried out in the "real world?"

The checkers game

Lin, a therapist and one of her patients, John, are talking together in one corner of the spinal cord therapy room, a large square area lined with mats, mirrors, and parallel bars on one side for the physical therapists, tables and adaptive equipment for occupational therapy on the other. This is one of the homier spots in the hospital. A dozen to fifteen patients are doing different activities in this room, all in electric wheelchairs driven more or less expertly. Windows line two sides. The view isn't much, but it helps give the whole place the feeling of a functional gym, undermining the hushed hospital tone so prevalent throughout many units. Therapists and nurses move through the room, stopping to say a few words to patients, calling out to one another as they pass by.

Along one wall, shelves are lined with that peculiar collection of adaptive apparatus found in any occupational therapy setting. Among these mouthsticks, reachers and splints are also shelves with games, mostly worn editions of checkers and backgammon. Scattered throughout the room are complex machines, what look to be adapted versions of gym equipment, metallic structures full of pulleys and chains and bars to pull on. Small groups of patients form and disperse as they drive over to one another to socialize.

Lin, the therapist, calls over to Mat, an eighteen-year-old handsome Irish boy, who wheels into the camera's view. Together with two research assistants, I have spent several months observing and video-taping sessions in this ward. Today Lin has the idea to treat both Mat and John in a single session, having them play a checkers game. Lin is trying to recruit Mat to this activity. She broaches this subject with them both.

LIN: (to Mat) OK, you wanna come over here, Mr. Reilly?
MAT: Mumble (in protest) Ah, ahm, ahm, why?
LIN: Just so you can chat with us while we do this. Come on over. Hello, there. Oh, he's a smart driver (proudly, to Mat). Do you have a license? (she laughs) Do you have a driver's license?
MAT: Should get one.
Mat pulls alongside Lin and John. They all pose for camera, giving silly grins. Mat waves. Lin then turns to face the two men, ignoring the camera.
LIN: (to both) I'll tell you what I was thinking, and let me know what you think. Ah (to John) do you have anything else scheduled for this afternoon?
JOHN: I was gonna go see my hair stylist, but . . .
LIN: (laughs) What time's your appointment? (challenging voice, with teasing mixed in)
JOHN: 2:30.
LIN: (startled, slightly uncertain) Do you really?
JOHN: No. (grins)
LIN: (laughs) Oh, God. Um, I thought it may be fun if you guys played a game of checkers (question intonation) or something, where I'd have you (turns to John) do it with a mouthstick . . . and have you (now turning to Mat) do it with your splint.
JOHN: Move the pieces?
MAT: Sure. How are we going to jump each other?
LIN: (gives him a look) Wise guy. (laughs) Well that's what I'm here for. I'll help out with that. But John has a pincer mouthstick that might work out for that too. So, we could try that. OK? (John shrugs OK)

Having secured their unenthusiastic permission, she returns to physically manipulating John's right hand. This manipulation, known as passive range of motion, is done to prevent stiffness and swelling in his hands. For John, who will almost certainly never have any capacity to use them again, it is largely a cosmetic exercise. Lin continues her conversation with the two men in the desultory mocking way characteristic of talk on the spinal cord unit.

The sheer physical stillness of the men's bodies, nearly inert in their chairs, seems to provoke this style of interchange, as though nothing on earth really needed to get done, as though this were an afternoon of beer drinking in the backyard. It is a style of muted desire, of anger turned into an informal omnipresent derision, of extreme truth-telling in the jocular mode. One gets the distinct impression that people are hanging about, lolling in their chairs, because they have chosen a different tack on life. They have recognized the futility of aggressive acts and are relaxing in their chosen spot. It is an air reminiscent of a neighborhood bar on weekday down time, comfortably settled by the unemployed regulars. Lin, John, and Mat are careful to preserve this atmosphere in their conversation. However, Lin's eyes and the energy of her manner belie her nonchalant style, revealing her determination to organize things, move things along. Lin inquires how these two men are doing, deploying the correct bantering tone.

LIN: How are you guys today?
MAT: I'm wonderful.
LIN: Are you? Mahvelous?
MAT: Yeah, he took a shower.
LIN: To get all spiffed up.
JOHN: I took a shower.

Lin leaves to talk to someone. Only Mat and John are within the camera's gaze. Mat asks, "Are we still on?" Cumba (the camera person) nods. He announces to the camera, nodding in the direction of the departed Lin, "She's going to help someone else, as good OTs do." Lin returns, realizes she is being teased, but has missed Mat's remark. "What?" she asks, looking Mat in the eye. Mat replies soberly, "I was explaining why you left." Lin grins at him, "I got tired of you." Lin preserves her bantering tone but raises the stakes by asking a potentially sensitive question about Mat's up-coming prom.

LIN: So Mat what are you doing this weekend?
MAT: Going to a prom. Junior prom.
LIN: Gonna be in a tux?
MAT: No, just a suit.
LIN: Sherry a junior? (Sherry is Mat's girlfriend)
MAT: A senior.
LIN: So why are you going to a junior prom?
MAT: I don't know. They let us go.
LIN: (laughs) Do you want to go?
MAT: (small pause) Yeah.

This topic is casually interrupted by Lin herself who has just noticed that Mat's physical therapist has walked into the treatment room. Lin wonders aloud if the therapist has any flexibility this afternoon and could reschedule her time with Mat so that she could have a double session with John and Mat. This precipitates the following exchange.

LIN: Could you have her (the physical therapist) come over here?
MAT: I need a lift bad and pressure relief.
LIN: You need a pressure relief, huh? Alright. Well maybe she could do that and you could come back and see us. (small pause) What do you think about that?
MAT: It's just ducky.
LIN: Just ducky. So you're going to that prom, huh?

This interchange reveals the ordinary negotiations common to occupational therapy encounters. Lin requests that Mat ask the therapist about this rearrangement; he responds with a request of his own, telling her he needs a pressure relief. Lin is reluctant to perform this somewhat tricky physical task that requires her to lift his upper body, a skill she is not confident about. She counters by suggesting that perhaps Mat could then make two requests of the physical therapist. Having secured his agreement, "It's just ducky," she moves fluidly back to the delicate matter of his up-coming prom date. The talk between occupational therapists and patients often carries the ambiance of chit-chat rather than serious revelation. The quality of apparent non-seriousness is most striking when therapists initiate conversations about topics that patients are likely to find quite difficult to handle, as in the interchange that next occurs.

LIN: I asked if you were going to be in a tux, but I don't remember what your answer was.
MAT: Suit.
LIN: Suit. No monkey suit for him.
(John laughs, grins)
LIN: (to John) Do you own a monkey suit?
(John nods)
LIN: Yeah? You do? You own one?
JOHN: Of course.
LIN: (mimicking him) Of course. Like all good O'Shea's do. (teasing voice) (she is ranging his hands) Did you go to all your proms when you were a kid?
JOHN: No, I missed 'em all.
LIN: Did you really? Nobody wanted to go with you. (she laughs)
JOHN: (with small grin) I was afraid of rejection so I didn't ask anyone.
LIN: Are you really – are you serious? Kinda surprises me.
JOHN: You shoulda seen me in high school. Do you think I look young now?
LIN: You looked younger in high school? (short laugh at herself) Well, obviously, that would make sense.

JOHN: At 17, I looked about 12.
MAT: Tsk, tsk, tsk. (Lin looks at Mat, frowning) I hadda reject people.
LIN: You hadda reject people? (Lin looks at John, rolls her eyes, grins)
JOHN: High school wasn't fun.
LIN: No? My high school wasn't always fun. Mat liked high school, huh?
MAT: Yeah, up till January. (his accident)
JOHN: (short laugh) Yeah.
LIN: Something happen in January that changed your mind?
MAT: Yeah.
LIN: Yeah?
MAT: I left school for a while.
LIN: Yeah? The truant officer come get ya?
MAT: No, now my teachers come here.
LIN: (seriously, dropping all banter) That's pretty nice. Do you (John) know
    that? That his teachers come here to tutor?
JOHN: Oh, yeah.

Lin triggers another conversational turn, focusing suddenly on John's
body and the physical manipulation she had been carrying on during the
earlier conversation. She looks at John.

LIN: Your hands – what's the spasm story today?
JOHN: It must be 'cause I took a shower. (laugh) I don't know.
LIN: You're not spasming at all! (surprised intonation) (they talk about the
    physical therapist who will come over to talk with Lin about letting Mat
    double up with John)
LIN: Actually, do you (Mat) want to go over and ask her if she – no I don't
    want her to feel like I'm pressuring her. (to John) Hold on for just a sec,
    OK?
JOHN: Alright.
LIN: Chat, you guys.
MAT: (mugs at the camera) Hi, mom.
MAT: (to John) So, how was your shower?
JOHN: It was most refreshing. It's different, 'cause they have to lay me down.
MAT: I'm leaving now. I just heard the news. (he goes over to the physical
    therapist) Bye!
LIN: (to Mat on the way) OK, sport, we'll see you later. (Mat will get his physical
    therapist appointment now)

With Mat's exit from the scene, Lin proceeds to negotiate afternoon
therapy with John, and then to ask him, in a much more serious manner
than she used when Mat was present, about a training session given to
his mother and sister the day before. As they broach the touchier subject
of John's missing legs, their comportment shifts again, back to the
flippant tone characteristic of the most fragile matters.

LIN: (to John) You know what I'll do, though, I'll show you, I don't know if I've
    shown you, 'member when you played cards with that mouthstick, do you
    think that mouthstick opens wide enough to fit checker pieces?

JOHN: I can't remember.

LIN: OK. So how did your mom and sister do yesterday with the teaching?

JOHN: Good.

LIN: Yeah? Excuse me. (she moves in front of him to his other side)

JOHN: They um, last night . . .

LIN: (talks briefly to maintenance man in the clinic) Yes? (back to John) This is not even causing a spasm! Did they increase your medication?

JOHN: Yeah.

LIN: God! John! Oh! Wise guy! (he got a spasm) Much different than yesterday.

JOHN: They put me back to bed last night –

LIN: (concerning spasm) But that's not still as bad . . . (trails off) Your sister and mom did?

JOHN: Yeah. And my mother, right (he spasms), they set up the slide board, (spasms again)

LIN: (notices that her massaging seems to be causing John's spasms) I won't do it (the massage to increase passive range of motion) while you tell me. (with a laugh)

JOHN: My mother picked me right up over the slide board! (he is grinning)

LIN: (laughs)

JOHN: (whispering) She's strong.

LIN: She's strong? She didn't need to –

JOHN: Wicked strong. Yeah, she don't need it.

LIN: She didn't really need the slide board. I wonder how much you weigh now.

JOHN: Hundred.

LIN: Do you really? That's a pretty good amount of weight for you.

JOHN: (disbelieving) It is?

LIN: How much did you used to weigh?

JOHN: With or without legs? (he looks at her sideways mischievously)

LIN: With legs. (they both laugh)

JOHN: About 130.

LIN: 'Cause I think legs are more than 15 pounds a piece.

JOHN: Maybe yours are. (both laugh, she mock-slaps his hand and he whispers) Just kidding.

LIN: I know, but it's a sensitive spot for me. (they both have wide grins)

JOHN: I know. (grins)

LIN: (laughing) You do know, don't you? Like the time you told me that skirt made me look fat? Remember that?

JOHN: No *couth*, I'm sorry.

LIN: None, not a bit of it. God! (sigh)

There is no mistaking the sting in John's smile as he tells the story about his mother lifting him over the slideboard. Former bartender and drug dealer reduced again to a child in his mother's arms. Lin deflects the cruel image his story creates, turning the humor on herself. If John has too little body, Lin has too much. She encourages John to tease her about her own imperfections, even reminding him of earlier barbs he has flung her way.

The physical therapist comes over to announce that Lin can have Mat back again if she likes because, as it turns out, the mat space is taken up. Such trading-off is characteristic of the informal atmosphere of the room, and also the power relations between staff and patients. Patients can be sent here and there, only having a definite say if they are willing to protest strongly. This lack of control over their time adds to the sense of waiting that is endemic to patient life.

While Lin and John look for Mat's return, Lin asks John more about the training session with John's mother and sister. As she speaks, it becomes apparent that she was also there and thus that she has not been asking for information from John but engaging in another kind of speech act, one prevalent in therapy sessions, a reminiscing and reflecting upon events where both patient and therapist have been present. She tells a brief story about his sister, which they both laugh about. This narration of earlier hospital events is commonplace, particularly in wards like the spinal cord unit where patients may stay for several months. The present is always saturated with anecdotes from shared past therapy times.

LIN: Anyway, so your mother did well, they put you back to bed. (he nods) They seemed a little exhausted by the time they were done out here.
JOHN: Uh, huh.
LIN: How do you think they feel about learning all this care?
JOHN: Alright.
LIN: Yeah. It seems like they're feeling more confident. Your sister said something funny. We're talking about the suctioning and she said, it wasn't the suctioning she minded. (pause) Oh! it was getting the gloves on.
JOHN: Oh, yeah. (they both laugh and grin)
LIN: I thought that was pretty funny.
JOHN: Yeah, 'cause it's the way you gotta do it, keep 'em sterile . . .
LIN: Yeah, she had a hard time doing that. She had her thumb in the finger and all that.

Suctioning patients who have had tracheotomies, as John has, is a task patients hate to do for themselves, hate depending upon family members to do for them, and a task others are likely to mind as well. It is messy and frightening. Joking about the gloves is Lin's way of reassuring John that the really difficult part is not going to be such a problem. They might have said more, but Mat returns and the tone of things changes once again, as Lin accommodates to the broad humor Mat favors. Mat and Lin set off on a joking exchange that accompanies Mat's need for a pressure relief, a task ordinarily carried out by the physical therapist or nurse but left today to Lin, who happens to be available. She allows Mat to instruct her in how she is to carry out this task. A comaraderie develops as they work out together on how to handle his body. Mat instructs her to take off his lapboard and unfasten the straps that keep

him upright in the wheelchair. When she has done this, he tells her how
to bend his upper body for the pressure relief.

MAT: Lean me forward. I might spasm, so watch out, gotta be strong . . .
LIN: (stamps a foot on floor and asks with exaggerated injury) Do you doubt me?
MAT: Yeah.
LIN: Yeah.
MAT: (grinning) Never.
LIN: You're awfully trusting. Now what about if I lock the brakes first?
MAT: Oop. Forgot. Uh-oh.
LIN: Good idea . . . What? Is that a spasm?
MAT: Minor one, minor one. I'd jump out of my chair if I could, but . . .
LIN: Now what do you do with your arms when I do this? Do they get all
    mangled when you go over?
MAT: I dunno.
LIN: You don't know? Great. Ready? (lets him lean forward) Now, do I have to
    hold you here?
MAT: No, just all the way down to my knees.
LIN: Are you kidding?
MAT: Nope. Whooa, I'm gonna fall out of the chair.
LIN: Thank you. That makes me feel great. (John laughs) John, tell him how
    neurotic I am. Oh, you know how nervous I am . . . I really just let you go
    down like this? I love doing this. And I just keep . . .
MAT: You can let me go as long as I don't fall.
JOHN: (laughing) As long as I don't fall.
LIN: And if you do?
MAT: Then, ahm, I sue the hospital and (grinning at the camera person
    conspiratorially) – can you bring the camera down here?
LIN: (laughs) How long do you do this for?
MAT: About thirty seconds. Maybe forty.

Mat's body becomes an object apart from Mat himself. It emerges in
their discourse as an unwieldy but precious commodity in the elaborate
series of jokes about whether Lin will really be able to prevent him from
falling or not. "Now what do you do with your arms when I do this? Do
they get all mangled when you go over?" Lin asks. Mat replies "I
dunno." "You don't know?" she repeats in her ironic way. "Great." The
joking also reinforces a certain practical attitude toward one's new and
broken body. The brokenness becomes an irritating impediment, like a
car that has gone on the blink and must be coaxed and reasoned with to
get started. The very prosaicness of this attitude gives a certain message
about disability. Disability not as horrifying shame, not as existential
drama, but as inconvenience – something that calls for clever practical
sense rather than deep anguish.

The same attitude is carried into the next activity of the session. Lin
announces that they are to approach the set-up of the checkers board

and table as a collective task. "OK now, it's gonna take a little problem-solving to set this up." The two men band together, giving her instructions about how the chairs might work, what table would be best to use. She contributes some suggestions of her own but primarily she drops into the role of physical extension, the one body among the three that can freely move. She asks them what to do, they offer ideas, she tries to carry the ideas out, when these fail she announces the problem and solicits more ideas. In this way they eventually put together a system that will allow John to move pieces with the aid of a mouthstick, since his head is the only part of his body he can move, and Mat is given a splint so that he can, in a fumbling way, use his hands.

LIN: No one has any suggestions for me, huh?
MAT: Yeah, you should put us over on that table.
LIN: On what table? That one?
MAT: On the corner, yeah.
LIN: Well, see, that table has to be certain height, so John can do it with his mouth. But if –
MAT: That table moves. (Lin laughs)
LIN: I know but you won't be able to be facing each other. I'm thinking, if I get you a bedside table, so that you can go to one side and you can go to the other . . . Hold on a minute . . . (she leaves and Mat and John joke between themselves while awaiting her return)
LIN: (returning) Uh, what are you guys . . . ?
LIN: Well, improve number 2. Can I . . . (all three speak at once)
JOHN: Nice nail polish (she's drummed her fingers, painted bright red, on the table)
LIN: You like that? It's a little – oh, OK. (realizes he is teasing her) It's a little on the bright side.
JOHN: A little.
LIN: To match my glow-in-the dark pocketbook. (she happens to move suddenly toward his chair)
JOHN: Watch my feet!
LIN: (inadvertently looking down and then laughing) Watch your feet?! Ahmm. (looking back at the board) This is not going to work, folks. (sighs) (John laughs) C'mon, somebody, give me a suggestion. Well, Mat maybe we could try your idea?
JOHN: Katie, how about a suggestion?
LIN: (to Katie) Any ideas? No?

Though claiming she intends to set up this long awaited checkers game, Lin continues to veer off in other directions. As she dumps a pile of mouthsticks on the table to look for one that might work for John, she asks him about plans for excursions out of the hospital. He is not anxious to answer and avoids the conversation, in that usual way among spinal cord patients, by ensnaring Lin into believing he will disclose something and then offering a ridiculous answer. Lin pursues the topic anyway but she is outwitted by the combined efforts of John and Mat. She gives up goodnaturedly with a laugh and moves back to the immediate problem of situating them for the checkers game.

LIN: So, John, have you started to talk about going on a day pass yet?
MAT: Maybe next weekend.
LIN: You or John?
JOHN: Yeah, maybe next week.
LIN: Really?
JOHN: Yeah.
LIN: Wow. With who? Whom?
JOHN: What do you mean with whom? With Mat.
LIN: Will you go out with your mother and your sister?
MAT: I'm gonna do his care.
Lin laughs.
JOHN: Yeah, I'm gonna go with . . .
LIN: (interrupting) No, I meant like is a staff member going also? No? (she sets up the board) I don't think you're going to be able to reach that.

A near accident with Mat's joystick on his wheelchair precipitates another short narrative burst by Lin. Again she tells a one sentence tale of an incident all have already witnessed, the time Mat's mother accidentally hit the joystick.

LIN: Remember the first time your mother took her coat off?
MAT: Yeah.
LIN: Were you in the room? (to John)
JOHN: Uh, huh.
LIN: She took her coat off and it caught on the joystick, and (laughs) and Mat starts to *whip* around, the TV starts to go.

John grins but Mat ignores her, concentrating on the current logistical problem. She congratulates him on his capacity to figure out which table would be best to use and finally, twenty minutes after they have begun, they are nearly ready to start the game.

LIN: Look at that, Mat, you get the points for the day. Lucky I'm secure and don't feel threatened by you knowing more than me. (she looks at him, he doesn't seem to react) OK.
MAT: (then, in dry humor) I'm not after your job.
LIN: I don't think so, either. I don't blame you. OK, how's that?
MAT: Close enough.
LIN: Hmm?
MAT: A little bit closer.
LIN: I'll pick up this hand here, you pick up the other one . . . What do you think?
MAT: It's good.

LIN: OK. Now, John, this is my question to you. Is this one going to work? (referring to the mouthstick she has given him)

JOHN: Ahh . . . (he considers but trails off as Lin interrupts)

LIN: I'll tell you what . . .

MAT: (interrupts Lin) See if you can touch me (unclear) spot 31. (on the checkerboard)

LIN: Can you reach here?

JOHN: Ahh . . .

LIN: OK, Mat may have to help you over here. I'll set up this one, oh, no, that's not gonna work. Alright.

(Mat wonders how he's going to reach the other end of the board.)

LIN: That's what I was wondering! (she laughs) Well, we'll problem solve as we go along, how's that?

I end here, at the start of the checkers game, to examine this interchange as it has unfolded thus far. Here is a strange healing practice, one in which three grown people work for twenty minutes to prepare to play a game from childhood. What kind of healing is hoped for here? What is the possible point to the whole enterprise? And what does narrative have to do with it? In what sense does clinical time take on the qualities of a proto-narrative structure?

I have given a detailed account of interactional minutiae, quoting directly from a transcription of the videotape, partly to capture the overwhelming inelegance of this session. Anthropologists who have described lived experience as chaotic, haphazard, formless, and humdrum could find plenty of material in this example. Here is a treatment space full of noise and activity, wheelchairs criss-crossing from one end of the room to the other, people calling out to one another, activities of every sort occurring simultaneously, a kind of Grand Central Station of health care. There is an unruly, ungoverned quality to time as well, particularly from the patient's perspective. For all this chaos, there is also plenty of waiting and no clear sense that moving is taking anyone anywhere. Patients are shunted to and fro depending on such practical exigencies as whether there is sufficient mat space to do the physical therapy session or whether the occupational therapist has a treatment idea that involves two patients at once. Among the three key actors in this example, there is some clever joking, some friendly comaraderie and even a few moments of painful revelation by John, but much of the time is spent in dull interruptions, minor difficulties (how to adjust the table height? where are the mouthsticks?) and side tracks. As for the activity itself, for which all this preparation is ostensibly taking place, there is little enthusiasm for a game of checkers. Where is the drama? The suspense? The excitement? The sense of beginning, middle, and end? In short, any of those elements which would characterize an experience we might think of as a dramatic moment, the enactment of a narrative?

While no elegant plot structure can be found in this twenty-minute segment, there are two important ways that the actions of therapist and patients come to take on narrative meaning. First, time, while it may display a certain random quality, is definitely not "clock time," as literary theorists would have it. The structure of small events is more complex than mere "brute sequence." Although things happen one after the other in a kind of desultory fashion, the meaning of this order is less linear or additive than it is narrative. The therapist, in particular, struggles to create a sense that each small therapeutic event points toward a much larger time horizon, and is but a moment in a "three-fold present." Second, the therapist works to make therapy a time which is about "becoming," about transformation. This theme is deep to Western narrative and it also runs deep to notions of healing. Recovery, in the world of rehabilitation, rarely means a return to a life one once had. It means, rather, the remaking of a life.

Time as a three-fold present

Against the prevailing descriptions of experience as chaotic, inchoate, an on-going "buzzing, blooming confusion," I offer the following view. Lived experience, our life in time, is not a sequence of "nows" following in some linear series; rather it is a time which is always situated between a past and a future (Heidegger 1962). The present has meaning not only or even most importantly as an extension of the past; it particularly has meaning as part of a story toward which we are heading. For occupational therapists, practical concerns and commitments keep them oriented to ends they mean to accomplish and much of the meaning of any particular "now" is shaped by its place in this unfolding story which they are anticipating.

Present experience is configured by remembrances and anticipations – therapists seek to change their current situations to more desirable ones. Practical imagination guides their perception of unfolding events as they seek to move things along in some directions rather than others. It is not merely that the therapist, somehow "pictures" a future state which he then tries to attain, but that the very sounds and sights and smells of the current moment are saturated with meanings given by these future images. Perception itself is an imaginative act colored by dreams of past and future. Their concern with a future strongly organizes the meaning of the present and makes therapists vulnerable to a disjuncture between what they have wished for and what actually unfolds.

In this checkers game, the concern to place the present within a remembered past and anticipated future is evident in Lin's interactions with Mat and John. There are several ways time takes on narrative depth. At the simplest level, there is some narrative aspect to this segment because a particular event (a checkers game) provides its ostensible focus. This event, like any commonly played game, is governed by a culturally understood narrative script with a clear sense of beginning, middle, and end. Even the lengthy preparation for the game is lent a certain narrative quality in the sense that it is attached to, and makes possible, the game which is to follow. Many of the "moves" in the preparation sequence (finding mouthsticks, adjusting the table, finding the physical therapist) take their meaning as part of this event. These preparation activities have a sequential quality (just one thing after another) but the game itself, with its inherent dramatic qualities (conflicts, suspense, tricks, and the like) structures time in a way which is more like narrative and less like sequence. The relationship between dramatic time and play time has often been noted (cf. Gadamer 1975 for an extended treatment of this point).

But checkers, for the players in this therapy session at least, is a children's activity. It holds little inherent dramatic interest for them, and the struggle to play it with their immense physical liabilities overwhelms the paltry drama of the game itself. The deeper narrative meaning in this segment lies elsewhere. It concerns the way playing this particular game, with these particular actors, connects to a more sweeping narrative vista, encompassing a past before disability and a future which is quite possibly too terrifying to contemplate.

Lin and her patients do several things to place this particular checkers game within their current life situations. They reinterpret it in adult terms. When Lin suggests the game, Mat replies by asking "How are we going to jump each other?" and his manner, all wide-eyed innocence, suggests the many adult meanings of "jump." The violent and especially sexual innuendoes which are ever present in the spinal cord unit become part of their game. Lin acknowledges the double (or triple) entendre. "Wise guy," she says and laughs.

Lin asks her patients to apprehend therapeutic time narratively, and in several senses. She repeatedly directs their attention to the meaning of any particular activity, no matter how minute, as an episode in a larger life story. She also alludes to other therapeutic moments, asking John and Mat to "read" the meaning of the present activity as an element to be interpreted by past stories. These three actors, usually at Lin's prompting, make forays into past and future. This is intimate conversation, laced with teasing barbs. It ranges easily from future to past, as Lin looks for openings onto the difficult vistas of sexuality. It all happens, as things do in this unit (and in much of occupational therapy) through an apparently trivial exchange over "monkey suits." Hints of future important events, Mat's first prom date in a wheelchair with his girlfriend, lead to John's revelations about fears of women, about the aversion to high school of a seventeen-year-old boy who "looked about twelve." The delicacy of this communication is most apparent in Lin's efforts to find paths to both these men, and to keep a balance between the extremely handsome and irrepressible Mat, still the star of his high school, still with girlfriend in tow and teachers who visit him, and the gloomy strength of John who offers pictures of a life that Mat carefully steps around. When Mat responds in typical jockish humor to John's confessions of high school failures, Lin counters protectively, and in the most careful way. She only looks at Mat warningly, and mimics him with a collusive grin to John. Her body position is also protective of John; she leans instinctively toward him as he mentions high school.

Therapy time as a place of becoming

Lin has tasks that quite clearly center on physiological deficits, injuries to the physical body. There are pressure reliefs to be given, table heights to be adjusted, skills to be taught about how to manipulate objects using adaptive equipment. In the midst of this physical focus, the framing of the clinical problem is continually expanded. For Lin is not satisfied to keep matters at the level of skill and technique. Her concern to widen the reach of therapy is most evident in the conversations she initiates. Stories and snatches of stories become a predominant means by which the clinical problem is reframed to include the patient's experience of his body and his renegotiation of the social world given this new body. It is in this sense that storytelling does essential referential work. It allows therapist and patient to *refer* differently, subtly recasting a physical problem into a phenomenological one.

Lin asks Mat and John to consider their own physical impairment as these enter their lives beyond the therapy session and beyond her encounters with them. From John she elicits a story about how his mother and sister responded to a training session the day before. Through this storytelling, Lin asks John to consider his spinal cord injury as it is experienced by mother and sister, who will be lifting him, suctioning him, feeding him. From Mat, she requests a kind of anticipatory narrative about his prom date. She asks him to imagine the story he will be in. She tells him a story of his mother's unfortunate encounter with his wheelchair joystick, nudging him to join in this recounting as a way to contemplate his own family's responses to his injured body. Mat and John belong to very different social worlds, and Lin must also reckon with the loneliness John experiences as compared to Mat's continued popularity in his high school world. This narrative sense-making is inextricably intertwined with Lin's perlocutionary motives, her concerns to persuade these men to see their bodies in particular ways and to recognize a place for occupational therapy within the larger unfolding drama of their radically changing lives.

Lin orchestrates most of the storytelling in this session. When brief tales are interrupted, as they inevitably are, she takes charge of returning the narrator to his story. By the end of the session, several storylines have developed, some about past events, some about events yet to come. Lin thereby historicizes the checkers game; it becomes a therapeutic interchange placed within the life situations of these two men, wedged between past and future events that spill out of the confines of the hospital ward into the domain of families and friends which constitute the real social world of these patients. Even apparent irrelevancies within therapy precipitate short stories; when Mat nearly bumps the joystick on his wheelchair, Lin recounts the time his mother caught her coat on that same joystick and sent him spinning. What is the point of this determined narrative exchange? What is Lin trying to persuade Mat and John of? One rhetorical focus is disability in phenomenological terms, especially those embarrassments, difficulties, and changing social relationships triggered by changed bodies. John is far more open to this invitation than Mat who skirts Lin's attempts to engage him in such revealing and potentially dangerous storytelling.

Storytelling is fragmented, interrupted, abbreviated, teasing, marked as non-serious, even anti-serious. The more frightening the content, the more likely it will be framed as play, and as optional play at that. This fragmented storytelling, couched most often as a joke or a casual reference, leaves open a range of responses. John is more likely to turn the conversation in serious directions despite Lin's teasing cues while Mat studiously confines his conversational gambits within play bound-aries. The joking story is more prevalent in some occupational therapy encounters than others. Spinal cord wards are especially likely to be characterized by this form of social interaction. Yet even among thera-pists who are not the teasing kind or who work with very different patient populations, phenomenological matters are often handled lightly, and the joking or casual story is a common entry into these sensitive issues.

But the subtlest way narrative enters this session is not through the storytelling at all, taken as a series of isolated acts. It is through Lin's attempts to create a significant experience through the patently insignificant medium of a checkers game. Therapists I studied were quick to mention the necessity of ordinary activity as a focus of intervention. They spoke with relief about the value of having something to create besides talk, the freedom this gave them and their patients to opt for the level of truthtelling they preferred. Lin probes, using apparently casual inquiries into proms past and future to invite revelations about sexual worries. She is wondering, no doubt, how Mat is handling the idea of taking his girlfriend to a dance in a wheelchair. But there is no insistence. John opts for one level of talk, Mat for another. Lin moves between the two, encouraging John but allowing Mat a lighter touch. Fleeting storytellings take their meaning as part of a larger whole that Lin works to employ so that therapy has some useful place in their lives. A narrative is being made through the combined efforts of all three players, but with the therapist very much in charge.

Checkers also plays a role in this storymaking. Checkers makes possible training in mouthsticks and splints, asks patients to judge the physical needs and limits of their bodies in relation to a physical task. Yet it is checkers all the same, not just mouthsticks and splints. The game is not incidental to Lin's sense of what she is up to. For there is always the idea that physical training is training for a purpose and that purpose is to do something one wants to do in the real world. In this case, desire and purpose come not so much from checkers but, if anywhere, from Lin herself. She asks them to care about the game, not in itself, but as an indicator, as an excuse to collaborate on their own rehabilitation. She asks them to care about their bodies and their abilities to move their bodies, to accomplish things, no matter how shrunken their range of motion, no matter how distant their accomplishments are from their desires. She asks them even to care about the creation of a temporary social world, a threesome in this case, two hospital roommates with little in common and one therapist whose world is more distant still from their lives, past or present. Perhaps they ask her to care as well, Mat with his charm, John with his painful honesty. This is the power of the drama which is not a talking therapy but which is still, in the doing, a fundamentally social endeavor.

What is the story Lin hopes to create by playing checkers with two quadriplegics? Checkers is the occupation of children, of old men on old country porches, not young men at the beginnings of adult life in Boston. Lin, John, and Mat all work to mask these associations. Jokes, aided or even incited by the therapist, serve as contraindicators. But no masking can disguise the fact of a checkers game, the current occupation of a former bartender and a former star high school athlete. Here is tragedy showing its plain (and ironic) face. Two men, one just a boy really, whose lives are confined, whose bodies are "silenced," in Murphy's eloquent phrase, by their disability. John may not live very long, a few years is considered lucky. Mat is, physically speaking, in better shape but he has perhaps fallen farther. Prior to the January accident, just a few months before this checkers game, he was recruited by a major league football team. Players from this team have come to visit him in the hospital. He is extremely handsome, a beautiful boy who still exudes physical energy. One expects him to spring from the wheelchair at any moment. His careless grin comes effortlessly, as does his easy humor. Not even bitterness is yet etched on his face but one expects, looking at him, that despair and bitterness are unavoidable. Perhaps he cannot yet believe his own monstrous bad luck, knocked down in an ice hockey game.

A therapeutic story is being constructed, but its meanings are unstable. Checkers has its place in this unfolding therapeutic narrative, but the therapist hopes for a place that is more than an ironic comment on the reduced circumstances of these men. Checkers is intended to offer the sense of a beginning, not the ending to adult lives barely started. Lin hopes for a story of social power, the possibility of action, however awkwardly facilitated by splints, adjustable tables, able-bodied others. This interchange, built on a slowly constructed checkers game, is a therapist's attempt to open narrative vistas that go beyond the hospital walls, that use checkers as a beginning to occupations that truly matter, a school prom, a visit home.

From a narrative perspective, social life is not cultural rule-following or habitual acting so much as a process of becoming. To consider life narratively is to consider how actors form and attempt to carry out commitments in their lives. The philosopher Bernard Williams (1981) contends that our sense of identity is deeply constituted by our commitment to carrying out certain projects in our lives, what he calls "ground projects." These are deep, narratively organized commitments. They might look from the outside like playing the appropriate social roles or conforming to appropriate cultural rules but from a more experience-near perspective they are on-going struggles to become something other than (or more than) who we currently are. Heidegger (1962) is profoundly right to notice that the fundamental issue (for a human life) is not being but becoming. Social roles (being a hockey player, an occupational therapist, a boyfriend) are, from the actor's perspective, not a matter of slotting oneself into the relevant social category but attempting to become a certain sort of person (a famous or at least well-paid hockey player, a brilliant therapist, an admired lover). This attempt is rarely completed, for the very movement generates new visions of who one might become. Speaking less individualistically, these ground projects might encompass a social group rather than an individual. One's deepest desires may be located not in one's own becoming but in hopes for one's children or one's clan, for instance.

Our practical perceptions are narratively guided because they are organized around a set of practical concerns: identifying the on-going social dramas in which we find ourselves, searching for an appropriate place in those dramas, and so far as we can, attempting to direct them in desirable directions. Our attempts to both locate ourselves accurately in a larger social story, and to steer that social story (or our place in it) in desirable ways, generates obstacles, surprises, the on-going suspense that characterizes much of life experience. Hope, in other words, is a narrative thing.

Where does the hopeful therapeutic plot come from? Rarely does it emerge from the particular events of therapy. These are, often enough, trivial, difficult, and mundane, taken in themselves. What gives therapeutic events significance are their connections to life plots, the extent to which they open onto much broader narrative vistas which lead far beyond therapy. Effective therapy must successfully address the question of why someone should care to engage in activities and exercises which are routinely dull or painful. A therapeutic plot only seduces to the extent that it emerges as an episode in an unfolding life story, gives some hope for a life that is still to be lived. Even therapy directed to the dying must offer something desirable for a future, a better ending to a life or a gift to pass along to those who remain. Therapeutic plots must connect the therapeutic plots and life stories. But not just any connection will do.

A therapeutic plot occurs in a kind of gap, a space of desire created by the distance between where the protagonist is and where she wants to be. A *narrative* possibility cannot be within easy reach. Narratives involve confronting obstacles, taking risks, facing enemies, overcoming dangers and the like. On the other hand, a narrative possibility cannot be too difficult. There must be something worth doing. A gap, in other words, is only of *narrative* import if there is suspense about the outcome and that means some hope for success, some reason to take a risk. Of course, to hope at all can mean taking a risk, making oneself vulnerable to desire. Sometimes the riskiest thing therapists ask of patients or family members is to hope that their actions can lead to some better life.

Narrative time is time that matters, in which something is at stake. It might seem that serious, life-threatening or disabling illness or injury would necessarily propel a person into narrative time. But sickness and tragedy have their own curious effects, not least of which is a sort of detachment, a leave-taking of the body, a disinclination to care about anything or a disowning of one's troublesome parts (Sacks 1984, 1995). "The arm won't move," patients declare, looking down at their useless limb as though wondering where it had come from. Even when patients discover they are in a state of emergency, a time when things are very much at stake, they may not see any place for action, at least not for any action they can take. "I wish God would do a miracle on me," a patient tells a therapist forlornly after a stroke has partially paralyzed his left side. This patient expresses desire, even a faint hope, but no faith in any efforts *he* might carry out. Certainly no interest in learning how to navigate his wheelchair so that he does not run into all the objects on his left.

A therapeutic plot which occupational therapists are willing to promote requires that patients desire something therapists can help them achieve through their own efforts. Miracles are not part of a rehabilitation program, especially not miracles which only require waiting. From a therapist's perspective, work, work and more work is the usual key to any compelling plot. Patients must also be willing to create a future self the therapist can embrace. "Can't you make me something so I can hold a gun?" a patient with a spinal cord injury asks his therapist. When he goes home he wants to shoot the rival gang member who shot him. His sense of the life story he was living out and to which he was committed was not one his therapist was willing to further. In short, for patients and therapists to be committed to a therapeutic plot, they must share some level of commitment to a particular version of a patient's life story. But this is inevitably a commitment to a life story which is deeply uncertain. The practical concerns which drive occupational therapists in these narrative directions and the role of imagination and desire in this storymaking are further explored in the following chapter.

4   Therapeutic plots

In each new clinical situation, the occupational therapist must answer the question: What story am I in? To give an answer is to make some initial sense of the situation on which the therapist can act. Discovering an intelligible story is often helped through analogy. Therapists may say to themselves, How is this situation like others I have been in? Or, put narratively, How could I retell, in a new way, an old story? As a way of framing a practical decision about what to do, stories offer an account about what has happened which gives a view of which actions make sense as appropriate next steps. Stories place events within a temporal context and in order to know how to act therapists often need a historical sense which locates them in relation to some past and some anticipated future.

This need for narrative framing as a guide to practice is suggested by a nurse quoted in Benner's study of clinical reasoning in nursing. This nurse, who works in an intensive care nursery, describes what she considers the most essential kind of thinking she wants her newly graduated students to evince at the end of their three-month affiliation with her.

To my mind, moving the child from Point A to Point B is what nursing is all about. You have to perform tasks along the way to make that happen, but performing the task isn't nursing. I wanted to see a light going on – that OK, here's this baby, this is where this baby is at, and here's where I want this baby to be in six weeks. What can I do today to make this baby go along the road to end up being better? It's that kind of thing that's just happening now. They're [her student nurses] just starting to see the whole thing as a picture and not as a list of tasks to do. (Quoted in Benner 1984: 28)

The process of treatment encourages, perhaps even compels, therapists to reason in a narrative mode. They must reason about how to guide their therapy with particular patients by images of where this patient is at now, and where this patient might be at some future time when the patient will be discharged. It is not enough to know how to do a set of tasks which have an abstract order. Therapists need to be able to picture a larger temporal whole, one which captures what they can see in

72

a particular patient in the present and what they can imaginatively anticipate seeing sometime in the future. This picturing process gives them a basis for organizing tasks.

The nurse quoted above emphasizes both the imagistic character of what the clinician needs to know, contrasting it with the knowledge of tasks, and the context-specific nature of those images. Occupational therapists I have studied speak in a similar language about picturing the patient, and especially about having "future images" of who the patient could be. They feel that what they often hold most vividly in mind when treating patients are not plans or objectives but quite concrete pictures of the potential patient, the future patient. One pediatric therapist said, "You know when I treat that eighteen month old child, I see the child at three, then I see the child at six, learning to write her name. I mean I have all these pictures in my head." They describe their difficulty when the patients or their families hold different images of the future and their own dilemma about the extent to which they should give patients or families their own pictures, which are often more pessimistic. (Therapists characteristically find themselves in the difficult position of trying to give hope to a patient while also gradually letting the patient know a very dark probable future. Patients and families are often extremely depressed about conditions which are worse than they imagined.) Therapists speak of these images as necessary but dangerous, necessary because therapist and patient need some guiding pictures, dangerous because these can blind therapist or patient to what is realistically possible.

Therapists I have studied are also, like Benner's nurse, conscious of the need to create quite specific images appropriate to a particular patient. General treatment goals devised from general knowledge of functional deficits and developmental possibilities are insufficient guides to practice, in the therapists' view. They work with much more concrete guides, images, and stories which are the "wholes" that allow them to selectively choose what aspects of their knowledge base are appropriate to the situation. These images are organized temporally, teleologically, giving the therapists a sense of an ending for which they can strive. Medical histories, of course, are also organized temporally and also provide therapists with a larger temporal context of past and future in which to locate their interventions. The particularly narrative character of this temporal placing is prompted by the therapists' need not only to understand the history of the physiological body but to locate their interventions within a history of illness experience as well as the on-going clinical experience.

This narrative temporality is also necessarily social. What Benner's nurse misses is that it is insufficient for the professional to see where a patient should "go." What is also required is that any effective clinical image-making must take the patient's future images into consideration. The social nature of therapeutic emplotment is fundamental to the rehabilitation professions. Emplotments which disregard the patient's narrative sense-making are unlikely to succeed. While occupational therapists do not speak of creating therapeutic stories with their patients, they are intensely aware of the need to bring the patient into the therapeutic process in an active way. Their effort to motivate patients and to have "active patients" is the single most important factor in creating a therapeutic structure which has a proto-narrative form.

The social construction of clinical plots

The structure of therapeutic practice drives therapists to attend to patient motives (and thereby to narrative contexts) and to try to match their therapeutic commitments to those of their patients. Occupational therapists say, "Nurses do for patients. We help patients do for themselves." "Good nurses" are ones with the patience to let the patient do what he can. "Doing with" patients also means having patients practice exercises in the hospital or at home during the times they are not seen by the therapist. Clinical reasoning in practice means reasoning not only about what is wrong and how to fix it but also about how to engage the patient in that fixing process. This, in turn, involves understanding enough about the meaning of the disability from the patient's perspective to develop a shared account of what "fixing" the problem could amount to in terms of their lives.

Therapists thus find themselves constantly confronted with the interpretive task of translating between their way of seeing and the patient's. If the goals the therapist pursues are too far afield from the patient's perception of their functional needs, therapy is sure to falter. Even therapists who prefer to avoid delving into a patient's life and try to restrict their practice to more narrowly construed physiological problems find themselves taking on the "whole person" as the quest for collaboration makes this unavoidable. If therapists cannot succeed in getting the patient to collaborate with them, they may discontinue treatment. So, for instance, one therapist tells the staff in a planning discharge meeting, "If Leo doesn't make some treatment goals, I'm going to discontinue therapy."

The need therapists have to involve patients as active partners (real people they sometimes say) in the therapeutic process is reflected by their intense drive to have patients communicate with them. While occupational therapy is very much an action-based intervention and doing takes priority over talking, therapists work to combine both, often using the doing to raise sensitive issues in which they ask patients to communicate their own personal experience of disability. When therapists ask patients to become partners in ordinary conversation they rarely relinquish control of interchanges. There are many markers that the setting is professional. "We are not equals here," is one indelible message of the hospital setting. And yet there are moments, often initiated by the therapist, when the patient is asked to participate in an activity or conversation as a "whole person," as someone who brings some part of a personal self to the interchange. Therapists make an extraordinary effort to talk with patients, to find some way of making contact no matter what their physiological status. This therapeutic commitment to communication is expressed in a practical capacity which any experienced therapist has. Experienced therapists learn to understand patients on respirators or with tracheotomies who can only mouth words or who have such severe speech impediments that, to my untrained ear, they are unintelligible. Even comatose patients are not exempt, as illustrated in the following example.

A therapist who works with neurological patients is seeing a patient for the first time. What is telling about this example is not what gets said, which is very little and strictly medical, but the therapist's sustained efforts to make contact with a comatose patient. This session involves an evaluation of the head injured patient, a 29-year-old female who was in a car accident the week before. The therapist begins by approaching the patient and saying, "Hi, I would like to look at your eyes." After lifting her lids, touching her chin and the bandages on her head, the therapist tells the patient, "I am going to look at your arm." She then tells her, "I am going to move your arm a little bit." After ranging the patient a few minutes she says, "Ginger, see if you can lift up your arm for me." There has been no discernable response by the patient to any of this, but the therapist continues to speak to the patient. The following day the therapist again sees the patient, this time in the company of a physical therapist. She begins her second day's work by saying, "Hi Ginger, it's Susan. We are going to work with you and move your body." She continues to speak directly to the patient as she works with her, though speaking of her in the third person when she discusses her with the physical therapist. After this session, the occupational therapist was interviewed and asked about why she talked so much to the patient when the physical therapist did not. She replied:

In general the OTs do more talking and interacting with the patient. I am dealing with the cognitive-sensory aspects of the person. OTs do a lot more problem solving with patients. For OTs, technique is secondary. She [patient] responds to tactile stimuli, that is why I touched her when I talked to her.

The therapist "overreads" what the patient can offer as a partner in conversation. She acts on the assumption that the patient may be able to understand her and she continually probes, watching for responses. She does not know, of course, whether this patient can hear her or not, but makes the most positive assumption; on the chance that if the patient can hear, she should be treated as a person and talked to as a person, not as a mere body. The therapist justifies her communicative attempts, in contrast to the physical therapist who speaks directly to the patient only once during the session, by saying that occupational therapists need more mental involvement from their patients. Although the therapist only addresses the patient in what (if the patient were awake) fits narrowly into a biomechanical mode, her persistence in attempting to establish contact with this comatose patient, on however minimal a level, exemplifies the pervasive concern among occupational therapists to bring their patients into the therapeutic process.

Though therapists attempt to control the unfolding story, its fundamentally social character is best revealed by the therapists' improvised revisions in their interventions, based on their concerns to enfold patient responses into a favorable storyline. Small revisions also reinforce the therapeutic value of involving the patient as a person while not subverting the overall direction of treatment. Therapists often revise their planned treatment activities in small ways as the patient voices concerns which they had not anticipated prior to the session. In fact, they often insist on interrupting their plans to respond to such concerns, as in the following example of a session between a therapist and a spinal cord patient. The therapist opens the session by initiating an evaluation on a paraplegic patient she has only seen once or twice before. The evaluation involves a standard set of questions intended to provide information on the patient's cognitive, motoric, and self-care status.

THERAPIST: Do you remember what my name is?
PATIENT: No.
THERAPIST: What letter does it start with?
PATIENT: Donna.
THERAPIST: What did you have for breakfast?
   (patient replies)
THERAPIST: How is your back doing?
PATIENT: It's giving me some pain.
THERAPIST: Remember how I was going to ask you some questions? We can do
   that or we can do some relaxation exercises first.
PATIENT: You're the doctor.

THERAPIST: Well, I'm not the doctor. Which do you prefer? How about the
    relaxation first, to help with the pain?
PATIENT: OK.

In this interchange, the therapist interrupts her evaluation when she
asks the patient how his back is doing. He tells her he is in pain, and she
stops to teach him how to do a relaxation exercise, an interruption
which lasts for about ten minutes (including the exercises) before she
returns to her evaluation format. She takes his pain seriously, and seems
to expect him to demand that she do so, as when she tells him, "Well,
I'm not the doctor. Which do you prefer?" After telling him he is to
choose, she chooses what she believes he ought to prefer, relaxation
exercises to help relieve his back pain. She implies that being a good
patient for the occupational therapist is not the same as being a good
patient for the doctor. Good occupational therapy patients are ones who
make choices – albeit choices within a list presented by the therapist.
Good patients are also those who take their experiences and the feelings
related to their disability seriously. The therapist later tells the patient to
"know that when you have pain, it's telling you something. You can
separate yourself from the pain, but you also have to take care of it."

Later in this session, they discuss his medications. He tells her, "I
don't give a crap about what a medicine's for but I guess I should." She
replies, "You do need to know about your meds' side effects. Suppose
you start getting a reaction of some kind, you'll know that it's from the
med. You have to be your own pharmacist. Know what to do when you
start feeling side effects." The therapist again picks up the themes that
being a good patient – or a competent disabled person – involves taking
responsibility for one's condition, coming to know your body and what
it is telling you, knowing how to treat yourself. But this time she asks the
patient to attend to his body as the medical professional might, learning
to read his body so that he can recognize the effects of medication. In
both instances, but especially the latter, the therapist wants the patient
to use his bodily experience as a source of information that will help him
to care for himself just as a medical professional might. Competence
here means learning to "be your own pharmacist."

The high need for collaboration is not confined to occupational
therapy but belongs more generally to the domain of rehabilitation. In
Murphy's (1987) autobiographical account of his own illness experience, a degenerative disease caused by a spinal cord tumor gradually
paralyzing him until his death, he offers an apt description of the
difference. He was struck with the irony that neurosurgery and clinical
neurology were among the most prestigious medical specialities while
rehabilitation medicine ranked among the lowest. The irony was that

neurology, as Oliver Sacks (1984) has also noted, "is essentially a passive science" because neurologists can only examine and diagnose. Rehabilitation, on the other hand, is an active science, where both patient and therapist work together to discover the patient's real limitations and to continually try to transcend those limitations. Because of the problems occupational therapists tackle, they deal not only with physical ailments but also with the patients who have them.

Murphy experienced rehabilitation therapy as a kind of game where therapists "urged, cajoled and nagged" him and his fellow patients to push harder than they felt able and where "today's painful overreach may become tomorrow's routine accomplishment" (1987). He tells of one day when

a young paraplegic woman was helped to her feet, given a walker, and told to walk. After about five steps, she told the therapist, who was walking just behind her, that she was tired and wanted to stop. The therapist told her that she was giving up too soon and ordered her to continue. The other therapists and their patients echoed him, telling her that she could do it, forming a cheering section as she struggled onward. She soon stopped again, this time begging to be put back in the wheelchair, but the therapist was adamant. Finally, after she broke down in tears and showed signs of collapsing, the chair was brought up behind her and she fell into it. Everybody in the gym applauded, and she wiped away the tears and grinned in triumph.

This happens to be a story about physical therapy but it belongs just as surely to occupational therapy. Rehabilitation medicine in general and occupational therapy in particular fit precariously in the medical mold, requiring so much more active and collaborative a relation between clinician and patient than is the norm in biomedicine. In rehabilitation, patients are very much involved in their own recovery. They must claim their disability rather than separate themselves from it. The powerful autobiographical accounts given by vivid and informed writers like Murphy and Sacks about their own experiences of disability, as well as the everyday talk of patients to their therapists, emphasize over and over again the assault to one's sense of identity that deep injury to the body causes. To become disabled is to become disembodied, alienated from one's own body. Therapists' efforts are directed, in part, toward a patient's "re-embodiment" – a reclaiming of the body – and this involves helping patients articulate a new sense of self.

Commenting on his own resistance to therapy and his enormous depression as he faced a deteriorating body, Murphy notes that "(rehabilitation) therapists must breach imposing psychological barriers to reach their patients and enlist their cooperation in the long tedious process of reconstructing their bodies" (1987). Effective therapy requires that patients be committed to a long path where gains are so slow they are difficult to perceive or are counteracted by a faster rate of deterioration. This means that therapists must address the problem of motivation. They must tap into commitments and values deep enough within patients to commit them to such a process. No matter what the technical and physiological expertise and orientation of the therapist, or what practice theories she relies on, effective collaboration requires treating the disability as more than a biomechanical matter which can be separated from the experience of the patient.

Therapists are prompted by their own professional need to create stories about who patients have been and how they experience their disabilities. Therapists work to create success stories as Murphy's wonderful example of the woman in the wheelchair shows. They presume that patients will not become committed to therapy without success, for success breeds hope, and hope is essential. But devising a session which ensures success is quite a tricky business because easy success is no success at all. Therapists can discuss at length the need to structure activities so that they can push the patient as far as he can reasonably be expected to go without pushing him so far that he fails. Occupational therapists speak of needing to discover what Csikszentmihalyi (1975) calls the "just right challenge."

Success depends not only on correctly judging the patient's physical abilities but also on assessing his own internal attitudes toward the disability, toward therapy, toward the therapist. All this matters in assessing how far any particular patient will be willing to push himself, how many risks he will take, how much failure he can tolerate. Such clinical judgment becomes extremely fine-grained and necessitates sensitivity to subtle cues from the patient. It requires a close reading of the context. For instance, a pediatric therapist working with a child who was performing an activity improperly had to decide how much she should correct the child. Here was the interchange:

THERAPIST: You know how to make a square, right?
PATIENT: Circle! Square!
THERAPIST: Uh oh, we're losing our square.
   (patient seems to be veering from square to circle)
PATIENT: Is that better?
THERAPIST: Much better.

The therapist decided to correct the first time, and not to correct, but validate, the second. She was asked after the session how she learned to judge when to correct and when not to. She said:

It's something you learn by trial and error, by reflecting on the sessions that went badly afterwards and trying to isolate what went wrong and correcting for that the next time. In correcting a child, you have to set your acceptable limits, have an idea of the child's limits, what you'll accept for now, what you think they can do. As you get to know them, you learn what they can tolerate, how much they can stand to be corrected, and how much you have to let go for now. It varies with the kid. With some, there's always a contingency plan, "OK, five more, then we'll do something else."

Therapists describe such reasoning as an intuitive and haphazard or even mystical aspect of practice. Sometimes they refer to it as the "art of therapy." I would say it requires a trained ability to construct a narrative of the situation accurate enough to be reliable. It also requires the ability to recognize cues which tell you when your judgment is incorrect so that you can respond midstream. The considerations involved in making this kind of small, ordinary decision are quite elaborate, based on the therapist's understanding of the patient's inner world of motivations, commitments, and tolerances. In this example, the therapist had to refer tacitly or explicitly to a number of interpretations of the child and her abilities, answering such questions as: What are her limits for this task, based on past experience with her and other children like her? What can the child do in the context of this task? How much can the child stand to be corrected? How much do I have to let her go for now? The answer to these questions depends upon a reading of the narrative context.

At times, a patient's uncooperative response to the therapist's desired therapeutic story is answered by a simple assertion of the story the therapist wants a patient to "buy into." She may announce the success of therapy. The following is a typical example. Patients are regularly told by therapists that they were performing successfully and they are often asked to validate that success. Validating success is a typical strategy, sometimes an explicit one, for trying to induce the patient's commitment to therapy. In the excerpt of a single session given below, the patient is initially willing to validate as requested by the therapist that he is improving but then in a heartfelt sigh asserts his own, quite contrary, view of the therapeutic (and life story) he has entered, one in which the future is dismal.

THERAPIST: At first you couldn't sit up at all. Now you've learned to sit up by yourself.
PATIENT: Yes, yes.
THERAPIST: Is that as hard as it was?
PATIENT: (response unclear)
THERAPIST: Not too bad. Because you really couldn't do it for the longest time.
PATIENT: I wish God could do a miracle on me. I can't use my arm as I should.
THERAPIST: Well, you are doing much better. You can give yourself a lot of credit. You and others have been working hard.

The therapist was asked after the session about these validation points. She felt that his agreement (as in the first two interchanges) was an important confirmation from him that things were improving and that such a confirmation mattered because it showed some active involvement on his part. She recounted her description of the session. "I was saying to him, 'Last week you had more difficulties. Now it is easier. You must be feeling better.' Before, everything was lousy in his view. I want confirmation from him that things are improving." The concern for confirmation is a narrative concern. The therapist asks the patient to participate in creating a particular kind of story, one in which progress is being made. She also appears to hold the theory that his participation in this story will further his improvement, that to believe he is improving will make it more likely to be so. In the last interchange, the patient declines her invitation, wishing for miracles rather than believing his own efforts are producing effects. The therapist responds to his despairing declaration by simply reasserting her own position.

The therapist is not so much reading the motives of her client as struggling to get him to take on a kind of narrative commitment which better fits her own. But narrative structure may be refined when the therapist's decision does not give her the results she had expected – if trouble arises. The pediatric therapist with the circle/square problem is clear that much of her learning comes from past problems. However, what she characterizes as a "trial and error" method appears upon closer examination to be more systematic: What she tries is driven by theories about the patient and what the patient can handle; she is not merely randomly experimenting.

These slight therapeutic forays into the intentional world of the patient only point toward the real work of narrative in the therapeutic process. Storymaking, most fundamentally, concerns the creation of significant therapeutic experiences.

The narrative shape of significant experience

Arendt (1958) recalls a maxim of ancient Greece: to fully live a life is to have experiences worth telling stories about. The occupational therapists I studied followed the same dictum in their assessment of therapeutic practice. The best practice created events worth telling stories about. Therapists were concerned not merely to know where they were going, not even merely to control where they were going, but to make of therapy something which was memorable *as an experience*.

Healing, from the perspective of occupational therapy (and probably many other therapies), is not merely in the goal but also in the journey.

Transformative events must transpire along the way. These, more than some end point, give therapy its efficacy, at least from the perspective of the therapists. In their work to create significant events, ones which would in their power persuade patients to view disability and healing in particular ways, therapists relied upon narrative.

In understanding their work, I draw upon "experience" as understood in the German hermeneutic tradition. The formedness of significant experience has been discussed by German hermeneutic philosophers since the nineteenth century (Dilthey 1989; Gadamer 1975). Powerful experience, the kind remembered long after events have passed, offers a sense of unity, a sense that something has occurred which is distinct from an unmarked flow of time. Experience, at least memorable experience, is not merely passively received but actively created. Narrative is one of the primary aesthetic modes therapists use to shape experience. They attempt to give unity and coherence to the succession of clinical episodes – to give a plot structure to what would otherwise be a sheer succession of doings. This is a rhetorical act of complicated social proportions for it requires much subtle negotiation and persuasion among the actors.

Therapists work to create significant experiences for their patients because if therapy is to be effective, therapists must find a way to make the therapeutic process matter to the patient, to make it meaningful to that patient. Beyond the need for active cooperation within the therapy session, therapists need patients to become staked because therapy is only successful if patients "take up" therapeutic activities – and the therapeutic vision – and incorporate it into their own lives. Therapists are with patients only a short time, often a few weeks or less. They might teach a few skills or improve the patient's strength a bit but generally their effectiveness depended on using therapy as a catalyst to help patients begin to see how they might "do for himself" even when the therapist was no longer there.

If the patient is to become committed to the therapeutic process, both patient and therapist must share a view about why engaging in any particular set of treatment activities makes sense. Coming to share such a view requires the therapist and patient to see how these treatment activities are going to move the patient toward some future he can care about. Such a view is not reducible to a general prognosis or even to a shared understanding of a treatment plan. Therapist and patient must come to share a story about the therapeutic process, must come to see themselves as "in the same story." This is a kind of future story, a story of what has not yet happened, or has only partly happened, an as yet unfinished story.

How is such a story constructed? Generally not through any explicit storytelling. Rather it is constructed through sharing powerful therapeutic experiences which point to a prospective story – a path therapy will take. Clinical reasoning involves seeing possibilities for creating significant experiences in which the patient will be staked, making moves to act on these possibilities, responding to the moves the patient makes in return, and, if the therapist is lucky and can get something started – can get the patient "in" – building on the experience by showing the patient a future in which this therapeutic experience becomes one building block. Or, in the language of narrative, the experience becomes one episode in a much longer story. The therapist tells the story not in words but in actions that create an experience the patient can care about.

Therapeutic efficacy depends upon patient and therapist finding some way to actively construe and connect clinical actions into a larger, cumulative process – making a larger story out of a series of on-going actions. The clinician's narrative task is to take the episodes of action within the clinical encounter and structure them into a coherent plot. This can be translated into more familiar clinical language through a narrativized reading of treatment goals. When an occupational therapist makes an assessment of the patient, the outcome is a set of treatment goals. Goals, to follow Ricoeur (1984) are not predictions of what will happen but express the actors' intentions of what they prefer to happen and intend to try and bring about. These goals express a therapeutic commitment. They capture what the therapist intends to accomplish over the course of therapy. Treatment goals are an expression of what the therapist has committed herself to care about with a particular patient.

As occupational therapists have argued (Rogers and Masagatani 1982; Rogers 1983), a primary task of clinical reasoning is the individualization of treatment goals. To speak narratively, individualization involves constructing a particular story of the treatment process rather than relying on a generic line of action which strings together standard goals and activities. For occupational therapists, cumulativity and coherence are not the main drives to create narratives out of clinical time. The biomedical organization of therapeutic time already satisfies these concerns, offering a goal directed linear structure in which treatment activities take their place as cumulative milestones in a progressive path from assessment (where goals are specified) to discharge (in which goals are finally met or fail to be met). A narrative structure is a different temporal form, one built on desire and drama as well as cumulativity and coherence. The need for emplotment is evidenced in occupational therapy because in this practice healing is linked to dramatic therapeutic experiences.

Six features of narrative time

The notion of plot, and of emplotted time, is most understandable by reference to its opposite – linear or serial time. In arguing for the fundamental role of plot in ordering our remembrances of times past and even our understanding of times present, Ricoeur (1980, 1981) and White (1980) contrast emplotted time with chronological time. A succession, that structure of linear time, of clock time, of one thing after another, is transformed by a plot into a meaningful whole with a beginning, middle, and end. Any particular event gains its meaning by its place within this narrative configuration, as a contribution to the plot. This configuration makes a whole such that we can speak of the point of a story. Yet this is an always shifting configuration for we live in the midst of unfolding stories over which we have a very partial control. Life in time is neither predictable nor highly controllable. We are readers as well as makers of our lives and the stories we think we are living through are subject to surprises, twists of the plot we never even imagined. We may find ourselves at any one point contemplating an array of foreseeable endings, uncertain which will come to pass, scarcely knowing which we ought to desire. The actor's commitment to a plot does not translate into the capacity to bring about a particular plot.

What is there to say about clinical time demarcated by plot that distinguishes it from clinical time not so marked? Or even from time marked predictably, one moment progressing smoothly to the next? One way to answer this question is by looking at the way narrative time is structured when stories are told. For if there is a basic homology between lived time and time structured within narrative discourse, as I am claiming, an analysis of how time is organized in the told story should make key aspects of lived time visible. I propose six features of narrative time. These features, culled from a broad reading of Western literary theory, emphasize notions of agency, contingency, and drama.

(a) *Narrative time is configured.* Events belong to an unfolding temporal whole, an evolving movement toward a telos. But the telos is not located in the literal ending, as a final stage of an action sequence. Rather, it emerges through the figure as a whole, the form of beginning, middle and end. This figure may be an intricate webbing of multiple figures, like the many smaller forms that comprise a complex dance. While built upon the relation of part to whole, no plot simply subsumes the parts such that they are merely episodes contributing to a single coherence. Narrative depth derives from a part–whole structure where episodes have their own authority; they, too may be memorable. A single glance in a single moment can have its own unforgettable character, conveying an image that sweeps across the surface of all other events, and is never simply swallowed in a larger action chain. Narrative form is based on the vividness of events in themselves as well as on their contributions to the plot.

(b) *Action and motive are key structuring devices.* Narrative time is human time, one might say, time in which human actions are represented as central causes for the outcome of events. Multiple actors with multiple motives are operating upon the same stage and through their interactions, narrative time is created.

(c) *Narrative time is organized within a gap.* It is configured as that place of desire where one is not where one wants to be, where one longs to be elsewhere. Another way of saying this is that movement toward endings dominates the experience of time.

(d) *Narratives show how things (and people) change over time.* While change is central, not all change is narrative. In narrative, the movement from one time to the next is not linear; it is full of tricks and reversals.

(e) *Narrative time is dramatic.* Conflict is omnipresent. There are obstacles to be overcome in reaching one's desired object. Enemies must be faced, risks taken. One almost never hears the story of how things went without a hitch from beginning to end, just as planned. Stories are told about difficult, even frightening situations. Desire must be strong because danger is also present and one faces danger only when one wants something badly. In this time marked by conflict, there is an implicit dialogue of points of view played out by the key actors, or even, by the same actor when the narrative scene moves inward.

(f) *Endings are uncertain.* Narrative time is marked by suspense, by surprise, by the recognition that things may turn out differently than one wants or anticipates.

In the following example, there is a shift mid-session from a series of interactions in which therapeutic time looks like a linear succession of discrete acts ungrounded in context or in a picture of the patient, to the narrative shaping of therapeutic interaction in which therapeutic time has been emplotted by the clinician's picture of how to create a significant therapeutic experience for a patient. The analysis is based upon field notes. An interview was also done with the therapist but not the patient about what occurred in the session. No claim is being made that the therapist's efforts at emplotment *necessarily* yielded a meaningful experience from the patient's point of view or that the patient's way of making sense of the session mirrored the story told below. Nor did the therapist speak of plots and stories, a language entirely foreign to the conceptual framework of occupational therapy. She did speak, however, of her concern to motivate the patient, to give him a picture of what therapy would be like, and to solicit his interest and cooperation in future treatment. The therapist can be seen to make a number of interventions which are directed to setting a certain sort of story in motion, and the patient's observed responses strongly indicate a willingness to take up the therapist's storyline at critical junctures, at least for the space of this initial session. One of the most interesting features of therapeutic emplotment is that while it can be guided by the therapist, it cannot be dictated. The "untold story" that unfolds is not created by any simple imposition of a preplanned treatment script but structured from unanticipated responses by the patient to the therapist's interventions.

The work of therapeutic emplotment is not necessarily obvious; treatment can appear as nothing more than a set of procedures. I purposely chose a quite ordinary therapy session because there is nothing narratively interesting or of any particular moral import which is immediately evident. While sometimes encounters between occupational therapists and patients are quite dramatic, more often they resemble the interaction between Donna and Steven recounted below. Quiet and, at first glance, uneventful. Just a therapist wheeling a patient through the hospital corridors. But a small encounter such as this begins to take on significance when recognized as an episode within a larger therapeutic story which is in the process of being constructed. Any therapeutic narrative, in turn, is but a short story in the larger life history of the patient, a life story which is under radical reconstruction while therapy is on-going.

The tour

The session begins in the hospital room of Steven, a twenty year old who has only awakened from a coma a few days earlier. Steven is between one and two months post-trauma from a car accident where he suffered a brainstem contusion. He cannot talk but communicates through signaling and writing. The occupational therapist, Donna, has seen this patient only twice before but very briefly since he was not yet ready for an "OT" (occupational therapy) session.

As Donna comes into Steven's room, a physical therapist and a nurse are getting ready to transfer him from his bed to a wheelchair. This is the first time he has been out of bed since the accident and he is reluctant to get up. Donna brings a student occupational therapist with her and they join the others around Steven's bed. So, as the session opens, Steven lies in bed surrounded by four medical professionals. During the first several minutes he is simultaneously treated by each of them. He (a) is given a shot; (b) is introduced to the student occupational therapist who puts on his sneakers; (c) has his lungs listened to by the physical therapist; and (d) is asked questions about his height by Donna.

The occupational therapists, nurse, and physical therapist have previously decided that he needs to stand up and then spend an hour sitting in a wheelchair. They are all there at the same time to help in transferring him from bed to wheelchair. The patient cannot speak but he is given a pad and marker and writes notes to them. Donna and the physical therapist tell him they realize he does not want to get out of bed. When given a pad and marker, he writes "Be careful of my back." All four professionals work together to stand him up. They give him instructions about how to help, for example, "Don't forget to put your elbow down and lean" or "Lift up your head. Straighten up your knee. Bring the right foot up." Two of the professionals congratulate him on how well he has done. The physical therapist does some more checking of his breathing while one of the occupational therapists tries to help him get more comfortable in the chair and asks him questions about pain. (Most of the questions directed at him are yes or no questions to which he simply puts thumbs up for yes, thumbs down for no.) The nurse and physical therapist then leave the room while the two occupational therapists stay behind.

The initial medical checking of Steven and the transfer to the wheelchair form a sequence of actions with little narrative integrity. This is most evident during the first minutes of medical check where each professional is doing something different, paying as little attention as possible to what the others are doing. The patient is treated primarily as an injured body, and is often referred to as "he," as in, "He is writing with his right hand. Was he a lefty? That's good writing." The professionals are primarily doing "to" the patient rather than "with" him. Minimal cooperation is required on his part during this phase. Neither do the professionals need much cooperation from each other since the tasks they are carrying out are quite discrete and distinct from one another. They make no effort to build on what the others are doing because accomplishing their task does not require cooperative action. They are quite simply carrying out a preplanned set of fairly isolated activities. Their tasks are certainly not meaningless and the physical therapist in a minimal sense "emplots" her actions by informing the group, including the patient, that his breathing capacity is improving and so is his ability to help transfer himself to the wheelchair. She says to him, once he is seated, "That was so much better than yesterday, excellent." And, when instructing him to breathe she says, "Yes, good breathing. A little more. That's better than yesterday. We want to get up this high. To the red line. See how close you can get. Two more times. Good."

This bare chronicling can be contrasted with the more fully narrative emplotting which subsequently occurs between Donna and Steven. When the nurse and physical therapist leave, the following dialogue ensues.

Donna hands Steven a comb and says "Try to comb your hair." He does not want to do it and hands her back the comb. She then tells him this will help him improve balance; it's a kind of exercise. She says, "It's good for balance practice." At this explanation, he combs, but with great effort. When he stops, Donna points to places he has missed. "Try here," she says, "Nurses can't do back here when you are lying down." As she touches spots on the back of his head for him to comb she says, "I'll guide you a little bit." She compliments him several times as he is combing. "Great job." "Nice." "Great."

Finally, they are done. The patient motions for paper. He writes, "Mirror." The therapist gets a mirror and sets it up on a table so he can see, correcting the angle just right. She asks him jokingly, "Going to make yourself look good for your girlfriend?" He signals for paper again. This time he writes, "Want to go for a ride." The therapist agrees enthusiastically. "Great! You want to check out your new place." Their tour begins. She takes him directly to the main occupational therapy room and she wheels him in. "This is the OT room. You will be spending a lot of time here," she tells him. She points to the mat and tells him that they will be working together there. She says, "You will learn to strengthen your trunk."

As they are about to leave, Steven expresses discomfort and Donna stops to investigate. He indicates that he has pain in his left shoulder when he moves his head. The therapist supports his arm and begins moving it. She explains the movements she is doing, asking him to hold and then let his arm go again. She notes, "Your left shoulder seems OK but that pain makes you not want to move it. But moving it is good. Moving will get it stronger and reduce the spasm."

They leave the occupational therapy treatment room, and the patient writes, "I want more of a tour before I go back to bed." The therapist

says, "You've got it. This is University Hospital." As they wheel down
the hospital corridors the therapist says. "Today is Friday. Saturday and
Sunday I am not here. But as you get stronger, your family will take you
out." They come to a large window looking out over the city. The
therapist stops to let him look out. She says, "Do you recognize the
Prudential?" He motions for paper and writes, "Open window." She
explains that the windows can't be opened, which she also demonstrates
to him by going over to the window. She takes him past the nursing
station and looks around to find any nurses who know him. The patient
writes, "Is Beth here?" Beth comes out and they have a quick, warm
conversation. The nurse tells him she's glad he is up. He writes down
"Please visit" on a note to her. Then the occupational therapist and the
patient proceed on their tour for a few more minutes. The therapist asks
him if he is getting tired. He indicates yes, thumbs up. As they return to
his room the therapist asks, "Do you remember which is your room?"
The patient indicates thumbs up when they reach his room. And there
ends the session.

A   Time governed by plot

Emplotment of this session begins when Donna asks Steven to comb his
hair. He does not want to do it. She persists, handing him back the
comb and giving him a biomedical sounding rationale – improving
balance – that apparently satisfies him enough to accept the comb and
do the task. When he finishes and she asks him to continue combing,
pointing out missed places, she subtly changes the meaning of the task
from a balance activity to a self-care activity by telling him that "Nurses
can't do back here when you are lying down." It may be more accurate
to say she adds a meaning, giving the activity a polysemic character.
Hair combing becomes both a balance support exercise and self-care.
And she decides to extend the task so that by the end he has not just
carried out an exercise, he has, in fact, combed his hair. By the end of
this activity, he seems to accept this meaning because he asks for a
mirror to see himself, as one might do after combing one's hair but not
after doing an exercise for balance practice. The therapist builds on his
request by not only getting him a mirror but in carefully adjusting it for
better viewing while simultaneously joking to him about fixing himself
up for his girlfriend.

Donna emplots her actions by defining them as part of a therapeutic
story she wants to carry out. The meaning of combing his hair as
preparation for being seen by others, a meaning he acknowledges by
asking for a mirror, is given emphasis by the therapist's joke. If you are

able to comb your hair, her joke implies, you can feel ready to be seen by people you care about.

The patient initiates the next phase of the session by requesting to go for a ride. Again the therapist not only agrees but builds on his request by announcing to him the meaning of his request. She tells him he wants to check out his new place. She thereby turns a ride, which might have meant going up and down the hall, into a chance to see his new surroundings, a chance to see and be seen.

By the point where the ride begins, a "sense of an ending" is also emerging. Discrete actions are coming to take on a unity; a figure in time is being sketched. For this whole session plays upon the theme of reentry into the public world. The therapist builds on her success at getting the patient to comb his hair, which succeeds not only in that he does it but in his subsequently asking to see a mirror and then to go for a ride. In her response to both his requests she not only enthusiastically agrees but explicitly marks them as requests to move out into the world. She "reads" them as moves within a story of reentry, and does so aloud so that the patient hears her interpretation. To his request for a mirror she replies by joking about his girlfriend, signifying that he is getting ready to be seen. She interprets his second request for a ride as his wanting to see and in seeing, to take ownership, to "check out his new place." She "emplots" his requests with a plausible but strong reading of the desires motivating them.

And she emplots his requests through her actions as well, not only bringing him a mirror but adjusting it, not only taking him for a ride but giving him a tour which includes stopping by the occupational therapy treatment room and stopping at the nurse's station to find a nurse he is friends with. She is personalizing the hospital. She is showing him "his" particular version of the hospital, the version that includes a visit to a friend and the occupational therapy room where he will be working with Donna to get stronger.

She also uses his request for a ride to give herself the possibility of showing him what he will be doing with her. While both gaze toward the mat in the occupational therapy room, she quite literally points to a future story. She sketches, in the barest phrase, what kind of story they are in. In this prospective story they work together and he becomes stronger. She reiterates this same prospective story when he complains about his shoulder. She says that working, even working in pain, will make him stronger: "That pain makes you not want to move it. But moving it is good. Moving will get it stronger and reduce the spasm."

She uses his requests as places of possibility to indicate a second story in which work, though it will take time and cause pain, will finally make him stronger. At this juncture of the session, the plot thickens. Two sub-plots are interwoven and embedded into a more complex causal chain. The first story of reentry, of return home, of freedom from an immobile body and an institutionalized existence, is connected to a second story about work and pain. The first story offers the hopeful ending. The second, however, emphasizes the difficult path which the patient will have to travel if he is to attain that ending. For before there is the return home, there is work, work which may be unpleasant, painful, work he may not want to do, but then there is strength and along with strength, there is the possibility of seeing and being seen, of reentering what Arendt (1958) describes as the public world of appearing. Arendt takes it that our urge to appear, to see and be seen, is essential to what it means to be human. She writes, "To be alive means to be possessed by an urge toward self-display which answers the fact of one's own appear-ingness. Living things make their appearance like actors on a stage set for them" (1958: 21).

The figure of the session, then, opens with the patient combing his hair, rather against his own wishes, and ends with a hospital tour. By the end, everything that has happened, from the initial taking of the comb to the end of the tour, becomes an extension or elaboration of a story of making himself presentable and thus reentering the public world. And by doing the tour after he combs his hair, the therapist also extends the meaning of that hair combing. What can look trivial to him becomes the very thing that makes it emotionally possible for him to leave his room for the first time.

One thing after another becomes, in narrative logic, one thing because of another. In what Burke (1966) calls a "temporizing of essence," earlier events become the causes of later events. Because the session links one small activity – hair combing – to another activity which the patient requests and clearly cares about, leaving his room for the first time, the session becomes an argument in story form about why occupational therapy activities should matter to this patient. Through the experience, the therapist is saying that something that might seem to him small for a large amount of effort on his part is really worth the trouble because it makes it emotionally possible for him to feel present-able and venture into the more public world of hospital hallways.

B   Human time and the centrality of motive

Story time is human time rather than physical time; it is shaped by motive and intention. To see myself as in a story, or a series of stories, is to see my life in time as stretching out toward possibilities (both hopeful and fearful) which I have some influence in bringing about. Even in serious illness, constrained by a physical body largely out of my control, my illness story concerns how I and the other actors who surround me respond to the physical stress of disease and deformity. Narrative time differs from biomedical time because it is actor-centered rather than disease-centered. While from a purely physical or biomedical perspective, the "main character" in illness is the pathology, from a narrative perspective the main character is the person with the pathology (Sacks 1987).

Because stories foreground the role of intending, purposeful agents in explaining why things have come about in a certain way, emplotted time is a time of social doings, shaped by the actions of oneself and others. In the therapeutic interaction described above, Donna's first task is to turn the patient into an actor rather than a mere "body" who is acted upon by others. She quite directly asks Steven to do something, to comb his hair, an undramatic habitual action, but an action none the less. The interactional play between the two is marked. Donna not only acknowledges but structures her own therapeutic actions in response to his. This gives a dialogical quality to their time together; it also, notably, means that carrying out a completely prescribed treatment plan is antithetical to emplotting a therapeutic narrative. How could one plan, for instance that the patient would ask for a mirror, or, more importantly, for a ride? And yet it was the request for a ride which structured the entire session and which allowed a reentry story to unfold.

C   Time governed by desire

The actions which form the central core, the causal nexus, of the narrative, are not motivated in some trivial sense, as when we are moved to make a cup of coffee or pick up the morning paper. They are driven forward by desire. A story is governed, the folklorist Vladimir Propp (1968) tells us, by a "lack" or a need which must be addressed. This lack may be caused by some kind of "insufficiency" (Propp 1968: 34) or created in response to the action of a villain who "disturb[s] the peace" (27). In either case, it is set in motion either by the hero's desire to attain something he does not have, or to right some wrong. The presence of desire brings with it a readiness to suffer. Our desire causes us to take risks (or pay a price when we fail to take risks) and this in itself causes suffering. Often our object will not be attained, or when attained it will not give us what we hoped for, and these things also cause pain. Our desire for something we do not yet have strongly organizes the meaning of the present and makes us vulnerable to a disjuncture between what we wish for and what actually unfolds.

Desire is even a central feature of our response, as listeners, to the well-told story. The essential place of desire in a narrative mode is particularly striking when we realize not only that the story hero but even the story listener is drawn to desire certain story outcomes and fear others. This point has been well discussed in reader response theory, particularly by the remarkable work of Iser (1974, 1978). When a story is told, if that storytelling is successful, it creates in the listener a hope that some endings (generally the endings the hero also cares about) will transpire. When we listen to an engaging story, we wonder what will happen next because we have come to care about what will happen next.

The parallel between the told story and lived time is easily drawn if life in time is characterized, following Heidegger (1962), as a present located between past and future. Our orientation in time, as Heidegger tells us, is an orientation toward a future. The meaning of the present is always a temporal situatedness between a past and a future which we await. We are not passive in this waiting, however. Desire in the face of an uncertain future plays a central structuring role. We hope for certain endings; others we dread. We act in order to bring certain endings about, to realize certain futures, and to avoid others. While we may not be (often are not) successful, we act nonetheless, striving as far as we can to make some stories come true and thwart others. In so acting we may come to decide that endings we thought we desired are not so desirable after all and shift our teleological orientation in favor of a different future. But always we are situated with an eye to the future and that future saturates each present moment with meaning. This is what Heidegger means when he describes us as always in the process of becoming, organized around care. It is not merely that the agent, somehow, "pictures" a future state which he then tries to attain. The future belongs to the present because we are, as Heidegger says, "thrown forward" in a stance of commitment, of care, toward a future. We are always "ahead of ourselves" (Heidegger 1962).

Returning to the case given above, the therapist attempts to shift the patient into narrative time by inviting the patient to be "ahead of himself." They take a tour into the future, both the future of therapeutic encounters and the future which matters, the one which leads out from the hospital back home. The therapy room she takes him to represents a temporary station, a purgatory, which, if endured and even embraced, offers a path to the outside. Or, at least, that is the narrative the therapist hopes will shape their clinical time together.

In this therapeutic interaction the therapist's concern to generate desire for therapy is evident in many of the actions she takes, including how she interprets the meaning to be made of the patient's own actions.

When the therapist asks the patient to comb his hair, he does not at first cooperate. Perhaps her fundamental task in this initial encounter is to create in him a desire to act and, quite specifically, a desire to act in therapy. Since there is no story where there is no desire, much of this initial session with the therapist can be seen as her effort at making therapy a place where there is something to care about. She begins to sketch out possible "endings" which she presumes the patient does, or will, desire – especially becoming free of his role as patient and reconnecting to those he cares about (family, girlfriend) outside the confines of the clinic.

D   Time of transformation – time dominated by the ending

In a story, time is structured by a movement from one state of affairs (a beginning) to a transformed state of affairs (an ending). In story time, things are different in the end. The structure of beginning-middle-end presumes, of course, that time is marked by anticipation of some end, one which, to make another obvious point, does not exist at the beginning. So narrative time is marked by change, or by the attempt at change. It is time characterized by an effort at transformation. Things may be changed in an outward, public way or there may be an inward difference. People may come to think and feel differently. But it is important that in the time of plot, the agency which most matters in creating change is human agency. Even if other factors are more determinant – physical and even structural conditions – these are background, the setting in which human actors take center stage.

When Donna and Steven take their tour of the hospital, the possibility of transformation is at the heart of the drama they are playing out. At first take, this point is so obvious that it goes without saying. If therapy is not about change, what could it be about? What is powerful in examining the thirty-minute interaction between therapist and client is how the topic of transformation figures centrally, and the sort of transformation that is emplotted.

Steven has awakened to a body horrifyingly transformed. Some further bodily transformations will occur as part of a natural healing process, apart from his own actions. And some will occur because of what others do to him. But none of these changes forms the core of the plot being sketched by Donna. This is not a narrative of passive awakening; there is no miracle cure and no magician healer. The plot is both more prosaic and more wrenching for it centers on the body transformation which Steven can directly affect through painstaking effort. Perhaps the greatest part of the pain will be Steven's growing acquaintance with his injured body, and his emerging recognition of the limits imposed upon him by that body. Through trying to heal himself, he will discover time and again the limits he must live with and will have to reckon with the loss of possibilities no longer available to him. This reckoning will precipitate inner transformations, changes of personal identity, perhaps even changes of character.

E   Troubled time

The very drama of narrative is based, in a sense, on the experience of suffering. Even the happy story, the one which ends well, takes us through a drama of plight – a lack or need which sets the story in motion, which propels the protagonist in a quest to obtain his goal through the overcoming of a series of obstacles. The process of over-coming, however happy the result, almost inevitably engenders periods of suffering for the story's heroes. This is such a pervasive feature of the structure of narrative that Propp (1968) made it central to his analysis of folktales and later narrativists expanded it to include many other kinds of narratives. And Arendt (1958) used it to characterize one moment in a dialectical treatment of the nature of human action. The "trouble" which marks narrative time is the necessary counterpoint, a required antithesis, to a causal structure dominated by the concept of human agency. Actions may be the central cause within narrative structure, but their causal efficacy is anything but sure. Nothing is guaranteed in the realm of human action. We do what we can but – in the narrative at least – there are always impediments.

The importance of trouble and suffering in the narrative is due to the sort of actions narratives recount, actions in which desire is strong and in which there is a significant gap between where I am now and where I want to be. If narrative plots turned on the everyday easy-to-accomplish actions which form habitual life (raising my arm to scratch my head, putting up my umbrella in the rain, heating a can of soup for dinner) suffering would not enter. The strength of our desire comes in part from the length of the reach required to attain what we want. Most stories we choose to tell feature difficult passages toward precarious destinations, journeys fraught with enemies who may defeat us at any moment. Upon examination, it is surprising how regularly everyday stories carry this plot structure; even tales of victory are set against this implicit backdrop of what might have gone wrong.

In attempting to set a therapeutic story in motion, the occupational therapist need not, of course, invent troubles or obstacles for the patient. These come with chronic disability. Suffering is paramount;

adversaries are everywhere. The difficult task for the therapist is locating a space for action at all. Her problem is how to offer sufficient hope to the patient such that the struggle to overcome obstacles becomes meaningful and bearable (Good et al. 1990). Occupational therapists speak often of their need to transform "passive patients" into "active patients." What they mean is that their patients are organized in the hospital to suffer, to wait, to be "done to," as they say. When Donna takes Steven for a tour, she is inviting him into a story in which he will not only suffer passively, as a victim of his injury, but one in which he goes out to battle, so to speak, actively incurring more suffering (certainly more physical pain) in a fight to overcome, where he can, the damage that has been done to his body. Within the therapeutic plot Donna hopes to initiate, the patient becomes an aggressor of a sort, engaging adversaries in an effort to become healed, and treating the therapist as a valued ally and trusted guide in this enterprise. Physicians often see themselves as engaged in a dramatic fight with disease, waging war against cancer cells, for example (Hunt 1994; Good et al. 1994; Sontag 1988). But in the occupational therapist's emplotment, it is the patient, in alliance with the therapist, who is designated as the narrative hero, the one who must fight the battles.

F   Suspenseful time: time of the unknown ending

The presence of powerful enemies, and of dangers and obstacles, mean that narrative time is a time of uncertainty. Our desire for an ending may be strong, but if our enemies are equally strong, or danger is prevalent, there is no telling what will finally unfold. Hence, the fifth characteristic of narrative time is that it is marked by doubt, by what Jerome Bruner (1986) and Byron Good speak of as "subjunctivity" (Good 1994; Good and Good 1994). If lived experience positions us in a fluid space between a past and a future, then what we experience is strongly marked by the possible. Meaning itself, from this perspective, is always in suspense. If the meaning of the present, and even of the past, is contingent on what unfolds in the future, then what is happening and what has happened is not a matter of facts but of interpretive possibilities which are vulnerable to an unknown future.

Life in time is a place of possibility; it is this structure which narrative imitates. For narrative does not tell us that what happened was necessary but that it was possible, displaying a reality in which things might have been otherwise (Barthes 1975a, 1975b). Endings, in action and in story, are not logically necessary but possible, and seen from the end and looking backwards, plausible. Ricoeur writes:

To follow a story, is to move forward in the midst of contingencies and peripeteia under the guidance of an expectation that finds its fulfillment in the "conclusion" of the story. This conclusion is not logically implied by some previous premises. It gives the story an "end point," which, in turn, furnishes the point of view from which the story can be perceived as forming a whole. To understand the story is to understand how and why the successive episodes led to this conclusion, which, far from being foreseeable, must finally be acceptable, as congruent with the episodes brought together by the story. (1984: 66–67)

Story time is not, at least in any simple or linear sense, about progress. It is not about building one thing onto another in some steady movement toward a defined goal. Time is characterized by suspense, both the suspense of not knowing whether a desired ending will come about, and the suspense of wondering whether the ending one pictures is the one which will still be desired or possible as the story unfolds.

In the therapeutic plot Donna enacts with Steven, the sense of uncertainty about the future is minimized. If there is one place where therapeutic emplotment in this case diverges from narrative time in the told story, it is over the issue of certainty. For Donna seems to point toward vivid and predictable endings. When they look out toward the Prudential, she speaks confidently of Steven's return home to family and friends. When they look into the door of the therapy room, she speaks of the gains he will make by working through pain. She does not raise doubts about what he will be able to accomplish, or what life he will return to. Her intent appears to be to offer him a hopeful ending, a set of desirable images, to which he might be able to attach himself. And yet, given the despair many patients feel over their ability to transform themselves and their lives upon awakening from a coma or serious operation, her cheerful certainty is set against the bleak, nearly silent uncertainty of a patient who, at the beginning of the session, did not even want to get out of bed. Her brisk assertions can be seen as a kind of whistling in the dark, an attempt to put a brave (or blind) face on a future which is anything but sure, one where things will never be the same.

Stories within stories

Therapists help patients make transitions from hospital to home, from sick role to active social member. They hope therapeutic activities connect therapy time to lives back home. They operate at the interstices, treating patients in settings apart from the everyday – the hospital or an unlikely corner of the grade school – but orienting patients to the ordinary world to which they will return. Therapists work to embed the activities they ask patients to carry out within patients' life stories and they often ask patients to discover connections between therapeutic activities and their personal lives. In all of these ways, their therapeutic activities take on a meaning that goes far beyond technical assistance at skill-building. Therapy sessions become microcosms of life which therapists hope patients will build upon and expand in the "real world" beyond the hospital or treatment room. It is thus that occupational therapists hope to aid their patients in the journey from hospital ward and sick role to the everyday world with its complex and responsible social roles.

In this task as transporters, therapists deal with the problem of "spoiled identity" (Goffman 1963). The disabled suffer not only a dramatic shattering of life stories through accident or disease, not only the imperative to revise their lives to suit those bodies, they also confront a society which views them as less than a normal member even though they have left the sick role. When therapists treat the "whole person," as they like to say, they treat a different person than the outside social world is willing to acknowledge. Goffman notes that the stigmatized person is one who has lost his wholeness in society's eyes. "He is reduced in our minds from a whole and usual person to a tainted, discounted one" (Goffman 1963). Enabling a person to "live on the outside" and take up an active life in society also means helping them to confront the enormous fears which accompany tackling the social world with a "spoiled identity." Competencies at specific activities of daily living become symbols of how to take on that frightening, dismissive social world.

Most patients occupational therapists treat have had their lives seriously interrupted by a disabling disease or trauma. They must imagine new lives for themselves, begin new life stories. Even the smallest routines of everyday life must often be reinvented. Therapists teach patients skills to assist in this reshaping of routines but skill-building is rarely the underlying goal. Therapeutic activities are not simply about building skills or strengthening muscles but about providing experiences through which patients might see how they can effect this transition to a life of comparative independence.

If therapists are to play this role of transporter with any effectiveness, they are compelled to construct narratives with their patients that place the therapeutic moment as a present situated in a shifting life story. The narrative meaning of any particular therapeutic episode must be embedded not only within the unfolding therapeutic narrative but also within a much broader narrative structure of a patient's life to which the therapist has not been privy. Even family narratives are sometimes imagined by therapists, who try to understand a family's past history and envision how that family history will change when the patient returns home. For the therapist to understand what story she is in, more than one narrative horizon must be reenvisioned. This is a matter of deciphering a complex narrative form, not the (comparatively) simple therapeutic story the therapist has been witness to. The "reading" task involves imagining a series of embedded stories in which the therapeutic plot is but one extended episode.

This story-within-a-story structure is evident in the following case about a therapist working in a chronic care facility with head injury patients. This case is, in effect, a story about creating a story. It depicts a therapist's task to take clock time devoid of significant meaning and transform it into story time. This process involves transforming patients as body parts, "all these little arms coming to group without any people attached", into "travelers" and eventually members of the "New York Subway Gang." Here is the story Madelyn O'Reilly writes.[1]

The New York Subway, by Madelyn O'Reilly

Monday, 9.00 a.m.
"I want you to take over the Upper Extremity Group that meets on Mondays and Wednesdays. It's a disaster, lots of absenteeism. Why don't you observe it today and let me know what you think?" These words came from the Rehab Program Director in what was called a nursing and rehabilitative facility, but, for most, was a long-term, chronic-care facility from which few individuals had been discharged in recent years. My first thought is, "That title has to go." It conjures up pictures of all these little arms coming to group without any people attached! I checked OT treatment cards to find that the group consists of 5 or 6 young adults, all head injured, all several years post-trauma and long-time residents, some of whom participate in an independent living skills program and 1:1 OT, all of whom I have noted to be cooperative and enthusiastic or at least feisty, during other activities.

Monday, 1.30 p.m.
I enter the large OT/PT treatment area where I see several residents scattered about at tables and exercise equipment. I think, "This looks like PT, where is the *group*?" At one table, a resident diligently puts small pegs into a pegboard. At the far end of the same table, the OT sits writing, and occasionally looks up to observe or give instructions, "Try that once more." Most memorable is the silence. Except for the clang of the pulley weights, a dropped peg or the therapist's quiet voice, there is not a sound in this room. I ask, "Where are Mike and Bobby?" The OT replies. "They didn't show up again."

Having observed the session for several minutes, I go in search of the missing members. Perhaps they need a reminder. Mike, a handsome, red haired and bearded young man responds to my inquiry about OT group, "That F— group is a waste of time. Bobby, even younger and, usually quiet and compliant, states, "Its boring." I let these fellows know that I'll be joining the group on

Wednesday, and would really appreciate their help in finding a way to make it less boring. They agree halfheartedly to come and to think about it. I leave wondering, what do I know about these folks beyond their diagnoses? Mike loves to talk. He has a terrific sense of humor, was into TV production before the accident. Bobby is so young, so handsome, so quiet, and often wears his college hockey shirt and sweats. Nancy is talkative, loves to socialize, talks mostly about home, family, jobs she had in the past. Eileen appears to be out of touch with reality most of the time, never complains about the pain of severe arthritis, is pretty hung-up on the Beatles' music. "Wow! What a group. Maybe I'll rearrange the furniture, get people closer together. How about music? Maybe games that require upper extremity exercise, checkers for fine motor, ball for gross, simon for speed and coordination. Will this infantalize them? *I'm stuck!*"

Wednesday, 1.30 p.m.
Only Nancy and Eileen come to group. Nancy comments on the radio that's playing, does a little dance in her chair. Eileen mentions the Beatles. I tell her that perhaps she could bring a Beatles album to group sometime, and ask if they have seen Mike and Bobby. "They're on C Ward," says Nancy, "They never come to exercise group anymore." The two women play checkers. I decide not to fetch the men. It is their responsibility to come, and their choice not to come. However, that does not change the treatment plan that says, "OT 2X's weekly in small group."

Later Wednesday and during every spare moment Thursday and Friday:
I wonder, "What is wrong with this group?" I make mental lists:
  1 *The name* – I'll talk to the residents about that.
  2 *The activities* – no meaning, no purpose, no life-related goals, not goals that belong to the clients.
  3 *There is no interaction* – among members with therapist.
  4 *Nobody is having fun* – the residents are bored – the therapist is bored (& boring).
  5 *Is there any progress that the residents experience?*
  6 *What are the reasons for attending or not attending?*
  7 *There is no direction and no theme.*

Theme! The group needs a theme! A theme about people – not arms – not extremities – not exercise, I think about the *people*. What do they want? What do they need? They are all so young; so far from home. They want to get out. They want to go home. Home! They're all from New York. That is it! New York! I have a theme with which to begin, but I don't know a thing about New York. The Program Director is from New York. I dash to her office. "New York," I blurt "The Upper Extremity Group. They're all from NY. Tell me something about NY, anything, everything." She lists: "Empire State Building, Statue of Liberty, Long Island Ferry, the subway." Laughingly, "You could have a New York Subway Group." I reply, "We could be *on the subway*. They can take me to New York. What does it look like; is there graffiti? We can do graffiti. I need a new room, away from the big treatment room, can we use the small meeting room?" Program Director replies "yes" and adds that she has a map of the NY subway and will bring it in. "I'll be the conductor. I have a blue blazer." She says, "I think I have a funny little hat that will pass for a conductor's hat." We laugh through all the possibilities of this activity. This is going to be FUN!

Monday, 9.00 a.m.
I go straight to Mike's room and ask him to make sure everyone comes to group today. "I have a different type of activity planned, and I'd really like to talk to everyone so that we can make some plans together." Mike states that he hates the d— group. I tell him that I understand that and that perhaps he could gather everyone for me, and come for awhile. "Then, if you are really unhappy with the activity, you can leave." He agrees. I hand him a small bag containing poker chips and ask him to give one to each group member on the attached list and have them bring the chips to group. "Okay, but what the h— are these for?" "It's a surprise. See you at 1:30."

Monday, 1.00 p.m.
In the room next to the OT/PT treatment area, I tape white paper to three of the walls, labeling various spots with street names and subway stops found on the subway map which I hang on the fourth wall. I put out materials, don my conductor's uniform and stand outside the door on which a sign reads: *New York This Way*

As I await the passengers, my stomach churns with anxiety and excitement, and I wonder where this ride will take us.

Monday, 1.30 p.m.
As the members arrive, escorted by Mike, I take their tokens, explaining that it is commuter fare for a ride on the New York Subway. Nancy grins, Eileen looks puzzled. Bobby shrugs. Mike says with a great laugh, "You are crazy." As these travelers enter the room, I hear snickers, and queries like, "What the h— is she doing?" and comments like, "It's better than the other room." Then, snickers, laughter and recognition. They go from stop to stop, reading, commenting – all smiling!

Bobby asks, "What's going on?" "Well," I explain, "You are all from NY, Right? This is a NY subway station. You've all ridden on the subway, Right? M. tells me that there's graffiti, words and pictures on the walls, in the subway. "We're going to do graffiti. You do remember graffiti, don't you?" "Yeah," laughs Mike, "but nothing I could write HERE!!"

With that, I close the door, and say, "You can draw or write anything you want in this room. The only rule is that you use the tools I give you." I distribute materials: Large colored pencils and wrist weights for Mike who has a tremor, but brush and paint for Bobby who's working on gross motor skills, crayons to Nancy who needs to strengthen wrists and fingers, markers for Eileen who can't tolerate resistance. Eileen asks, "Where are we supposed to be?" "Anywhere you'd like to be, and when you finish working at one place you can move to another. It's up to you." Nancy starts: "This is neat, just like when I was a kid." We're off!

From this point, drawing, writing, conversation and laughter are continuous. So much activity fills this room that it is difficult to remember details. Words, pictures, memories and feelings cover the walls: This place sucks. My ass is stuck in Mass. Home sweet Home, and on and on. I go from one participant to another, asking about their work or just watching. After 35 minutes, I ask the group to finish up their art work so that we can talk a bit and plan for our next group session. Stickball wins unanimously. Since, I admit, I know nothing about stickball, I ask the group to write out rules and equipment we'll need and get it to me on Tuesday. They agree, and, in fact, begin to work immediately. As I leave to see my next client, I tell the group, "You guys can hang out here for a while. Just be sure to take your words and pictures with you when you leave." Thinking, clean up can wait.

Epilogue

This New York Gang, as they came to call themselves, met every Monday and Wednesday, and informally, on alternate Saturdays for an OT Brunch. Other New Yorkers joined the group. Our activities included making giant pretzels and cooking hot dogs to sell from a make-shift push-cart, a trip to a simulated Central Park, filling of a photo album with pictures of the group, home, drawings, postcards, NY *Times* clippings. An unwritten rule, of course, was that every member tease me, at least once, about my ignorance regarding New York and my funny Boston accent!

Madelyn's case traces a journey (first hers, then the patients') that begins with the problem of patient motivation – the patients refuse to attend the group. The problem of patient non-compliance engenders a move toward narrative. There is a gradual narrative reframing of therapy initially conceived in narrowly biomechanical terms. Clinical time, construed in the narrowest physical terms, is remade as story time, in which the same biomechanical problems are addressed but rather than functioning as foreground, they are buried in a highly symbolic activity. Madelyn builds a therapeutic activity around "home." And she does not choose just any common New York experience as her starting point. She begins with a subway ride. Here is an activity which concerns movement, the journey. The theme of return is unavoidably highlighted.

Other images key to occupational therapy also find their place. For patients are not simply asked to ride a subway but to write subway graffiti, to use their own voices. There is a thematic continuity here which stretches from a therapist who speaks to a comatose patient, thus insisting on the socialness of their interaction and the personhood of the patient, to Madelyn's invention of an activity that requires patients to communicate, using words of their own choosing.

Finally, there is the theme of healing as creative act, initiated by the healer but taken up by the patients. What becomes clearer in this case than in previous ones is that the narrative elements of effective therapeutic sessions (danger, risk, suspense, transformation, trouble) belong not only to the patients but also to the therapist. She must take a risk, moving from the safe (if ineffective) role as director of an upper extremity group to conductor, dressed in foolish costume, of a highly unusual subway gang. When Madelyn told this story to a group of us, she described in more detail her anxiousness about appearing ridiculous in front of her professional colleagues. Her anxiety increased with her commitment. By the time she had finished planning this new group, she had come to care a great deal about its success. Her very hope increased the gap between where the group was when she began (essentially non-existent) and where she wanted it to be. Along with desire comes another kind of risk, potential failure in a situation that matters.

This case also reveals the fundamentally social and interactive nature of successful therapeutic storymaking. Madelyn is conductor only once. While nearly the whole case is told about creating a first session, one with a plotline, a beginning, middle and end, the important thing is what kind of ending this is. For the end of an effective therapeutic narrative is, of course, a beginning. If any particular therapeutic episode does not open onto other vistas there is narrative failure. Her epilogue is important in telling us that this emplotment opened new possibilities, leading the group from the subway to other places. Notably, her own role shifts as well. She initiates the journey, but then changes position, allowing the group to make their own next episodes in a story which has a definite beginning but only a sense of an ending. In her oral narration of these events, she also told us that three members of this group actually left the chronic care facility to live in a group house. This was the first time in several years that patients had left that facility. While I have no evidence that the New York Subway Gang played any part in the journey of these patients back into the real world, it is impossible not to speculate about the importance of an initial symbolic journey home.

Madelyn's case also underscores the fact that what makes a thera-peutic plot powerful and significant is its connection to broader narrative horizons – to life stories. In the following chapter I examine the relation between the therapeutic plot and the life plot more closely. How do a therapist's and patient's conceptions of the patient's life story influence the therapeutic plot that gets constructed? How are differing concep-tions negotiated? And how do therapist and patient tack back and forth between the emerging therapeutic plot and the emerging life plot?

5   The self in narrative suspense: therapeutic plots and life stories

At their best, therapeutic plots provide experiments in considering who one might be, even with a disability. But rarely do they offer decisive answers to the questions, "Who am I now?" or "Who will I become?" Their messages are fraught with ambiguity, images in the subjunctive mode (Good and Good 1994; Bruner 1986, 1990; Iser 1974, 1978). Illness trajectories are notoriously uncertain (Becker and Kaufman 1995; Casper and Koenig 1996). Diagnoses may offer some parameters which constrain what therapists, patients and kin may reasonably hope for, but treatment is often an on-going guessing game in which prognoses are revised as the illness is lived out (Good 1995). Bodily uncertainty is compounded by the phenomenological uncertainty which characterizes rehabilitation, often forcing even the reluctantly reflective to ponder the meaning of their lives. Illness can mark an intensely contemplative time, an irrevocable and unmistakable turning point. When illness or injury will be followed by disability, the turning point cannot be avoided.

This chapter takes up in a more explicit and careful way what has been reiterated all along, that therapeutic plots and life plots are irrevocably intertwined. In doing so, it addresses a number of central anthropological assumptions about what makes a self and what narrative has to do with it.

Narrative and the coherent self

Anthropological thought has taken some rather complicated turns in considering the self as narratively configured. Anthropologists have followed in the steps of such forefathers as Durkheim and Mauss in trying to elucidate a particular society's conceptions of the self (or, more often, the person) and in attempting to differentiate a Western conception of self from that held by others (Collins 1985). The Western self, as it has most often been anthropologically designated, is an autonomous, unified whole with clear boundaries between self and other. Narrative has been deeply implicated in the development of this Western self, particularly the Western stress on the self as a unique individual. Individualism as a Western concept is tied to the growth of a particular narrative genre, the autobiography. "Individualism, with all its contradiction, is inconceivable . . . without its literary expression" (Freccero 1986: 29).

The Western self has generally been construed by anthropologists as a dualistic whole, split between an internal private self and a culturally constructed, socially governed public persona. Mauss offers an evolutionary picture in which the development of an "inner self" emerges only in Western societies (Hollis 1985; Carrithers 1985; Collins 1985). More recently, particularly within American anthropology, the problem of the relationship between the "subjective experience of the self" and the "intersubjective world of the social person" as offered by Mauss has been taken up, and recast as the problem of the social construction of both person and reality (Roseman 1990a: 228; see also Shweder and Bourne 1984; Geertz 1984). This relationship has also been provocatively considered in discussions of the embodied self (Csordas 1994). In one way or another, most discussions about the Western self presume a division between a public self, identified by roles, institutions or public symbols, and a private self, an internal experiential essence which is mysterious and unknowable.[1] With the emergence of a bifurcated individual, the inner self is painted as a kind of interior space full of emotions, wishes, streams of consciousness, delusions, and other vague and unstable items.

While any lengthy discussion of these points is beyond the scope of this book, I sketch them here because the dualistic self has provided narrative with a confused and even paradoxical place in anthropological thought. Sometimes narrative is linked to a publicly knowable self, a cultural or scripted person who can be distinguished from a private, inaccessible inner self. But scholars have also recently turned to personal narrative to explore their informant's sense of self as this relates to, or contrasts with, culturally shared meanings. Anthropologists have been drawn to study the self as characterized by emotions, personal histories, unique experiences, private ruminations, tacit knowledge, even the "unsaid." Here, narrative emerges as a vehicle for exploring just that inner experienced self Geertz (1984) (and many others) have declared out of bounds to the anthropologist.[2] Life history narratives have gained a new, much improved status in this investigation of the self as something personally experienced.

On the one hand, narrative is elevated to the very thing which guarantees us the ability able to have a self, at least in the sense of something we perceive as unified and whole. On the other, it turns out to be a kind of trickster, a rhetorical ploy by which we disguise the genuine nature of ourselves – as splintered and discontinuous. In phenomenologically inspired explorations, narrative may play an odd part. For if narrative helps make an inner phenomenological self coherent, this suggests that there exists a pre-narrated self which is, in its primal state, not coherent. The inner self as something *experienced* is very often depicted as fractured, a point discussed in Chapter 2. The coherent self emerges conceptually as an "illusion," a "fiction" which is part of our Western ideology but is not borne out in individual experience (Ewing 1990, 1991; Kondo 1990).

Ewing is especially clear in making this argument and I quote her at some length here. She argues that the illusion of coherence is produced through discursive strategies. Individuals provide inconsistent accounts of themselves which allow them to believe they have a coherent self. "In all cultures people can be observed to project multiple, inconsistent self-representations that are context-dependent and may shift rapidly" (1990: 251). People may not be aware of these inconsistencies or shifts and "may experience wholeness and continuity despite their presence" (1990: 251). She equates wholeness with timelessness, with sameness. The perception of self continuity comes, she argues, not from life experience but from our culturally informed representational capacities. Presentations draw from "selected 'chains' of personal memories," as well as culturally available constructions. These highly edited versions of events and experiences are tailored to situations and abandoned in favor of other (presumably inconsistent or highly variable) self presentations when contexts change (1990: 253).

This depiction of an incoherent inner self has predecessors in Nietzsche and Hume. Nietzsche emphasizes the mediating factor of language in the constitution of the self. Self construction is also self deception: "everything that reaches our consciousness is utterly and completely adjusted, simplified, schematized, interpreted, the actual process of inner 'perception,' the relations of causes between thought, feeling, desires between subject and object, is absolutely concealed from us, and may be purely imaginary" (in Ricoeur 1992). Hume, too, wonders why we want to impose something like a coherent or continuous self identity on what he saw as simply a diversity of experiences, a kind of stream of consciousness. Identity is a land of illusion, he argued, which drives human imagination. We are able to have the notion of ourselves as continuous (the same) over time because our imagination allows us to see different experiences as the same if differences are slight (in Ricoeur 1992: 127).

Many would not be prepared to argue to this extreme, but the pervasive assumption in narrative studies of illness is that narrative provides coherence to a self which might otherwise unravel in the face of enduring affliction or a radically altered body. Narrative is often perceived as the prime strategy by which the meaning of a life-altering ailment – and the meaning of a life – is created (Frankenberg 1986; Frank 1995). The central task of narrative, according to most theorists, is to provide coherence to the confusions and chaos generated by illness. The effect of narrative is "to make over a wild, disorderly natural occurrence into a more or less domesticated, mythologized, ritually controlled, therefore cultural experience" (Kleinman, quoted in Kirmayer 1993: 162). A major theme among those studying what one might call the "suffering self" is "the need to preserve or reconstruct some semblance of continuity in the wake of disruption to the body" (Becker 1994: 385). Narrative often figures as that form of discourse which makes it possible for us to see ourselves as continuous over time. It has been given a dominant place in some anthropological discussions of the self precisely because it is viewed as a privileged rhetorical strategy which allows us to transform the discontinuity of experience into a continuity.

The widely held idea that narratives concern a breach from the expected (Price 1987; Linde 1993; Bruner 1996; Carrithers 1992) reinforces the importance of narrative in making meaning out of illness. Dominant narrative theory argues that because stories concern "breaches" from cultural convention, narrative helps us create order out of the discontinuities engendered by ruptures from the normal course of events.

By emphasizing the incomplete, sketchy quality of therapeutic and life plots, I mean to complicate the pervasive assumption that what narrative offers to the structure of experience of the self is primarily coherence. Throughout this book, I have tried to complicate or challenge anthropological assumptions which turn on a strict dichotomy between experience as narrated and experience as lived. I have also suggested that coherence is not, perhaps, the most significant thing narrative offers to the afflicted or their healers.

In my studies of clinical work, I have found that the drive to create a compelling therapeutic plot has less to do with a need to find continuity or coherence than with a need to locate desire. Therapists battle hardest with despondency, times when their patients evince a loss of direction, even a loss of interest in their lives. As MacIntyre remarks poignantly:

When someone complains . . . that his or her life is meaningless, he or she is often and perhaps characteristically complaining that the narrative of their life has become unintelligible to them, that it lacks any point, any movement towards a climax or a *telos*. Hence the point of doing any one thing rather than another at crucial junctures in their lives seems to such a person to have been lost. (1981: 202)

Powerful therapeutic plots may foster hope by pointing toward some new telos when the old directions are no longer intelligible. But this new telos is always in suspense.

Uncertain actions and possible selves

Even small exchanges reveal therapy as an exploration of multiple possible selves. The most pervasive way this exploration occurs is in the on-going naming of therapeutic activities as actions of a particular sort. Naming an action can occur quite explicitly in language, or in non-verbal ways as when a therapist responds to a patient as *though* he had acted with a particular intention in mind. In trying to bring about certain therapeutic plots, therapists are continually labeling their client's behaviors as actions which contribute – or fail to contribute – to their preferred plotlines. At one level, there is nothing special about this labeling which sets occupational therapists apart from anyone else. It is simply something we humans do, part of our fundamental sociality (Carrithers 1992). Most basically, this labeling is part of our very human need to "read other minds," that is, to infer intentions and motives from observable behavior in particular contexts. We accomplish this mind reading through the creation of narrative contexts which render particular motives intelligible.

Speaking from philosophy, MacIntyre argues for a narrative construal of our representation of action. He contends that the philosophical notion of basic action is wrong, that action is fundamentally narrative in character. When we want to understand what somebody is doing, he points out, we are not simply interested in the "basic act" (turning on the computer) but in the intentional contexts which give it meaning (writing a book or, more broadly, getting on with my career, even, in grander moments, changing the way anthropologists think). These are narrative contexts. "Narrative history of a certain kind turns out to be the basic and essential genre for the characterization of human actions" (MacIntyre 1981: 194). Jerome Bruner, who has made an extensive case for the narrativity of this inferential work, describes it as integral to "folk psychology." He writes, "Folk psychology is about human agents doing things on the basis of their beliefs and desire, striving for goals, meeting obstacles which they best or which best them, of this extended over time" (1990a: 42–43). And this, of course, is the very stuff narrative is made of. Not just any event will do as material for a story. Stories deal in motive. There are, of course, unmotivated dramas, great astronomical and geological and biological processes, for instance, bursts of hydrogen, meltings and coolings of an entire planet, the invisible warring of genes. We often refer to these as stories, as when we speak of "the story of the universe." But these "unguided doings" (Goffman 1974) however eventful and dramatic, are not the stuff of stories proper. When the gods left the scene, so did the stories. Stories always show what happens as *action*, so that even if fate seems to prescribe a certain direction of the plot, the specific events which occur are always linked to the intentional actions of the characters.

You cannot have stories without action and you cannot understand action without stories. Kenneth Burke offers a particularly subtle discussion of narrative (drama, as he calls it) and action. Dramas, he says, are about acts and "As for 'act,' any verb, no matter how specific or how general, that has connotations of consciousness or purpose falls under this category" (Burke 1945: 14). He illustrates:

If one happened to stumble over an obstruction, that would not be an act, but mere motion. However, one could convert even this sheer accident into something of an act if, in the course of falling, one suddenly willed his fall (as a rebuke, for instance, to the negligence of the person who had left the obstruction in the way). (1945: 14)

Stories are investigations of events as actions; they are, to use Burke's vocabulary, "dramatistic" investigations. Drama stands for the paradigm of action in its full sense as distinct from motion with machine as its paradigm. Galactic, planetary and other "inhuman" events do not provide material for stories not because they lack drama – they are certainly dramatic enough – but because they do not require any look behind the movement for the motive.

Looking for the motive does not mean climbing into someone's head so much as scanning the scene to see what the actor could possibly have been up to in doing what he did. Put differently, the search for motive required just to name an action demands more than a simple assessment of individual intentions; it requires placing what others do within plausible narrative frames. Intentions are only intelligible within a situational and cultural context, that is within a narrative context. To understand an act in its motivational fullness, one must have some hints about the situation in which it occurred. There must be clues to such question, as: What happened? How did it happen? Who did it? Where and when did it happen? But naming an action or an event in one way rather than another also furthers the on-going reading of a situation as the playing out of a particular narrative. So, naming acts helps in naming plots just as identifying the plot is necessary to name the action. Actions and narratives are interpretively dependent, locked in the familiar hermeneutic structure of part to whole.

It is often unclear in therapeutic interactions just how a patient's behaviors should be named. Intentions may be difficult to infer and narrative contexts are often uncertain. And of course, the multiple actors engaged in therapy bring different interpretive perspectives: these too, create ambiguities and even struggles over how a patient's behavior should be labeled. Patients, therapists, and other key actors routinely designate the "same" behavior differently, each seeing what is going on as part of a different unfolding narrative. These different narratives not only say something about different perspectives on therapeutic activities. They inevitably point toward different perceptions of what kind of life story the patient is living out. They offer different answers to the question: Who is this person becoming?

The following case illustrates just such contested puzzling. It concerns a single pediatric session with three key players: the therapist, Julie, the patient, Patrick (an eighteen-month-old infant), and his foster mother, Bernadine. In ascribing different intentions to the child, mother and therapist contest something at a much deeper narrative level, namely what sort of life story the child is in, and what sort of life story is possible for this child.

This case also displays how therapists emphasize, even exaggerate, some aspects of a patient's behavior rather than others in order to promote a particular version of the patient's potential self. When family members are present during therapy, therapists often demonstrate and model to families how they should relate to the patient. As part of this performance, they label a patient's responses through a myriad of verbal and non-verbal gestures so as to further a particular "reading" or "interpretation" of who the patient is and what his possibilities are. In this case, the endemic "overreading" of a child's behavior (characteristic of pediatric practice) sets the stage for a complex negotiation between therapist and foster mother concerning who Patrick's future self is.

Patrick has tested positive for cocaine exposure. When this session took place, in the middle eighties, cocaine-exposed infants presented a comparatively new diagnosis and little was known about the kinds of developmental damage such children might suffer. While Patrick had been a quiet enough child, he had suddenly developed a lively personality and this worried Bernadine, who speaks of him in this session as "hyperactive." It became clear from a subsequent interview that Julie feared Bernadine was taking too negative a view of Patrick. In her work with Patrick, Julie faces a subtle rhetorical task. How to persuade

Bernadine to see Patrick in the best light, to read his behavior in the most positive ways? In the vein of "actions speak loudest," Julie tries to do most of her persuading through creating images-in-action, small moments that belong to one sort of life story rather than another. She works to create experiences in her play with Patrick that show Patrick the lively and socially adept boy rather than Patrick the pathologically frenetic boy.

The session follows a typical three-part segmentation that characterizes out-patient pediatrics where family members are present. Sessions always begin with an opening sequence in which therapists ask questions and families "report in" about how the child has been doing since the last visit. This is followed by the session proper in which the therapist directs most of her attention to the child, though occasionally offering comments to family members or sometimes asking them to assist in treatment. The closing piece returns the focus to families as therapists summarize what they have observed about the child's activities during the session and outline "home programs" they ask families to carry out until the next visit. Therapists serve as interpreters of a child's behavior during therapy, reading the meaning of what they see in light of the diagnostic problems they are addressing. This reading, while centered around diagnostic issues, goes far beyond a simple report about pathology or progress. Questions about a child's future possibilities are what are most at stake.

After some introductory discussion between Bernadine and Julie about Patrick's progress at home, the "hands-on" portion of the session begins. The foster mother fades into the background, serving primarily as an audience while Julie engages Patrick. Julie is, in effect, staging a drama which Bernadine is to witness. She seats Patrick between her legs on a floor mat, both facing a large mirror. Patrick, a social child, gurgles and smiles into the mirror. His arms have a pathology-driven tendency to move up and behind him, causing his body to tilt backward until he falls over. Julie's task is to train his body to move in more appropriate positions. She struggles to teach him to lean forward, propping himself up by putting his weight on his two arms down on each side, hands flat on the mat with palms down. But he doesn't want to stay in this position long. She keeps a running commentary as she positions his body.

JULIE: Uff, did you just pop up? Did you just pop up? (She says each time an
    arm comes flying up, while laughing and smiling at Patrick in the mirror.)
JULIE: Pop goes the Patrick. (she sings to him)

Julie sets a tone of cheerful dialogue in which Patrick "talks" with his body and Julie answers back. In her answering, she also defines what he is doing. When his arms fly back involuntarily, Julie asks him if he "popped up," as though he was pretending to be a Jack-in-the-box. "Pop goes the Patrick," she sings softly to him, reinforcing this association. When, a few minutes later, Patrick starts to squirm and Julie struggles fruitlessly to keep his flailing hands down, she tells him, "No, I don't want to fight, I don't want to fight." And then, when his body responds in an instinctive stressful pattern (arms stretched taut, back arching), she concedes, "Ohh, OK, alright," and stops. In response, his body begins to relax.

Julie's efforts with Patrick's body are characterized by her attribution of a broad range of fictional motives to him: playfulness ("pop goes the Patrick"), anger ("I don't want to fight"), and stubborn insistence ("Ohh, OK, alright" in concessionary tones). These attributions are offered in a frivolous tone, the therapist marking their fictional status. She and Patrick continue to smile and laugh together facing the mirror, which further distances Julie from any harshness in her teasing statements. While she clearly maintains her "this is just play" tone, she also insists on offering Patrick an array of volitional states, suggesting that she is engaged with the cognizant Patrick and not with a body whose movements are emptied of personal intelligence.

At one point, Julie shifts momentarily, introducing a language of involuntary action. She notes, "That left hand doesn't want to go down, does it?" This language is accompanied by a dramatic change of manner, a disconnection with Patrick. She speaks in an adult tone, as though talking to herself, or perhaps directing her comment to Bernadine. Her remarks are brief and quickly abandoned. She immediately redirects attention to Patrick, laughing and smiling as he smiles back at her. "Such a handsome guy!" she tells him several times over. But Bernadine takes up Julie's comments, clearly ready to elaborate. "He doesn't want to put that hand down. He just doesn't want to put that hand down. He also tends to . . ." Bernadine's train of thought is interrupted by Julie who speaks over her to Patrick. Julie finds she is now able to position him properly, arms down. "There you got it!" Julie cheers. "Yeah, you got it! Annd puush. Aand puush" she instructs in exaggerated tones. Patrick (or Patrick's body) has gotten the knack of this, and Patrick gurgles and grins at himself in the mirror. Julie is ready for her next move. "Yeah!" she cheers and then, taking his arms and stretching them toward his feet, "Let's go get some toes. Let's go get some toes." Patrick starts to laugh as she does this. "C'mon," she urges.

This welcome interlude is halted as Patrick starts to lose his position, again arching his body back. "Nope, nope," Julie admonishes and Patrick scrunches up his face and starts to cry. "You're not quite sure, should you be laughing or crying," she tells him. She quickly shifts tone, starting a game with him. As she moves him back into the position she wants, his hands grabbing onto his toes, she lets her hands fly off his arms and then quickly brings them back to hold him, a kind of variation of peek-a-boo in which her hands, which he has been watching in the mirror in front of him, disappear out of view and then magically reappear. He looks intently in the mirror, surprised and pleased by this turn of events. Julie laughs "Who's doin' that?" she asks him. "Who's doin' that?" she repeats. Patrick responds with a big delighted laugh as he looks at himself straight in the mirror. His deep belly laugh is so infectious that everyone in the room joins in, even the quiet camera person who has been taping the session. Bernadine also gives a small smile and she is not one to laugh at Patrick's antics. But Patrick cannot stay in this position for long and in another moment his left hand starts to rise of its own accord, one finger pointing in the general direction of the mirror. Julie jokes, as she takes his arm to try to bring it back down, "Oh, but I need to make a point! Yes, I really need to make a point!"

During the final moments of the session, Julie instructs Bernadine about what to do at home and she announces to Bernadine how Patrick's actions should be labeled and evaluated. Julie tells her, "When the kids are playing with him at home and he is standing, and you see his toes curling up, you can just flick them so they go flat. Even just when he's playing with the kids, even with starting to get him to straighten with his toes like this." A moment later, as Julie watches Patrick bob enthusiastically up and down with his head on a large ball, she remarks: "He's really working hard." Then again, as Patrick fusses when the ball is removed and joyfully resumes bouncing when Julie puts it back in front of him, she says to Bernadine: "Is he able to tell us what he wants?" Bernadine nods enthusiastically and replies, "Yeah, he's telling us, he's definitely telling us." Julie replies with approval, "He's maybe not as good at it as other kids because of all the physical involvement but he definitely lets you know what he likes and what he doesn't like."

While Julie and Bernadine have temporarily converged on this reading of Patrick's behavior, they again diverge in their subsequent interpretations.

JULIE: (to Patrick who continues to bounce his head on the ball) You're a wild man! Yes, you are! (Laughing)
BERNADINE: You don't call that hyper?
JULIE: No. (thoughtful pause, slows words down) He just started to move, Bernadine. That's one of the things we're seeing. He, when you first came in, he didn't move at all, remember? So, he's really improved.
BERNADINE: Now its like from one extreme to another.

JULIE: He's not as well organized as some other kids, I know. He's very active. When he's awake, he's very active, very busy. But I don't see that as negative yet.

(Patrick pauses and looks at himself in the mirror)

JULIE: And he does have moments like this, where he can really focus on something. He does have moments of calm.

BERNADINE: Those looks, it's like he's getting to the staring pattern.

JULIE: Even when I've seen him stare, it's just like this, where he seems to be focused.

BERNADINE: Well, we've seen the other.

JULIE: You've seen that mindless stare, like you think it's brain seizures?

BERNADINE: Yes, that's what we've seen.

JULIE: Well, huh. I haven't seen that but then maybe it's definitely time to make an appointment with the neurologist.

BERNADINE: OK.

While it is clear that the two of them have different diagnostic opinions about Patrick, how is this a *narrative* difference? One could say that both are constructing a story about Patrick, an incipient life story, in which his disability plays a major role. This is very much a potential story, for Patrick is very young and the diagnostic category is very fuzzy. This story is being created, and socially negotiated, partly through words – the ways that the therapist and mother name the behaviors they see – but also partly through actions. The therapist is, in a sense, trying to make a case for Patrick as a baby who, whatever his motor impairments, is proving himself to be full of life, full of fun, ready to make social contact. In her story, this is still a baby with many social and cognitive possibilities. She argues for these through her own social engagement with Patrick, with the pleasure she takes in the games she and Patrick play. She unfailingly "overreads" Patrick's actions, playfully attributing intentions, and complex intentions, even to behaviors that are clearly not intended at all. In her play she creates an image of a baby who is able to captivate an audience, play games, make her laugh. Bernadine, on the other hand, underreads the intentionality of his actions, at least from the therapist's perspective.

The different labels they ascribe to Patrick's individual behaviors place Patrick in very different narrative contexts. The foster mother sketches a child in a dismal story, one in which he shows increasingly pathological symptoms. In addition to a kind of "mindless staring" (which she believes is related to brain seizures) there is the matter of his hyperactivity. What Bernadine calls "mindless staring," the therapist calls "calm attention." And what the mother refers to as hyperactivity, the therapist calls "Patrick being *very social*, engaging in the world around him," a healthy sign. There is no question that Patrick has suffered brain damage and that this has affected his motor centers, but there is a question about whether he is cognitively damaged. The therapist is inclined to give him the benefit of the doubt at this point, and to encourage others to see him as socially and cognitively intact. The foster mother presumes differently. Both recognize they could be mistaken. As Bernadine tells Julie at the session's close, "Well, we'll just have to see."

Therapy as a "little plot"

If therapy time becomes narrative time, the *sort* of narrative it becomes is less like a well-rehearsed cultural script and more like what Lyotard calls a "little narrative." Lyotard differentiates two kinds of narratives which ground our understanding of how to act in the world, the grand narratives of "traditional" society and the little narrative of the post-modern era. Traditional stories offer positive or negative apprenticeships into the fundamental social practices which constitute a culture, and Lyotard argues, through these accounts, these narratives legitimate the practices they describe. They "allow the society in which they are told, on the one hand, to define its criteria of competence and, on the other, to evaluate according to those criteria what is performed or can be performed within it" (1984: 20). For Lyotard, this traditional narrative accounting is what has been called into question in a postmodern world, being replaced by the "little narrative" which does not purport any certain moral position or any definite handle on reality.

Little narratives offer no possibility for a unified or complete picture of the world. For Lyotard, little narratives are the incommensurable local stories which have replaced creation myths and grand teleologies in the postmodern age, when one no longer lives in a total reality with its epic vantage point. Said differently, the little narrative creates desire in a particular way. The seduction of the good story can be produced by quite different, even opposing impulses. Stories can entice through offering an authoritative rendering, a truthful account of the world. Their allure is a promise of certainty, of realness, as though they allowed us to glimpse the world as it truly is and, further, as though the world were unambiguously some particular way. These are, for Lyotard (1984) and Jameson (1991), myths or master narratives. Bakhtin (1981) calls them epics. But some stories interrupt this act of seduction, or cast a shadow over it. The interruption works its own seduction (as in Barthes' [1975b] "text of bliss") but what we are enticed into is uncertainty. We identify with the narrator and his hero, but this hero is fallible, and we come to wonder whether he, or anyone, has got the story right. Some essential meaning seems to escape the hero of the story or even the narrator retrospectively recounting.

Powerful therapeutic plots invite this same puzzlement. Without necessarily adopting Lyotard's postmodern vision or his rather fanciful depiction of the "traditional society," his depiction of the halting, skeptical, little narrative gives a compelling picture of much of the everyday storymaking that pervades clinical life. Therapeutic plots are very often little narratives, self-conscious in their incompleteness, in their elusiveness, in their being just one take. Or, to follow Bakhtin, they are dialogical narratives. In the clinic, incongruities and oddities abound and any narrative composition, any plot structure, is likely to feel temporary. Above all, therapeutic plots rarely work, as Hayden White (1980) says of traditional histories, by "telling themselves" as though there were no narrators behind the scene organizing, persuading, struggling to make the right sort of story come true. The most important characteristic of the "little" therapeutic plot is its moral uncertainty. In literary narratives, particularly the Western novel, moral ambiguity is created by several narrative devices relevant to therapeutic plots, particularly: (a) a depiction of time as something still open to future revision, including moral revision; and (b) the presence of multiple voices which offer different moral perspectives.

In the "little" therapeutic plot, what is offered by way of beginnings and endings alludes to significant absences, as though one had walked into a play in the middle of an act and exited early. This sort of narrative is about "life without beginning or end" (Bakhtin 1981: 20). The plot is offered in a provisional way, cuing the reader that other beginnings could be found and that the end is still uncertain.[3] Narrative uncertainty is compounded in the novel by the presence of multiple voices who offer multiple versions of the world. While the "epic world knows only a single and unified world view" (Bakhtin 1981: 35) the dialogical narrative offers a world threatened by its multiple renderings, tenuously held together, precarious. This is an important narrative difference. The epic has individual heroes who bring their differing perspectives, but it does not have, as Bakhtin says, "varying truths." "In the epic, characters are bounded, preformed, individualized by their various situations and destinies, but not by varying 'truths.' Not even the gods are separated from men by a special truth: they have the same language, they all share the same world view, the same fate, the same extravagant externalization" (1981: 35). In the dialogical narrative, however, one never forgets that other stories could be told and that these represent alternative moral readings.

Point of view can be rendered ambiguous through another literary device, the juxtaposition of multiple narrative elements which offer different interpretations of the meaning of the story. This creation of meaning through juxtaposition is explored by Kenneth Burke in his brilliant "grammar of motives." He analyzes the way motives are conveyed dramatistically through five generating principles: act, scene, agent, agency, purpose. Each of these principles carries messages about what motives govern the actions of agents, what the merits of those motives are, and how they reveal the central vision offered by the text. Messages are modified or complicated through an interplay of principles; moral complexity and uncertainty is easily assured by this means. I illustrate with one of Burke's examples, the relationship between action and scene in Ibsen's *An Enemy of the People*. Sometimes the scenes in which events occur lend credence to the actions of the main character. So, for instance, when the main character, a Dr. Stockman, announces his plan to found a school for the education of society, this pronouncement is made in his study. But in the dramatic finale, essential ambiguity is introduced when Stockman declares "The strongest man in the world is he who stands most alone," but makes this claim "surrounded by a loyal and admiring family circle" (Burke 1945: 5). Neither the statement offered by Dr. Stockman nor the implicit statement offered by the scene can be taken at face value; they each modify the other. We hear the words uttered with sincerity at the end of a long internal moral struggle, we envision the cozy family gathering where they are declared and realize that the meaning of the play does not rest in any stable place.

Lest all this seems a catalogue of over-subtle devices confined to Western high literature, I return to my ethnographic data to underscore the open time and multiple perspectives characteristic of therapeutic plots. In the case of Julie, Bernadine and Patrick, the "openness" of therapy time and the multiple perspectives offered by Julie and Bernadine, are obvious enough. These factors, taken by themselves, do not give this session its deep ambiguity. Rather, it is Julie's actions which are deeply ironic and provide the plot with its "littleness." Julie does not offer one sustained perspective and Bernadine another. She tells Patrick (and Bernadine) that he is "making a point" or "fighting" or "playing Jack-in-the-box," but she does this in a therapy session using treatment techniques designed to discourage these movements. The therapeutic techniques carry one message – Patrick's body movements are pathological and involuntary. Julie's pronouncements to Patrick carry another; she is acting out a drama in which she and Patrick partake of a wide range of subtle cultural exchanges and Patrick means everything he does. In this drama, his movements are not unruly nature at work. They are social gestures, and he is offering clear statements in the culture's kinetic idioms. Like Ibsen's Dr. Stockman, Julie says one thing in a scene that says something else. What makes this irony "unstable" (Booth 1974) is that neither message cancels the other. Both are, in some important sense, true. Or, and this is a hope Julie tries to sustain, both may very well be true. Patrick's body movements are pathological but he may have all the capacities for subtle communications that any child has. His body, as Julie argues to Bernadine, may prevent him from using it effectively as a medium for the social messages he is (cognitively) capable of giving.

What this case does not reveal so clearly is a dialogue of moral codes about how one ought to live or who one ought to become. The final case reveals the therapeutic plot as "little" in the most important sense, namely as a morally ironic and contested place.

Little plots and the question of self continuity

Everyone would agree that we present ourselves differently in different contexts. But do our variable personas suggest that our perception of having a single self is a mere representational fiction, a by-product of our narrative ingenuity? Severe illness or injury which results in sudden disability poses a particularly potent challenge to self-identity and raises a host of interesting conceptual questions about what it means to have a self, as well as the role of narrative in self-construction. If our sense of self is ensured, in part, by the continuity and sameness of our body, how do we know we have the same self if our body is suddenly, unalterably changed? Does this self come to an end in some way? How does this situation of radical bodily change provoke a search for self, for some new self which can fit a new body? And finally, where does narrative enter into this process of self-searching?

The case given below is one of the few in this book in which *storytelling* plays a key role in the plot which unfolds. Because in this example there are stories told and a therapeutic plot which is created (a story of stories, so to speak), this case makes it possible to consider the broadly held view that stories which are told about illness give coherence to that experience and to the sufferer's life. I want to suggest that narratives told about the self are not as orderly as they are often taken to be and the self in action and experience is not as disorderly. While there is a difference between self-as-narrative and self-as-lived, the difference is less oppositional than has been portrayed. In the case that follows, action and stories told about actions interweave, each playing parts as episodes of a larger, unfolding narrative. Storytelling is only one way selves get constructed and communicated. Actions too, may not only speak louder than words, they may provide a more readily accessible vehicle for communicating, negotiating and even reflecting upon one's self identity, an argument compellingly made by Wikan (1995). And, therapists and patients operate with multiple storylines, multiple possible plots which point toward different possible selves, and they experiment with a variety of self understandings through the actions they take and the experiences they try to create for themselves and others as much as through "the stories they tell" to selves are in suspense.

Drawing upon this final complex case, I will also argue that narrative deserves a privileged status in relation to the self, but this is not because selves are a mere flux of experience which narratives render orderly. Such a position equates the self with *sameness*. I follow Ricoeur in arguing for a very different notion of self. The self is composed of two antithetical qualities. There are those aspects which ensure sameness over time (including habits, roles, even "fidelities" and promises). But there are also those which ensure discontinuity (shifts in context, the accidents of fortune, human development). A narrative is precisely suited to revealing both these qualities.

The ability to connect events through narrative plot allows the self to be revealed not only in terms of sameness, but in terms of discontinuity, instability and the like. As Ricoeur states, a story is, on the one hand a "demand for concordance," and on the other, a portrayal of discord, of disruption to this order. Discordances are the "reversals of fortune" that threaten to overturn any order which presents itself. These discordances make of the story "an ordered transformation" (1992: 141). A story, to borrow another phrase from Ricoeur (1984, 1992) is a "synthesis of the heterogeneous." It has the capacity to pull into it discourses of various kinds. To meld together, to make as one, elements which belong to entirely different language games, creating a world in which disparate elements find their fit. Like metaphor, narrative brings together items which have no natural kinship. Through unique juxtapositions of what has not hitherto belonged, both narrative and metaphor make room for innovations in meaning. "With metaphor," writes Ricoeur, "the innovation lies in the producing of a new semantic pertinence by means of an impertinent attribution" (1984: ix). The innovative capacities of narrative are triggered through the vehicle of plot. "By means of the plot, goals, causes, and chance are brought together within the temporal unity of a whole and complete action. It is this synthesis of the heterogeneous that brings narrative close to metaphor" (1984: ix). There is always the "manifold of events" on the one hand and the "temporal unity of the story" on the other (1992: 141).

The four story roller coaster ride

This example concerns an encounter between an occupational therapist, Lin, and John, a spinal cord patient treated by Lin. This therapist
and patient were introduced in the "Checkers Game." This particular
session occurred during a four-week period when John had become
very ill and had begun to give up his struggle to live. Lin and John had
known one another since his entrance into the hospital two months
earlier when he had been hit by a car while crossing a major highway
at midnight, very drunk. He had not been expected to survive. At the
time of this session it was still uncertain how long he would live. While
a week or so earlier he had been well enough to be moved from bed to
wheelchair, and thus socialize with others in the "big room" – the
large, open rehabilitation room on the spinal cord unit – he had again
been confined to his solitary hospital room due to a bout of pneumonia. Even his roommate, Mat, had been discharged a week earlier
and no new person had yet come to occupy the neighboring bed. The
doctors had just recently asked John if he wanted to be resuscitated
should he go into another medical crisis. Had he agreed, they would
have been willing to let him die. It is not an exaggeration to say that
Lin was the one (or one of the very few) who kept John alive during
this critical period, offering a different message than he was receiving
from members of his largely absent family, the physicians, or his own
body.

Thus the ordinariness of their interchange in the session described
below must be placed in the context of a very literal life and death
struggle. Therapists often treat people at times when nothing is ordinary
for them, even when the patient questions whether it is worth living at
all. Occupational therapy is very likely to occur at horrifyingly special
junctures of a person's life, ones from which there will never be a full
retreat. The strangeness of these junctures is also marked by unusual
relationships among people who, under more ordinary circumstances,
would never know one another. The relationship between Lin and John
is rather like this. Lin, a middle-class Jewish woman from suburban
Philadelphia and John, a working-class Irish man from South Boston,
are an unlikely pair. And yet, they have become close.

The particular February morning session I describe here was videotaped and transcribed. Lin was interviewed afterward and asked to tell
her story of what happened. This is one of many sessions I observed
between this therapist and patient; their developing relationship became
a key case for the study as a whole. Many of their sessions were
videotaped over a six-month period. I draw upon the data from the

video transcript, my observations of their relationship and work together over time, interviews with the therapist about her work with John, and my own rather elaborate knowledge of this case, to analyze how the narrative plot which emerged in this session can be seen as one episode in a larger therapeutic struggle which Lin and John engage in as they attempt to recreate a new sense of self for John.

As the session begins, Lin walks in and slouches over John's bed, resting her arms on the guard rails. She speaks jokingly to him but more gently and softly than the words alone imply. She begins in a manner at once offhand and kind. "Hi sport. Whadaya want? Want some water?" He nods, almost imperceptibly, and she goes to fetch a large plastic cup with a bent straw which she places near his mouth so that he can sip. As he drinks she continues in her same jostling style, all the while leaning near so that she faces him at nearly even level. "Thirsty?" she asks. "Is [the water] cold enough?" He says nothing and nothing seems to be expected. She continues, "How are ya buddy? Buddy boy. You OK?" She persists in her inquiries while stretching his left hand to keep it limber, a therapeutic technique called "passive range of motion." Finally John replies, "Yesterday was a lousy day." She then asks, "What was wrong about it?" With his answer begins the drama of the session, built around his growing hopelessness. "No one came to visit," John announces. "Not a one?" Lin echoes sympathetically and then changes the subject, commenting that he seems to have fever spasms in his hands (a good sign). She asks about his pneumonia. The news from John is dismal as they discuss his secretions and the level of oxygen he is on. Lin remarks of his relapse, "Well then, up and down, huh, in a big way." This metaphor – illness as roller coaster – will be repeated in other iterations throughout the session.

John grows angry as he talks about his condition. "You can swear," Lin suggests helpfully and grins. John grins back, the first smile he's offered since Lin walked into the room. "Uhh," Lin groans. "I need ta lean against something. My stomach. Ever since I came back from Mexico, hasn't been great." She looks down at his hands which she has continued to range. "You're tight today," she says of his hands. "You know what happens, because your spasms go this way (she illustrates) it makes your joints tight coming in. That make sense to you? That's called flexion, inner flexion. Do you know the names of the joints in your hands?"

She is now clearly poised to launch into an intervention strategy therapists refer to as "patient education," and John responds accordingly. "No," he tells her grinning, "but I bet you do." Lin says, "I do indeed. Do you want to know them?" John mouths a sarcastic response which Lin ignores as she proceeds to describe various distal and proximal bones and joints. John continues to mouth sarcastic asides but Lin is unflappable. She concludes her five minute lecture with a laugh and a sardonic comment of her own which acknowledges the unwilling-ness of her student, "Next week we'll do the thumb." And then she asks, "So is anyone coming here today? Who's coming?" John ignores the question. "I'm bored," he announces. Lin echoes, "You are bored." "Well not all the time," John replies, "Sometimes I put on a good act." He speaks, then, about missing his hospital roommate, Mat, who has recently been discharged, was expected to visit but hasn't yet turned up. Lin counters, in her usual way, by apparently agreeing and sympathizing with his plight and then changing the subject completely. "You missin' him I know. We don't even have admissions in the near future. So I don't know." She looks down at his thumb. "John, did you ever? Is this an old scar on your thumb? Where did you get it?"

Through this conversational gambit she gives him a freedom to speak as he will, while never fully relinquishing control of the overall tone, the developing narrative configuration. She interrupts the dismal illness story he appears to be developing with almost random comments, as in "Is this an old scar on your thumb?" an invitation to tell her about a past accident that has permanently scarred his body but not in the significant way he has recently been transfigured. Her interruptions nearly always ask him to shift his stance from present to past or future. From this point in the session, the storytelling begins, initiated by John.

First story: The gift

John tells a kind of "future story" about a surprise he is planning. He is going to give away his hockey equipment to one of the hospital staff with whom he has become friends. He has worked out a way to surprise the staff member with this happy idea and he describes how he wants it to occur. At first, John had considered selling the expensive equipment but by giving it away, he will honor an act of friendship because it was originally given to him and, as he tells Lin, "it would be just cheap of me to sell something that was given to me." Lin prompts him to tell his story of the planned surprise gift in even greater detail. When he finishes, both are smiling at one another as they anticipate the pleasure of the recipient. "What a nice guy you are," Lin tells him with a heartfelt sincerity. "That's a nice thing to do." John smiles more broadly, filling in more details as Lin questions him further. "Two hundred bucks for skates!" Lin says wonderingly as he informs her about the magnitude of this gift.

Second story: The non-visit

Lin initiates a second story by asking John about his sister who, as she already knows, has not come to visit. She inquires, "So where's the picture of you on the boat that looks like your dad? I've been waitin' for that one." John's sister, Sandra, has promised to bring him this picture, which Lin realizes full well would be prominently displayed on John's side table had it arrived. Lin has been following the rocky relationship between John and his sister, using therapy time to get caught up in the unfolding family drama and John's shifting family role which has been precipitated by his near fatal accident. Once a drug addict himself, John has been trying to convince his sister, also a drug addict, to seek help. Until recently, he had been hopeful that he might persuade her. Lately, his hopes have fallen. Lin asks, "So are you still convinced, are you still determined to help her out?" John shakes his head, no. His despair over his sister began a few weeks earlier when, Lin reports, "he had said that . . . he could never change her." He had a brief surge of hope a week before but during this session his despair has returned for she has not come with the picture as promised, and he knows she is trying to avoid him. The on-going saga with his sister is characterized by the same roller coaster ride that shapes his illness experience.

Third story: Remembering the ICU

There is a pause as Lin continues to range his hands. In this silence John says, "I have nothing to look forward to." At first, Lin does not seem to reply. Instead, she and John speak of a swelling in his arm caused by an infiltration, a minor problem which Lin explains. She then moves associationally from talk about his swollen arm which, she assures him, will "go down in no time" to his first days in the Intensive Care Unit when he was swollen almost beyond recognition. John has always been a slight, almost delicately built man and Lin graphically describes his metamorphosis: "You remember how swollen you were [in ICU]?" He shakes his head. "No? You don't remember up in the unit? You were a *big* boy. You were huge. Your neck was like this." She gestures with hands to illustrate his monstrous neck. "Your face, I mean, you looked obese!" John nods in agreement and Lin continues. "Yeah, remember I told you that joke up there? Remember, I went up to see you?" Her narrative style is sketchy, cryptic, events are etched as questions. Her tone is soft but there is a certain relentlessness. "And we did that thing when you were really stressed out? And I asked you if you wanted to do some relaxation and we did that thing to Hawaii? Remember that? I told you to close your eyes and relax and feel the warm sunshine. Remember that?" John nods, his face growing more and more sad as he listens. He has been following her intently as she describes these ICU scenes to him, as if reminiscing with her, though it is unlikely he actually remembers because they occurred when he was still critically ill, having just awakened from a coma. However, he has very likely heard this story of his first waking moments before, from family members as well as Lin. He knows it now from its retellings. "Do you really remember," Lin asks, "or are you just saying that to be nice?" She goes on without waiting for a reply. "And then I was telling you the joke about the bear and the rabbit and you knew the punch line. So I told the other joke about the . . ."

John interrupts to tell the rest of the story himself. He mouths his words while Lin reads his lips. Still ranging his hands, Lin exchanges places as audience, repeating his words aloud. She echoes, "You were pretty confused? You remember that you winked at Sandra [his sister]? That was the first thing you did [when you woke up from your coma]? First time you responded?" John nods again and tears start down his face. "What makes you sad?" Lin asks, leaning forward and quietly wiping away tears with a tissue as he continues to tell her his story. "Yeah," Lin replies to something he has said, "Hard to believe all that time has passed." Then she inserts her own voice, reassuming the dominant narrative position. She tells him "The members of your family were so determined for you to survive. And obviously they knew you well enough to know you would have been so determined. I mean people really didn't know if you were going to survive. As soon as you came to the determination really . . . What gives you the courage to do that?"

John's reply is inaudible and Lin chooses not to repeat it. Instead, she presses forward, "What do you look forward to?" she asks. John simply shakes his head. "Something, anything," Lin insists. "What's a real small thing?" She continues to wipe his eyes. John suddenly grins, breaking the intensity. "I can't tell you," he jokes. Lin laughs, "Well, whatever it is, it must be pretty good." Lin tries to probe further but John will have none of it. "Let's change the subject," he says. "OK," Lin concedes. "What shall we talk about? The Lakers' game on Sunday?"

Fourth story: Where are John's friends?

As John and Lin talk about sports, a fourth story develops about a benefit the Boston Bruins (hockey team) had for John's ex-roommate Mat who was being groomed for professional football before an accident playing ice hockey left him paralyzed. "Was the benefit for Mat last night?" Lin asks John. He nods. She inquires in more detail. "It wasn't on TV was it?" John shakes his head no and then begins to describe the benefit for Mat, mouthing words Lin follows but I mostly cannot understand. He looks visibly upset while Lin listens. "Wow!" she exclaims as he tells her that "over 600 people came" and "they had to turn people away at the door." She speculates about the money they must have raised. Mat, ex-athlete and still a handsome, charming boy of eighteen, has a starkly contrasting experience as a spinal cord patient to John, who cannot even persuade his sister to come and visit. Lin teasingly declares, "Oh sir. Too bad you don't have any friends to do anything for you." They both grin at this, but painfully this time, a joke which nearly tells the literal truth.

The plot: a story of stories

The session ends soon afterward. The four stories move as point and counterpoint on the themes of hope and despair. They have managed to shape the session into a narrative form that fits Lin's diagnosis of John's illness experience: a roller coaster with the patient on a downward slide. John's actions (not eating) have sent him plummeting dangerously downward. He is threatening to end the ride altogether in one final descent. Lin's "treatment" is a narrative counterattack, located in the few intense moments when she tells him the story of his first critical days after the accident. He listens with heart and soul, his eyes never leaving her face as he silently cries. In her storytelling she has found a way, for a brief moment, not only to remind him of his first days and how physically ill he was, but to introduce an alternative plot structure, a brave story in which he struggles to *will* to survive.

She follows a roller coaster of hills and valleys in her own guiding of the session. Her guidance is indicated in the curious way she lets the first hopeful story about giving away his hockey equipment (which he initiates), slide into his second despairing story which she, in fact, instigates by asking about visitors when she already knows that his sister has not come. While Lin mostly listens and only tells one of these stories, she plays a key role in shaping which stories John tells her by the questions she asks. But the shaping of this session is quite mutually guided. While there may be some sense here that the therapist is in charge, there is also a sense of teamwork, of patient and therapist being part of the "same story" which is still unfolding; one which neither has tremendous control over.

Though Lin does not dictate what gets said, her interventions help give a drama and a storyness to this session. She describes her goal as wanting to "touch base" with John and "touching base," like any complex action, requires a certain cumulativity of smaller actions. The session itself builds in intensity, peaking when she "touches" John with her own storytelling about the ICU experience. This is a kind of creation story; he awakens to someone he (and others) can barely recognize. She is tracing a narrative path. Once she has reminded him of this genesis, of immense courage at that hardest time, she then initiates her "Can you think of the future?" intervention. Here she locates his current situation with a story of beginnings and a pointing toward the future. Present is sandwiched between past and future, and in being so wedged, is emplotted in her story as a courageous movement forward. This reading is, in turn, taken up and then discarded by John who concludes this intense narrative exchange with a glum account of his roommate's wonderful benefit – a tale of too many visitors.

Though John has the last word, Lin's story of the ICU remains an unforgettable moment in that session. The intensity of that narrative interchange subverts John's dismal storytelling as surely as his final tale undermines any simple tale of progress. These two plot structures stand in uneasy relation to one another, allowing multiple and contradictory readings of John's unfolding illness experience to stand side by side. These contradictory readings are visited and revisited by Lin and John through the months of his hospital stay, both kept alive by the events that unfold, neither canceling the other out, each simultaneously cherished and cultivated by patient and therapist who simply allow them to co-exist.

From the therapist's perspective, emplotment involves configuring therapeutic activities which point to a particular reading of his illness experience. The reading is no passive matter; how John interprets his illness experience has become, quite literally, a life and death situation. Because John is so sick, the primary action left to him is talk and hence talk is the therapeutic medium through which emplotment occurs and an experience is created. Reading the illness story is accomplished by an apparently haphazard exchange of four small personal stories. Lin and John are at once authors and audience to their own stories. They tell different kinds of stories. Lin is more often the voice of hope and John the voice of despair. Yet it is not that simple. For Lin believes it essential that John voice his despair; this fits her own view of the necessary emotional response to the tragedy he confronts and her own idea of the paradigmatic illness story which requires a dark passage through grief and mourning. Patients like John who are willing to speak about their own fear and anger are ones she works best with, the ones she believes will survive. And John seems to ask Lin to voice a hopeful side as counterbalance to his own hopelessness. So while their stories seem to derive from different positions, they are in fact necessary counterparts to one another.

Taken together the story exchanges create a reading experience of John's illness which, quite remarkably, has the same up-and-down movement Lin believes characterizes John's illness experience as a whole. The narratives play off one another to create an image of John's illness experience in which the thematic configuration is "illness as roller coaster." And yet, at one pivotal point in the session, Lin interjects with a story of such intensity that it provides a wholly different narrative structure, threatening to overturn the roller coaster configuration with an against-all-odds emplotment, a battle in which John gradually wins a fight for his life. This narrative threat is, in turn, subverted by John who will not let Lin's story form the basis for images of his future. The plot, and the stories which make it up, are "little narratives," as Lyotard has used the term.

Who is John in this therapeutic plot?

How well do the dualisms of role versus inner self, or narrated self versus experienced self, hold up in this case? Both are challenged. Let us take the first dualism, and simply glance at John in the role of "brother." If we look at this brother role simply as a role, a persona governed by culturally shared norms, we do not begin to engage in his struggle over how to be a brother to his sister. There is the question of which kind of brother to be. Certainly he has been the "bad" older brother in the past, and now as he tries to convert to the responsible older brother, how much should he agonize over his inability to play this role effectively? That is, how hard should he try to influence his sister in good ways, and how closely should he tie his own emergent and changing sense of identity to this particular effort? To what extent should he try to become the "man" of the family? As responsible older brother, he might be expected to assume this role since his father passed away a year earlier. Notably, the picture he wants by his bedside, the one his sister has promised but failed to deliver, is one of his father, at some younger age, looking very like John. (Or rather, like John before the accident.)

But what does it mean to become the man of the family for the first time, when John now has a body which must be cared for as an infant, and his mother and sister are coming to the hospital to learn how to do this care? Can he be both brother and infant at once? Or brother and father and infant? Is one of these roles a mask while the others reflect an inner self? The dualism does not seem to carry us very far in sorting out the dilemma John faces of who he should now try to become as a member of his family.

As for the distinction between the experienced self and the narrated self, this also appears problematic. Lin and John tell stories which offer alternative (even inconsistent) messages about John's unfolding life story. No single coherent narrative structure is offered. But this inconsistency does not point toward an inchoateness or incoherence at the level of the experience of self, as some anthropologists have argued. Rather, these stories – including the way they follow one another – indicate a self in suspense.

Above all, John's case represents a self in moral suspense. Nussbaum describes narrative as the necessary avenue for coming to the question How should I live? For this question must be asked in recognition of the world's variety, its strange contingencies and elusive problems. One needs narrative to contemplate the world in its complexities and to decipher how one should navigate one's way in it. For narrative is just that form which is built on surprise, chance, contingency, the anomalous event. Its very form offers a vision of life as constituted by "significant surprises" (Nussbaum 1990: 3). Practical reasoning is narratively centered because, in the midst of life's strange turns and puzzling passes, our moral task "as agents is to live as good characters in a good story do, caring about what happens, resourcefully confronting each new thing" (Nussbaum 1990: 3–4).

John is struggling over how to transform himself, who to become. This is not a matter of chaos versus order but contemplation concerning a limited range of options. This contemplation is expressed and carried out not only in his stories (or in his reception of Lin's story) but in his actions. He plans a surprise party to give away his hockey equipment. This is not merely a story he tells, but an action he contemplates and later executes. He is, I would say, trying to create a story of a self transformed, from drug addict and irresponsible fellow to giver of gifts, honorable friend. He describes his plan with relish, with delight. Simultaneously, he is refusing to eat, therefore acting as a character in quite a different life story, one which ends in despair, and very soon at that.

His actions and his stories are of a piece. They point toward the self at a cross-roads, someone who cannot go back and who, in trying to see how to go forward, tries out several possible paths, and all at once. This case is not about an experienced self as chaotic on the one hand and a narrated self as ordered on the other. The actions which the stories recount express an exploration of self, provisional answers to the question "Who Am I?" among a limited range of historical possibilities.

6 Some moments are more narrative than others

Although clinical interactions are always guided by some underlying narrative (some answers to the question "What story am I in?") emplotment may be minimal and easily relinquished. Many of the narrative plots described in earlier chapters have been rich in images and clearly co-created among participants. Not all clinical time is like this. A narrative orientation to therapeutic actions is always in tension with another structure of clinical action which resists emplotment. One sees narrative interruptions – plots that begin, a story that seems to develop between therapist and patient but is subverted, and often by the therapist.

One of my first observations of occupational therapists took me by surprise as I puzzled over the odd nature of the therapist's interventions. I was struck by the therapist's willingness to abandon a group activity that, to my eyes, appeared to be highly successful. I draw from field notes and memory to tell this story. A vulnerable-looking young woman in her early twenties, a girl really, with long brown hair, sat surrounded by ten old men in their wheelchairs. She was conducting an "activities group," she told me later. The men drooled as they listed sideways in their seats, white legged in their white dressing gowns. I watched from outside the circle, taking notes. No one seemed to notice me. Is it possible to be partly dead, I wondered? The occupational therapist had a yellow foam ball that she told them to throw to one another. She pitched it underhand across the circle. One thin arm swung out, batting ineffectually. The girl got up, retrieved the ball, and tried again. Some swooped and thrashed in half-hearted attempts at catch, others stared into the distance, letting the ball bounce against them without even a glance. A few minutes later the girl announced cheerfully, "Although winter is coming, we are going to talk about spring. Soon we will plant some seeds in the window boxes so we can grow some flowers or vegetables. Did any of you ever have gardens?"

An odd thing happened. A man began to speak, straightening in his chair ever so slightly. "I used to drink beer in the spring," he said. "I watched baseball on TV." Then another man said, "I had a garden every year. I grew tomatoes, squash, peppers, zucchini." Others joined, recounting the wonders of gardens past. Someone talked about the fish he used to catch. Heads lifted. Eyes focused. I watched this awakening in amazement. They were not dead after all. And then the therapist, mid-story, announced to the group that it was time for the next activity, chair exercises. She set them off in a series of arm stretches. Heads drooped, eyes glazed, but she continued instructing in a clear sweet voice, showing them how to bend and stretch, though she was the only one moving.

The pain of this scene has stayed with me, the kindness in the girl's eyes when she retrieved that yellow ball, green gardens heavy with vegetables, younger men drinking beer while they picked red tomatoes and listened to the ball game on the radio. How could the therapist awaken these men to this storytelling and shut them down again at the prescribed time according to her treatment plan? How could she bear this daily demise as they returned to corpse-like inertness, knowing as she did how they could lift their heads when they told of their gardens and their beer and spring baseball? How could her brown eyes be so kind and so heedless all at once?

While in this early observation I had not yet developed a conception of the narrative structure of clinical action, I did wonder why the therapist relinquished an activity that seemed to be going somewhere, that awakened these sleeping people and allowed them to express their desires, and in such a way that one person's comments were listened to and built upon by another. Later, I came to analyze such segments in narrative terms, as the emergence of a "proto-narrative" structure. But at this time I simply felt the oddness of it, and the loss which came with interrupting an activity that had some heart to it, that went beyond a set of rote actions and addressed, in some way, the larger life horizons of these old and dying men.

For some reason, this particular session has remained vivid. But there is nothing unique about it. I have seen scenes like this again and again. What first looked like a curious carelessness on the part of the therapist later became evident as a tension deep within the professional culture. Put simply, this tension emanates from a need to structure clinical interventions in a way that fit a medical model of clinical work, on the one hand, and interventions tailored to the individual needs, motives and desires of the patient, on the other. While sometimes these dual concerns can be addressed at once, therapists often feel themselves pulled between competing conceptions of good practice, now veering toward directing clinical interventions in a way that somehow "fits" the particular patient (or the particular group), and then shifting toward clinical work that more obviously fits a "medical model," as the therapists say.

Even during the best of times, this dual focus is likely to result in a sort of jagged dance in which both the patient and the condition are addressed and in which therapeutic plots are created, interrupted, resumed, and sometimes abandoned altogether. The following is one such example. A therapist treating an acutely head injured patient is about to see her for the third time. The therapist, Elizabeth, anticipates that her patient, Mary Sue, will be able to do little active movement. Mary Sue is quite ill and her level of medication is toxic, increasing her drowsiness and inability to respond in therapy; also, she is neurologically unstable. A massive "insult to her brain," as Elizabeth puts it, has resulted in an injury where she could "bleed at any time." Elizabeth presumes she will have to watch her responses extremely carefully to avoid increasing intracranial pressure that could result in a bleed. Her main goals for the session are: to increase her level of alertness over time, to improve her trunk control and head control, getting her to a point where she can sit unsupported and move her right arm without falling over.

Elizabeth is known as an expert in her area of acute neurology, valued by colleagues because of her in-depth clinical knowledge rather than her bedside manner. More than many therapists, her emphasis is on diagnosing and treating the body. She is less interested in the "biographical self" presented by the patient than the self expressed through movement. In her view, the capacity for physical movement underlies the capacity to have a certain sort of self – to express functional independence, to have desires which one is able to carry out. Her stated objectives for the session reflect this. These goals, which provide some general notions of what to do, will be modified as Elizabeth observes Mary Sue's responses to treatment. They are by no means organized in narrative form. Yet even here therapist and patient will work to transform the interchange into a personal drama with the patient as hero struggling with her own body. How are these goals transformed from a series of generalized treatment objectives, named one by one, into a narrative complete with risks, desires, transformations and a plot structure? How does this narrative structure crumble in the face of the therapist's concern to investigate and address the pathological body? How is the interrupted plot again resumed, and for what reason?

The touch[1]

A very sick woman enters the room. It is impossible to tell her age accurately, though I guess her to be in her mid-twenties. She is wheeled into the treatment room by an occupational therapy student assisting in the session and brought over to the mat. One half of the room is dominated by a large orange mat (a plinth) which looks rather like a bright plastic double bed sitting on a wooden frame. The patient's head is completely shaved. There are stitches along one side. She is in the usual hospital gown. As she comes in, she seems almost expressionless, hanging awkwardly to one side of the wheelchair. Her bald head and her weary expression make her seem old. And yet there is something naive in her look and when she speaks, as she soon does, her voice sounds girlish. The sound of a fifteen-year-old in an old woman's body. Despite her rather desperate looking physical appearance, she greets me cheerily after Elizabeth introduces me. "Mary Sue, this is Cheryl and she is going to do the filming." "Hi Cheryl," Mary Sue responds immediately, giving me a grin.

Mary Sue is transferred to the plinth where she sits with feet resting uneasily on the floor as she sways slightly from side to side. The rhythm between Elizabeth and Mary Sue soon establishes itself. Elizabeth, in her low and firm voice, instructs and requests, accompanying her words with assistance from her own body. Elizabeth asks Mary Sue to reach out to her hand which she holds just far enough away so that Mary Sue must struggle to maintain balance while reaching to make the touch. As Mary Sue complies with the therapist's requests, Elizabeth cheers her on in her low, even voice, a well-muted enthusiasm. She also asks Mary Sue to let her know how her body feels as she moves, thus requesting that Mary Sue both carry out the task and reflect on the effect of the movements on her body. A snippet of dialogue in which Elizabeth talks, while Mary Sue bodily responds, serves to illustrate:

ELIZABETH: (speaking very slowly and quietly) OK, Mary Sue, you try to sit up the best you can. Do your absolute best. (pause to watch Mary Sue move) Not bad. You're doing it better than yesterday. (pause again to watch Mary Sue steadying herself in a sitting position) Good. See if you can sit straight, get your hand over to my hand. Good. Now, get this hand out to my hand. Reach forward (pause while Mary Sue reaches) you can do it. Try to catch your balance. (Mary Sue steadies herself) OK, reach out to my hand. (Mary Sue reaches) That's it, all the way to my hand. (pause to watch Mary Sue lean) There you go. (Mary Sue touches her hand) Very good. Now can you reach for my hand up here? Reach for my hand. (Mary Sue does) Great. Can you hold it there? (Mary Sue uses Elizabeth's arm to steady herself) Don't pull my arm down, just hold it. Hold it.
MARY SUE: OK?
ELIZABETH: OK. Do you feel a little bit wobbly?
MARY SUE: Yeah, a little bit.
ELIZABETH: OK, look for my hand up here. See my hand?

MARY SUE: Yup.

ELIZABETH: Can you reach for it again? (Mary Sue does) OK, great. OK. Let's see if you get this hand on top of my shoulder. But, do it very slowly, OK? I want you to really concentrate. Get it on top of my shoulder and try to hold yourself up at the same time.

MARY SUE: Like that?

ELIZABETH: Um-hum.

Most communication here is a kind of body fitting, as Mary Sue reaches toward Elizabeth and Elizabeth almost imperceptibly rearranges herself to guide Mary Sue's movement. Although there is little actual touching, there is an encircling, as though there were a literal thera-peutic space being drawn by their movements. The words themselves, almost but not quite incidental, offer a break in the silence but it is silence that prevails. This is a quiet rhythm, two women together, intent on their reaching, one hand trying to touch another; a very slow waltz. Elizabeth keeps a left hand outstretched and still above Mary Sue's head, waiting for Mary Sue's touch. Elizabeth's right arm is poised a few inches from Mary Sue, ready to right her should she get too wobbly. Mary Sue concentrates on the outstretched hand. Carefully and with utter seriousness she navigates her body. Her mouth is pursed.

These small touches to a hand or a shoulder are marked by small congratulations offered by Elizabeth, sometimes at Mary Sue's prompting. Pauses mark silences as Elizabeth watches Mary Sue struggle to carry out her directives. Progress is often noted.

MARY SUE: How's that?

ELIZABETH: That was good. And bring your hand down to your lap. And do it slowly, very slowly. (pause) OK, great. (pause) OK, super. (pause) That's fine. It looks wobbly to you, I'm sure, but you're doing a great job. Something you couldn't have done a couple of days ago.

MARY SUE: That's for sure.

ELIZABETH: Yeah! (a light, soft cheer) Try and get your hand on top of my shoulder again and do it again, super slowly, way up on top of my shoulder. (pause) That's it. (pause) Oh, not pulling on it, not pulling on it. Just reach up for my shoulder. (pause) OK, reach up. (pause) OK, almost. (pause) You're cheating a little bit, I must say. You're pulling on my shoulder a little bit. Try not to pull on it. I think you can do it on your own, it's just going to be a little harder. But I think you can do it. Want to try again?

MARY SUE: Sure.

ELIZABETH: OK! OK, reach on top of my shoulder, slowly.

MARY SUE: Was that better?

ELIZABETH: That was better. That was much better.

Elizabeth offers her quiet, authoritative voice to this pronouncement, countering any negative interpretation Mary Sue might be making. In effect she declares, as therapists so often do, that Mary Sue can safely believe Elizabeth over the evidence of her own senses for Elizabeth is the expert record keeper of therapeutic gains.

This gentle dance is finally interrupted by Elizabeth, who has other activities in mind. Elizabeth wants to do some diagnostic checking of Mary Sue's overall motoric responses to assess how they have been affected by her brain injury. She asks Mary Sue to lie flat while Elizabeth rolls her body from side to side, soundlessly observing the responses of Mary Sue's body to these maneuvers. A student therapist, Jennifer, who has been standing to one side, is now called into action. Elizabeth asks her help in moving Mary Sue into the proper positions so that trunk stability, muscle spasticity, range of motion and the like can be assessed. Elizabeth also turns to Jennifer, occasionally explaining what she is doing. Mary Sue becomes fretful and begins to complain.

ELIZABETH: (directing Mary Sue) Look toward the wall, turn your head to the wall. All the way. That's it, keep your head right towards the wall. Do you have your head turned towards the wall?

MARY SUE: Ouch, that hurts.

ELIZABETH: OK, let's try it again. I think I can do it without hurting you. Keep your arm way up over your head. (pause) OK. (pause) Is your shoulder up there or is it (inaudible)? (pause) Jennifer, see if you can hold her arm up for me (inaudible).

MARY SUE: Ow, that hurts.

ELIZABETH: Is it just the arm that hurts or is it something else?

MARY SUE: My arm and my shoulder.

ELIZABETH: OK. (to the student) There is a little bit of tone in that side. (back to Mary Sue) Can you stand it for two seconds?

MARY SUE: Yeah.

ELIZABETH: Look to the wall again, turn your head way over to the wall. (pause) Turn your head a little more. (pause) To the wall. (pause) OK. Are you worried you're getting too close to the edge? Let me move you a little bit.

MARY SUE: The pillows keep on sliding.

After less than ten minutes of this, Elizabeth shifts back to her earlier rhythm, ignoring the student, dropping the impersonal reference, and redirecting her communication to Mary Sue who is again asked to touch her hand from this new position. The change in Mary Sue is instantaneous, as though she was trying to reinforce this improvement in events. At her first compliance with Elizabeth's request, she enthusiastically congratulates herself, taking over the job of marking her achievements. Elizabeth now becomes the echo, as Mary Sue exuberantly cheers herself onward.

MARY SUE: I did it!

ELIZABETH: You sure did! Try it again, can you do it a second time? You have to get there somehow.

MARY SUE: Come on, stretch. I did it!
ELIZABETH: OK, I guess you did it again.
(They close this act as they did earlier, by noting progress.)
ELIZABETH: You have a lot more energy today as compared to yesterday.
MARY SUE: Yeah, this is one of my good days. You better take advantage of it.
ELIZABETH: I sure will.
MARY SUE: I think what helped is that the doctor changed my medicine.
ELIZABETH: I'm sure it made a big difference.
MARY SUE: It made a big difference.

Another shift is introduced when Elizabeth sets a final task for Mary Sue, the most difficult of all, a reach that throws her precariously off balance. Mary Sue, who sits for this reach, begins to slide off the mat. This slip frightens her. Elizabeth reassures her that everything is alright, that this slip is not a failure but was intended all along to teach Mary Sue how far she can lean without losing her balance. This segment demonstrates the line therapists try to walk, cajoling patients farther and farther, asking them to struggle through pain or physical fear, while not losing sight of a plot structure in which successful progress is being made. After Elizabeth and Mary Sue finish this last difficult reach, they offer a series of congratulatory rounds and Elizabeth calls a halt to the session.

ELIZABETH: I think you deserve a break.
MARY SUE: OK.
ELIZABETH: Do you agree?
MARY SUE: Alright. I'll take a break, sure.
ELIZABETH: You worked really hard, you know?
MARY SUE: Yup!
ELIZABETH: That's a lot of hard work. You did a great job!
MARY SUE: This is the best I've done all week.
ELIZABETH: I think so too. That's a good sign.
MARY SUE: Jennifer, do you think so too?
JENNIFER: Oh yeah!
MARY SUE: At least I stayed awake.
ELIZABETH: You stayed awake the whole time.
MARY SUE: Through the whole thing.
ELIZABETH: It looks like you have some energy left, too!
MARY SUE: Yeah.
ELIZABETH: But you know what, I think you should go back to your room and
    rest anyway.
MARY SUE: OK.
ELIZABETH: Take it easy for a bit.
MARY SUE: OK.
ELIZABETH: Then tomorrow, you are going to do it again?
MARY SUE: Sure.
ELIZABETH: Alright.

Mary Sue is soon helped back into her wheelchair and taken out by Jennifer. She says good-bye to me as she leaves.

The plot

In this session the therapist has been keenly tuned in to a neurological drama – a precarious diagnostic condition where the prognosis is in suspense. A clinical drama may be unfolding in Mary Sue's body but where is the social drama that places Mary Sue at the center? Where is time narratively configured in the sense I have used this notion? Where are plot, motive, desire, trouble, dramatic reversal and transformation, suspense? Clearly, this is a therapeutic narrative of minimal proportions. There are few words, no obvious transformations, no great dramas in evidence. The patient is very ill and very eager to please, the therapist very much in charge. And yet, this is not a session of rote obedience by the patient, or of rote directives by the therapist. There are moments in which it looks like a well choreographed dance, a choreography which is not the result of following a script but of improvisations in which the therapist responds to as well as guides the patient. However, these two women are not "in the same story" in the sense of wanting the same things from their time together. They enter the scene with different desires and, inevitably, different ways of understanding what therapy is meant to accomplish.

The plot begins when Elizabeth introduces me to Mary Sue. This bit of politeness is routine to Elizabeth. But it holds narrative import. It prefigures a plot in which Mary Sue emerges as a dance partner and, gradually, as a self-reflective performer. There is even a moment or two when she becomes the director of other actors on the stage. At one level, emplotment here is simple, a dance of desire in which a touch has two distinct meanings, satisfying the quite different concerns of these two actors. For Mary Sue, a touch is a social connection. For Elizabeth, this touch carries clinical weight. Any social meaning is secondary, a vehicle for clinically defined ends. More subtly, she plots to structure an interaction in which Mary Sue experiences her body moving in more normal ways and learns to evaluate the "goodness" of her movements. But the plot is also with Mary Sue's body apart from Mary Sue's intentional understanding. Elizabeth wants Mary Sue to intend a purposeful act, like touching her hand, but not to intend the many body movements (balancing, reaching and the like) necessary to carry out that act. This unconsciousness is, of course, integral to normal body activity. However, Elizabeth knows she must connect with the intending, conscious patient as well as with a tacitly experienced body.

Connection involves a transferral of desire. Elizabeth explains to me later that Mary Sue is too ill to care about her own body very much. Elizabeth must, in a sense "be the person" for Mary Sue, wanting improvements in Mary Sue's capacities for movement that Mary Sue cannot now care about. Mary Sue is not without desire, however. What motivates her is a "social interest," as Elizabeth puts it, in doing something together and in performing well for the therapist. Elizabeth draws upon this, asking Mary Sue to do things which Elizabeth hopes will begin an internal reconciliation – mind with body. This journey back to the embodied self provides the narrative frame within which Elizabeth acts; each of her actions takes its meaning as part of this journey. And, Elizabeth also hopes that Mary Sue will take up this same narrative horizon, will gradually see herself in this same story. "With more normal movement," Elizabeth tells me, "she'll become more aware . . . that this feels good."

Motives: The centrality of desire

Elizabeth's first task is to turn the patient into an actor rather than a mere "body" acted upon by others. One way she does this is through an introduction to me. This presentation is eagerly taken up by the patient who transforms in front of my eyes from a very sick body, a kind of biomedical disaster area, into a particular young woman – Mary Sue – with a certain amount of spunk, a friendly nature, and a palpable loneliness. While Elizabeth opens the door with her introduction the transformation is accomplished by Mary Sue herself when she lifts up her bald head, looks me straight in the eye and gives me a cheerful hello, carefully repeating my name. I like her immediately. Such a little thing, this greeting, but in the world of the hospital it is remarkably rare for a patient, especially one so sick, to be extended this courtesy and invited into the social world of the non-sick.

Although Elizabeth does not take the particulars of Mary Sue's life into consideration, she is intent on establishing a personal connection at the start of therapy. Even in this work with a very ill patient who seems stripped of her identity (head shaved, barely able to move, drugged almost into a stupor, adorned in hospital gown), when Mary Sue shows a certain spark in her personality, Elizabeth capitalizes on this. Nowhere is this more evident than in the choice of therapeutic goals. When the therapist directs Mary Sue in a reaching exercise, what Mary Sue must reach for is Elizabeth herself. This allows the session to take on the figure of a dance, a very fluid and graceful dance in which the two women move together to reach a shared goal. Elizabeth, slim and tall, bends her body toward Mary Sue so that she will have to work to reach her shoulder but, in doing so, can look Elizabeth in the face. Elizabeth lowers her voice so that her directives take on an almost musical lilt. Whenever she sees that Mary Sue is wobbling too far, that the reach is too much, she shifts her body almost imperceptibly, edging just close enough to allow Mary Sue to make contact.

Elizabeth's body becomes a technical tool, a very delicate one, which can respond and adjust fluidly, as needed. Elizabeth's movements are so slight and smooth in the interaction it was only later, upon examining the videotape, that it became evident Elizabeth was continuously in motion, modifying her own position in response to Mary Sue. Using her body allows Elizabeth to challenge Mary Sue to what she estimates to be the limit of her ability. Elizabeth's body also serves as a data-gathering instrument. By feeling Mary Sue's touch, she can continually reevaluate Mary Sue's motor capacities. But this fluid use of her body satisfies Mary Sue's desire as well. Elizabeth recognizes and uses Mary Sue's need for social connection, for person to person touch. She also draws upon Mary Sue's need to please. Elizabeth announces early in the session, "You're doing [the reaching] better than yesterday." The events of the session underscore this pronouncement. Elizabeth guides every movement so that Mary Sue experiences her body as competent. With her own body as target, Elizabeth can shift without Mary Sue even noticing and ensure Mary Sue's success.

Elizabeth hopes that the experience of these touches will reawaken Mary Sue's inclination to move. Mary Sue lacks appropriate concern for her body, is curiously detached from it. But Elizabeth needs Mary Sue to struggle to the very edge of her capacity, to reach beyond what is comfortable even when she becomes afraid. Her problem, from a narrative perspective, is how to inspire Mary Sue to make a journey that she wishes for more than Mary Sue does. The dance we see between these women is not only in their movements. There is also a dance of desires, each working to accommodate the other because neither can have what she wants without the other's assistance. For if Mary Sue is not so keen on the journey, she at least wants the guide, and the touch. And perhaps even more, the chance to present herself as competent, as having capacities which others applaud. For this, she needs Elizabeth's help as enthusiastic spectator.

The plot is quickly set in motion, then, from the first introduction. Mary Sue is given the chance to make social contact, which she does with a smile that lights up her whole face. And, she gives Elizabeth what she desires, hard work. For this, she is rewarded not only by Elizabeth's constant attention, her encircling body, but also by Elizabeth's approval of her efforts. Mary Sue plays her part in carrying this plot forward by making regular requests to which Elizabeth always responds. When Mary Sue wants more, she asks and Elizabeth complies. "How's that?" she regularly inquires. "That was very good," Elizabeth responds. There are even some congratulatory chants. "Was that better?" asks Mary Sue. "That was better. That was much better," echoes Elizabeth.

Troubles and transformations

Here is a young woman so very afflicted she may die at any moment. Her life has been an endless parade of illnesses. This last medical crisis, and the drugs she has been given to treat it, have rendered her body an alien thing. This is not the alienness of John, the man with the spinal cord injury who is keenly aware of his loss and is considering death as a possible response. Mary Sue is rendered indifferent. She is far too undisturbed. The therapist hopes to create trouble, to give her experiences which will kindle some commitment to her body, some willingness to take trouble over it. Of course, as we have seen, Mary Sue is not indifferent to everything. But she has lost interest in her body. Sacks' description of a patient who became "disembodied" may tell us something about Mary Sue's condition. Sacks writes of this patient, "She continues to feel, with the continuing loss of proprioception, that her body is dead, not-real, not-hers – she cannot appropriate it to herself" (1987: 51). Sacks goes on to say, "She has lost . . . the fundamental organic mooring of identity – at least of that corporeal identity, or 'body-ego,' which Freud sees as the basis of self" (1987: 52). This loss was so total that the woman Sacks tells us about became truly disembodied, "pithed." Mary Sue is not this profoundly lost in her body and Elizabeth hopes that a reconnection will be possible. When Elizabeth asks Mary Sue to reach for her hand, she is inviting her into a story in which she will be transformed from impassive observer of her own body to someone who has repossessed her "organic mooring." This return to a first home is no mere matter of relearning some lost perceptual motor skills. It requires a reawakening of bodily desire, the will to move, to reach out to the world, and to know that something of significance in that world is within one's grasp.

There are two clearly marked transitions in this session. One, triggered by Elizabeth, is a temporary abandonment of the plot they have been creating together. The second, which occurs after this, is a dramatic shift in Mary Sue as she takes a strong role in directing the evaluation of her performance. While at the beginning of the session, Mary Sue looks toward Elizabeth for confirmation that she is doing well, she later takes on this role for herself, informing Elizabeth of her good work. This shift is an important signal to Elizabeth that a therapeutic plot has been taken up by the patient who is now not merely acquiescing but judges for herself when she is doing well. And more heartening still, Mary Sue is quite accurate in her assessment. The final half of the session is, comparatively speaking, charged with energy. Mary Sue seems to gain strength from each successive try for Elizabeth's hand. Her voice grows more confident as she reaches again and again. Their dance becomes synchronous, the reaching and touching so smooth that they seem to have grown together, each anticipating the other's response. Their speech also has that feel, as they repeat one another in a kind of poetic incantation. "I did it!," cries Mary Sue. "You sure did it," replies Elizabeth. A moment later, "I did it," cries Mary Sue after her second success. "I guess you did it again," replies Elizabeth. Even a discussion of a change in medications follows this repetitive beat. "I'm sure [the change] made a big difference," Elizabeth asserts. "It made a big difference," Mary Sue replies.

Suspenseful endings

The final interchange of this session looks very much like the "evaluation" stage of an oral narrative. In Labovian analysis, the evaluation phase comments on a story just told. It is here that the narrator offers an explicit moral to the story (Labov and Waletzky 1967). So, too, this final segment comments on the events which have transpired during their session. Notably, this commentary addresses the "narrative" segments and skips over the diagnostic interlude in which Mary Sue plays no active part. Extended congratulations are offered, initiated by Elizabeth. She does not say it is time to quit but, evaluatively, that Mary Sue "deserves" a break. She then presses her point by asking Mary Sue to agree, which she does, but without self-congratulation. Elizabeth is not content. "You worked really hard, you know?" she says. When Mary Sue enthusiastically concurs, Elizabeth reinforces "You did a great job!" Roles reverse as Mary Sue takes over. "This is the best I've done all week," she announces. Elizabeth agrees. Mary Sue then invites the student therapist to applaud. "Jennifer, do you think so too?" The dance which marked the session is recapitulated in this evaluative moment, therapist and patient building on one another's comments. "At least I stayed awake," says Mary Sue. "You stayed awake the whole time," replies Elizabeth. "Through the whole thing," Mary Sue echoes.

This ending is, of course, also a middle, one episode in a therapeutic encounter that began two weeks earlier and will stretch out into the future. And it also represents a beginning, one episode in a more hopeful therapeutic plot – an imagined plot – where Mary Sue builds on her good week and becomes stronger and more capable as the weeks unfold. Elizabeth makes this narrative intention clear in her last question. "Then tomorrow you are going to do it again?" "Sure," Mary Sue tells her. Beneath repetition is the hope of history, movement through time marked by ever widening possibilities for action.

Narrative interruptions

While there is a sense of plot in this session, emplotment is fragile and barely developed. In narrative time many factors may precipitate a dramatic movement but those that matter most are generated by human agency. Human agency is foregrounded even if it has to do with how individual actors *respond* to events that need not be humanly caused at all (a "massive insult to the brain"). In therapeutic context, time is narrative when the body as lived and experienced, as called upon by the actor, is central to the intervention.

The implicit narrative pact is broken by Elizabeth mid-way through the session. There is an abrupt return to a non-narrative clinical time in which Mary Sue is a patient with an intricate diagnostic history and uncertain prognosis. The journey Elizabeth initiated is halted because Elizabeth wants to do some evaluation of Mary Sue, and also to teach the student therapist something about how to assess motor dysfunctions in a patient with Mary Sue's acute neurological problems. The ambiance of the session changes. Elizabeth shifts her tone, speaking in a clear, carrying voice directed as much to the student as to Mary Sue. Her posture changes as well. She straightens to her full, nearly six foot height as she circles the plinth, deftly shifting a prone Mary Sue into the positions she wants.

Mary Sue is also transformed, now a small bald bundle, helpless and fretful. Her hospital gown falls open in back to expose her pale and naked to the camera's view until Elizabeth, who has been concentrating on her head and neck, happens to notice and covers her. Nothing is asked of her; she is reduced to sheer body, a shift underscored by the conversation between Elizabeth and the student therapist in which, at one point, she is referred to in the third person. "Jennifer," Elizabeth directs, "see if you can hold her arm up for me."

In these non-narrative moments, the patient as actor recedes into the distance. In Burke's (1945) grammatical metaphor, the patient and her body become the "scene" upon which the play is enacted. From the healer's perspective, a plot may still be unfolding but the central character is a clinical condition. This abandonment precipitated by the therapist is protested by the patient who struggles to return to an emplotment that engages her desires and requires her participation as actor.

Emplotment and the double vision of occupational therapy

The clearest difference between clinical time structured in a "medical model" and time more narratively configured is the extent to which the patient is invited to be a human actor necessary to the unfolding plot, one capable of desire and motive. Clinical time which suppresses narrative generally does so in the name of treating the diagnosis. In these anti-narrative times, the clinical task focuses on the treatment of discrete body parts or functional skills. Note the following exchange between a therapist and an elderly male patient during a clinical session. They are working to improve the range of motion in his arms. At the beginning of the session, the therapist describes the purpose of their task to the patient: "We've gotta get the range for you to have the strength." The therapist directs the patient in stretching exercises. The patient is positioned in front of a mirror so he can watch his body move. He comments at one point that these stretches aren't making him sore, a fact that worries his therapist.

PATIENT: I'm looking for the pain and I can't find it.
THERAPIST: What we're really doing is . . . I'm doing all the work. Sometimes if I stretch my leg, it will hurt the next day. Maybe I'm not taking you far enough.
PATIENT: Well, I mean that pain you get when you exercise.

Here is pain no longer associated with the person, not *my* pain, but something external to myself even if in my own body, something I cannot find. This same dissociative stance is echoed in later exchanges between the two as the therapist offers a verbal commentary that serves as choral accompaniment to the patient's repeated efforts to lift his arms.

THERAPIST: C'mon, M., you can do it, c'mon, c'mon, let's go! Up! Up! Up! To the ceiling, out to the side, no cheating, Yes, yes, yes. To the side, all the way back. Good! Relax.
(The therapist gives him a bungee cord to pull on as she pulls the other end.)
THERAPIST: Pull! Pull! Pull! Elbows up. Back to your chest. Good. Now think up this time. Overhead! Think over your head. Think it's your shirt. Think shirt. We want to get it over your head. (practically yelling) We want this to go around your neck. Touch your forehead. I know you can do this. C'mon.

C'mon. Pull! Pull! Get it to your forehead! C'mon M., I know you can do this.
PATIENT: It won't!
THERAPIST: Don't say *it* won't. You *can* do it. (he reaches his forehead) *See*, you can do it. OK, relax.

The patient struggles with a bungee cord, crying out that "it won't" as he fails to bring the cord over his head. What is this "it" exactly which "won't"? Whether he is referring to the cord, his body, or the failed action itself, his language is passive. He is instantly countered by the therapist who retorts, "Don't say it won't. You *can* do it." While she is ostensibly returning the patient's personhood to the act (a very definite "you" is pronounced as the critical agent), she simultaneously undermines his role as agent because she flatly denies his own self-description. The ambiguous "it" is the deciding agent from the patient's perspective, but this perspective is just what the therapist disallows in her counter description.

Even when patients offer comments that reveal their experience of their bodies in a highly personal way, therapists may refuse to take up this phenomenological drift and reframe body problems in purely physical or technical terms. Avoiding the phenomenological permits a cause and effect relation to prevail which links discrete physical gains to overall life improvement. The need to skirt any questioning of this explanatory rationale can be seen in the common side-stepping of other framings suggested by patients. For example, during one therapy session, an elderly woman whose right leg has been amputated tells her therapist, "I used to be so strong, arms, legs, hands. I got weakness in my leg due to bypass surgery. I spent a year sitting. I got numbness in my hands from arthritis." She looks down at her hands. "They look like my grandmother's. There's so many things I like to do that I can't do. Even sometimes cooking – to chop – it depends on the day. I have a hard time chopping." There is obvious potential in this passing reflection on hands that now fail, symbolic now of one's transmutation into a family elder. Rather than plunge into a potential phenomenological abyss, the therapist chooses to read the woman's comments as a request for technical help and suggests a piece of adaptive equipment, a rocker knife, to aid the chopping problem.

These examples reveal that storymaking enters therapeutic practice in an uneasy way. Occupational therapy integrates (rather uncomfortably) a double vision of the body, a biomechanical conception which belongs to mainstream medical culture, and a phenomenological conception which arises in part from the professional culture as historically developed and in part the nature of occupational therapy practice (see also

Mattingly and Fleming 1994). The ability to help patients improve physical self-care skills ideally results in "measurable outcomes" which therapists are most comfortable reporting in staffings or in the medical charts. However, because therapists are also inculcated with a strong belief that disabled patients should return, as far as possible, to their primary occupations and carry them out as independently as they can, this agenda tends to propel them very differently. They are moved beyond a narrow physical focus on body improvement to consider the meaning of a disabled body for the life of the patient. They are further propelled in this direction, as illustrated in earlier chapters, because the structure of practice requires that patients become invested in therapy and patients very often demand to be treated as individuals with their own singular histories and commitments as part of this process.

Often, this leaves therapists in a highly conflicted position. In the following example, Joan who works with hand injuries, tries to sort out her role with a patient who has turned to her for help with life problems. She describes an extremely common predicament. Despite a concern not to neglect the whole patient, that is, to resist a mechanistic reduction of the person to a diagnostic category, when patients do develop trust in therapists and begin to confide deep personal problems attending the disability, this throws many therapists into a quandary. They feel they have strayed out of their depth, out of their role as occupational therapists, and are being called upon to assist in a way which they do not feel professionally competent to do. Thus therapists' concerns to treat the "whole patient" sometimes lead to a level of discussion which therapists then reject as no longer occupational therapy. Joan describes this dilemma to the interviewer (also an occupational therapist)[2] as it arose in her work with one patient, Charlie.

INTERVIEWER: Do you think that's one capacity of OT, that we go beyond a single hand to try and look at all . . .? (trails off)
JOAN: Yes, I think we do. I think it's important to look at the whole dynamics and I think it's not realistic to treat Charlie not looking at all these issues. But I think . . .
INTERVIEWER: But yet you said you felt as though you did step beyond [your boundaries as an OT].
THERAPIST: Right, because I think that the idea is for him [Charlie] to be seeking psychological and social support from a trained professional. If he wants to share what's going on in those sessions, sort of in a more informal way, that's fine, but I should not be that person. I can't be both roles. I can't be an objective therapist
INTERVIEWER: An objective occupational therapist knowing . . .
JOAN: Becoming very involved in all the dynamics. I know we have a lot of empathy for our patients. As OTs, I think we're like that. But, it's a hard

time drawing the line. It makes it more complicated to treat. Because rather than knowing he's going to get that support somewhere else and that I can really focus my treatment on that extremity, you find that you do a little work and maybe not as much work as you should have. You are spending time talking and you are still limited in time because you have another patient coming.

This discussion presents the dilemma of working within two different discourses, the examination and treatment of "that extremity" which involves a mechanistic discourse, and a second, very different kind of discourse in which the patient begins to reveal deep problems raised by his disability. In this case, Joan outlined these problems as sexual difficulties with his wife, drinking, and depression. The therapist described her problem as one of having "two roles." The first, treating the extremity, she referred to as "work." She also characterized her role here as being "objective," implying that her treatment of an extremity is a role with credibility. She contrasted work to talk when she noted that she didn't get as much work done as she should have because she ended up spending more time talking. Yet she could not abandon the idea that she was also responsible for initiating and carrying through discussions with the patient because when the interviewer says, "So the talking part of the treatment is not really the issue at hand. You'd rather be working on the activities?" she replies, "Talking too, and conversation."

In the case of this patient who has come to trust the therapist and to attempt to share personal problems which he has refused to take to a psychologist, the therapist faces the dilemma of feeling wrong no matter which direction she goes. She has presented herself as someone who is sincerely concerned about the patient as a person and he has responded by beginning to talk out his problems with her. Joan's response to Charlie's trust and openness is to feel uneasy and conflicted. While talk is important she is not, as she says, a "trained psychologist or social worker." Her stated strategy for avoiding the problem of having talk go "too far" is to try to maintain a precarious balance of "superficial personal conversation." She finds herself in difficulty when "the person goes deep into their interpersonal relationships." For Joan, storytelling has become a window onto an overwhelming array of difficulties. Though she meant to open this window just a crack, just for a comradely look, now she cannot shut the unwieldy thing. She states, "My responsibilities to him are to get his hand better, and to be very real, very open, very honest because he doesn't get – his doctor's a very closed-mouthed person." By attempting to be real, honest, and open, Joan allowed the possibility for the patient to confide problems to her, to reveal his experience of his illness. Perhaps a significant reason for the scattered

and non-directive questioning of patients which often characterizes
therapist–patient talk is precisely to prevent conversation from deep-
ening into serious discussion of the trauma associated with disability or
disease.

Even among therapists working in a psychiatric setting where talking,
and talking about emotional problems is a more usual aspect of therapy,
conversations often avoid stories of the profound kind. They tend
toward a superficial and broad noting of "facts" about the patient's life
rather than an exploration of the patient's concerns and meanings. This
was sometimes the case even when patients raised issues that were
particularly "occupational" in nature, such as major career changes, or
the horror of having to depend on others for self-care. Below, for
instance, is an excerpt from an initial evaluation done by a psychiatric
occupational therapist. She and a patient are discussing a leave of
absence the patient took from her regular job which gave the patient a
chance to work in a mayoral reelection campaign. The patient is
extremely concerned about her job situation and about what career
choices she ought to make, as she reveals at several points during this
initial assessment interview:

THERAPIST: Was the two-year LOA [leave of absence] OK with you?
PATIENT: No, but it was a good opportunity. (Patient is referring to her chance
    to go into politics and start a new career.) I love politics, just love it! Rather
    than quit, I took an LOA, because you never knew if the Mayor would be
    re-elected.
THERAPIST: When's the LOA up?
. . . (Later in the same interview, the therapist has been discussing the groups
    the patient will participate in.)
PATIENT: It seems so vague to me. It's like, I know it's important but it's hard to
    think of getting better.
THERAPIST: I know, you've been in the hospital a long time.
PATIENT: I don't want to build up to something else, because then something
    comes up, it's like protective devices. I know I have two options, working in
    the Mayor's office or going back to my old school job. I have a difficult
    major decision. (This is the second time she has raised this in the interview.)
(The therapist responds by describing in more detail the groups they have, finds
    out if the patient has schedules for the group.)

Here is an invitation by the patient refused twice over as the therapist
determinedly follows a checklist approach to a discussion of the patient's
life, even though the main issue this patient raised was one of major
career choices. Although occupational therapists are not usually vocational therapists, issues of work are considered central. Yet this therapist
does not ask for more detail, nor does she indicate that this will be
pursued in more detail at some later time. The first time the issue about

careers is raised, the therapist responds by asking a factual question about her work situation and the second time the therapist simply ignores the topic. She does not reflect on or express concern for the patient's feelings. This example illustrates the common therapeutic checklist approach to problems which allows therapists to stay very near the surface of the patient's life. Checklists help preclude storytelling from clinical interactions. Where stories are told, they are more likely to be the minimal affairs amply illustrated in previous examples in this chapter. While storytelling does not guarantee profound reflections on the meanings of disability, systematic refusals to encourage stories are very compatible with treatment that attempts to contain the phenomenological issues. This surface orientation to a patient's life issues is not merely a personal strategy of therapists but is built into the standardized assessment tools used by therapists to identify salient clinical problems during initial patient evaluations. The surface treatment of problems is guaranteed by a very long list of questions so that no one subject is dwelt on at any length. Important themes, such as that of work raised repeatedly by the patient in the excerpt above, need not be dwelt upon by the therapist. The superficiality of the initial evaluation in regard to the patient's illness experience and personal concerns is often duplicated in treatment in the level of conversation the therapist encourages.

The fear of entering too far into a patient's life story becomes understandable in light of how therapists conceive their professional role. Therapists will say that therapy is often a "damned if you do, damned if you don't" situation. To be a good professional in the eyes of non-occupational therapy colleagues is to stay within professional turf boundaries, which also ensures that services will be reimbursed by the government or insurance agencies. These factors drive therapists to narrow the scope of treatment goals and activities along specialized biomedical lines – to treat the physical body and minimize storytelling and storymaking. But being a good professional also means eliciting the strong commitment of clients. Here, therapists are drawn to broaden the scope of clinical problems, addressing many "real life" issues that do not yield neat, precise, or measurable outcomes. They spend time talking and listening to patients and searching for ways to create significant therapeutic experiences even at the expense of working on physically defined treatment goals. While therapists have doubts about the legitimacy of delving into deep life problems or spending extra time with patients to tailor therapy to patient preferences, this delving and tailoring is also what they tend to value most. Treatment which is dramatic, conversional, and deeply meaningful to patient and therapist overwhelmingly predominates in "best practice" stories I have heard.

Because many value this, they continue to try to make "something happen" in therapy. But because it is not "reimbursable" or legitimate, not "real OT," they do not document it (Lawlor 1994; Mattingly and Lawlor in press). The phenomenological and aesthetic aspects of their work thus constitute an "underground practice" (Mattingly and Fleming 1994).

Therapists I have studied neither reject nor comfortably accommodate to a biomedical model of disability, but uneasily attempt to straddle two very different approaches to patients. The power of the biomedical frame is demonstrated strikingly at those moments when patients directly ask therapists to deal with personal traumas associated with disability. These pleas for help, or sometimes simply for attention, often cause therapists to feel torn between doing what the patient seems to need and doing what appears most appropriate as a specialized professional within the clinical world. At such times therapists express their own anxiety in post-session interviews, often worrying aloud that they are "moving beyond OT" with a patient either by crossing professional boundaries, thus trespassing into the domain of social worker or psychiatrist, or by abandoning their professional role altogether and "acting like a peer."

The institutional context of the hospital is powerfully restrictive of the occupational therapists' practice, funneling therapy into an acceptably biomechanical channel and constraining the sorts of creative alternatives considered. In general, these constraints are maintained by means other than explicit rules and regulations. Where such rules exist (e.g. regulations concerning what can be reimbursed), they are easy enough to circumvent. The influence of the institutional context is more covert. Medical values and authority structures become internalized in the way therapists view themselves and their ability to treat patients. This internalization is evident in therapists' expressions of concern about how a particular treatment activity might appear to other staff members, about whether a treatment will cross turf boundaries of other professionals, and about whether a treatment will be seen as "professional" by the medical staff.

Clinical reasoning about best treatment for the patient thus becomes inextricably mixed with reasoning about the politics of maintaining respect and not causing trouble for oneself with other members of the staff. Therapists quite reasonably assume that if they flout institutional norms they may lose influential colleagues. A pervasive concern is to look sufficiently technical and specialized and never, under any circumstances, to be mistaken for lower caste professionals such as nurses aides or recreational therapists. Preoccupation with status directly conflicts with addressing phenomenological aspects of disability. For instance, a psychiatric occupational therapist decided not to give a patient a craft project to work on during non-therapy time because the request came from a nurse who requested in an inappropriate way. The nurse asked, "Why don't you give this person an activity to keep him busy over the weekend?" which cued the therapist that the nurse perceived psychiatric occupational therapists as "the fun people." This therapist saw part of her task as "staff education" of nurses and psychologists who seemed to confuse occupational therapists with recreational therapists. She said in a later interview, "The bottom line is that OT is not a department store and we don't have the funds also to be just giving things out." In deciding not to give an activity to the patient, she did not consider the particular patient and whether this made sense, but the attitude of the nurse requesting the craft activity.

A second example concerns a therapist who worked with respiratory patients. She had a patient who continually asked to be taken to chapel during occupational therapy time. In thinking through what to do, she considered her role as an occupational therapist on the floor. She felt that going to chapel would be very beneficial to the patient, who was quite religious, because this patient was extremely depressed, had been in the hospital off and on for two years and had not been able to go to church because of her physical problems. However, she eventually decided not to take her patient to the chapel, and explained this decision as follows: "I guess I thought in my own mind, is this something that I can do as an OT? . . . I didn't want to set any kind of precedent." She wanted to avoid creating the perception by either the patient or other medical staff on her floor that she did activities requiring "no skill," activities which could be done by an aide. It was not the patient's *need* which determined her action here, for she was clear that going to chapel would be beneficial. Rather it was her professional identity, especially her public identity within the hospital staff community, which she was concerned to preserve and which finally determined her decision not to comply with the patient's request.

Plots that threaten

The institutional context can also promote therapeutic plots that are dismissive of the patient's perspective – plots that threaten. A primary danger, well known to therapists themselves, presents itself when the professional presumes she knows which story she is in and does not heed warning signals which tell her she has got the story wrong. If the patient cannot identify with the therapist's hoped-for story and is allowed no

room to initiate a different one, the result is often a stalemate. Therapeutic time dissolves into a series of power struggles, stagnates into
repetitions, half-hearted therapeutic activities in which nothing much
seems to happen, or ends because either patient or therapist finds a way
to exit therapy. Mismatches between the therapist's hoped-for story and
the patient's – or family member's – easily lead to a mutual blaming and
to therapists' complaints about the non-compliance of their clients.

The following example illustrates this dangerous process and the
stalemate that ensued. A psychiatric occupational therapist, Mary, faced
a recalcitrant patient who remained passive in the face of her attempts to
get him actively involved in therapy and take responsibility for his
rehabilitation. Mary's prospective story is driven by a generic script, one
shared by other colleagues on the psychiatric unit where she worked.
The patient, a man in his mid-forties, with a diagnosis of depression,
was readmitted periodically to the acute care hospital where she worked.
Upon discharge he would appear to the staff to have improved, and yet
would be back to his previous condition upon his next readmission some
six months or so later. Readmitted chronic cases tend to frustrate
therapists who feel a sense of failure at not effecting significant change.
They are often angry at such patients, especially when they believe that
if the patient had only cooperated properly during the course of the
therapy, readmission would not have been necessary. Patients are also
often angry to find themselves back in the hospital, caught in a cycle
they cannot get out of and frustrated with medical professionals for not
being more helpful.

Mary shared the frustrations of her professional colleagues. Ordinarily
when she encouraged him to take responsibility for his own actions (a
key theme in this clinical milieu), he passively acquiesced. But on one
occasion, after several of these readmissions, he spoke up. Mary related
the conversation. "He said, 'It's not up to me, Mary.' He'd say, 'It's up to
God.'" Mary continued, "He had these delusions of religiosity. Not real
articulated, not real verbalized, but it would definitely come out when he
was confronted with what responsibilities he could take for his life. But
this guy was adamant about just resisting the whole idea of taking
responsibility, of doing anything to change his life. He felt like a victim.
A helpless, innocent victim, where what happened, was a result of fate,
or a result of God, and when this guy resisted so much, inside I would, I
would get like this turmoil. As a result, I confronted him with it."

The therapist described the escalation of increasingly direct and
hostile confrontation between herself and the patient in which the
patient would leave the room and the therapist would find herself
getting angrier and angrier. "He had been in the system, he had heard

all of this before, and I felt perfectly safe confronting him about it. So I would do so. And frequently . . . he couldn't handle it. He'd get up and he'd walk out of the room saying, 'There's nothing I can do about it.' And it would infuriate me. Because I thought, Mister, you know, you've been through this, you know, not that I want you to repeat what I'm telling you, but to help him . . . I really believed deep down that he had a responsibility."

Their hostile exchanges finally came to a head. Mary described the ensuing scene. "Anyway, one particular day . . . I made a comment to him [and] he couldn't handle it and he left the room. And I thought, this can't go on. I don't want this guy to think that I'm threatening him. I mean, if anything, I want to be supportive and I want to help him to realize that he has potential, just, how to actualize it. So I went to talk with him." For some reason, Mary listened this time, as they talked, and she came to see him differently. She described her change of heart. "I honestly felt that this guy was sincere in that he did not think that there was anything that he could do. Prior to that, I felt that he was denying any type of responsibility, just plain denial. But I actually felt that he was sincere . . . he had been in several times before and all of this information he had learned before. Somehow or another he couldn't follow through or it didn't work, and it resulted in the same thing, him coming back. He went into God. That's the only thing that he had to hang on to, and his family."

Mary finally confronts her own narrative expectations and, in this story, it is she rather than the patient who is transformed by the therapeutic encounter. Therapists often resist such conversion, however. They will exercise great creativity in attempting to maintain and further the plot they deem essential to healing in the face of conflicts or unexpected responses by the patient. They are particularly likely to cling to a prospective story if it is well reinforced by the institutional culture where they practice, as in Mary's case. For therapists also inherit narrative anticipations, and narrative proscriptions, from colleagues and the ethos of the institutional milieu. Here, the tension they may feel is not between a need to suppress narrative on the one hand and encourage it on the other. Rather, the clash is between the sort of therapeutic plot approved in the institutional culture and the plot any particular patient is willing to help create.

Therapeutic plots and professional tensions

The history of this profession reveals a long-standing tension between a collaborative, individually focused and highly inventive therapy that encourages the creation of powerful therapeutic plots as part of the healing experience and a practice that gains its power and legitimacy by standardizing interventions to conform to medically defined conditions and goals. Initially the occupational therapy movement was a response and a protest to the rising prestige of medicine, particularly to a physiologically centered approach to medicine which emerged power-fully in the first decades of this century (Starr 1982; Kielhofner and Burke 1977; Levine 1987). Occupational therapy grew, in part, out of dissatisfaction among some physicians with this narrowing of the medical perspective. Some dissenting physicians were concerned to develop medical therapies that preserved a sense of the mind-body unity and, even more broadly, recognized the role of social and physical environments in influencing mental and physical health (Levine 1987). Two social movements served as forerunners to the establishment of occupational therapy as a profession, the moral treatment movement in America (Kielhofner and Burke 1977; Engelhardt 1977) and the arts and crafts movement of the late nineteenth and early twentieth centuries (Levine 1987: 248).

The notion of "occupation," as it developed in the occupational therapy movement, connected health to a kind of occupational rhythm, a movement through time which balanced certain occupations funda-mental for human health. Health required not only productive work but recreation and rest (Zemke and Clark 1996; Kielhofner 1983; Rogers 1982; Meyer 1977). The occupation cure was intended to introduce a balance between work and play for those who had become "unbalanced," and to do so not primarily through talking but through doing. Occupa-tional therapists had the task of constructing environments, carefully graded to increase the challenge to the patient, where they introduced increasingly complex activities which asked patients to increase their capacities to perform complex, meaningful and socially appropriate tasks and, in this way, adapt themselves to the "real world." There was an emphasis on adaptation. Also a definition of illness as a maladaptive response to an external environment rather than an internal process, was one of the most important distinguishing marks that separated occupa-tional therapy from the medical tradition, both in physical medicine and in psychiatry (Bing 1981; Rogers 1982; Meyer 1977).

The beliefs of the early occupational therapy movement dominated practice until the 1940s when external pressures from physicians and other powerful groups led therapists to try to justify the efficacy and scientific basis of their interventions. Changes in the health care delivery system over the past decade, particularly the tremendous attention to fiscal accountability, has had a huge impact on rehabilitative health professions such as occupational therapy. Shorter hospital stays, the power of insurance agencies in dictating what kind of care is reimbursable, the need to produce quantifiable outcome measures and the like, have increased tension in the practice. Treating the "diagnosis" tends to be much easier to justify than treating the "illness experience." Hence, those aspects of therapeutic work which I speak of as creating therapeutic plots, and therapists label "individualizing practice" or "treating the whole person," are heavily under threat. Yet, increasing activism by the disability community and increased respect of "holistic health" has encouraged a less specialized and biomechanical approach to treatment.

When therapists depart from the medical model during a therapeutic session to treat the patient's "lived body," to treat the disability as it affects the patient's work, relationships, independence or other areas of concern, this is often done more casually, and less directly, and is easily abandoned if it interferes with therapeutic exercises intended to improve the biomechanical functioning of the patient. Perhaps the most striking and consistent evidence of a dichotomous practice is the demarcation of a clinical session into "work" and "non-work." "Non-work" is categorized as "rapport building," "chit chat," or things "not strictly OT" (Lawlor 1994; Mattingly and Lawlor in press). When therapists describe and analyze clinical sessions, they nearly always separate certain parts of a session which they label as marginal (e.g. "getting set up," "building rapport," "distracting the patient," "making the patient comfortable") from the "work" of the session, which is almost always identified with carrying out particular treatment modalities, most of which have a biomedical rationale.

Even when therapists help create powerful therapeutic plots which clearly matter to their patients they are likely to dismiss this aspect of the treatment in public discourse. For instance, after an intense session between John and Lin described in the previous chapter where John has announced that he has lost his will to live, Lin was interviewed and asked to describe what had happened. She replied, "I went in and he wanted some water, so I gave him some water. And I started ranging his right hand. I tend to say, I ranged his right hand, I ranged his left hand, I scratched his upper lip and that was the end." There was more than a little irony in this astonishingly understated description. She was prompted to say more. She then offered a much longer, more detailed account of the session. However, at the end of a ten or fifteen minute account of what was said and her nuanced interpretations of the patient's conversation in light of events within his family, she concluded by saying "You know, I pretty much ranged him." The message about what counts as "real therapy" in the public world came through clearly.

7   Therapeutic plots, healing rituals, and the creation of significant experience

It is difficult to speak of life as a storymaking venture without falling into a number of traps, portraying a world which is: (a) overly individualistic where single agents control their own destiny; (b) overly instrumental where attempting to create a story is equivalent to pursuing means to achieve ends and narrative endings appear as nothing more than instrumental goals; (c) overly coherent and free where we each, through our choosing, live out a single, unified life story; (d) overly self-conscious, where human agents act only on the basis of deliberate choices.

In developing a narrative theory of social action and experience, I have tried to avoid the illusions that we operate as individuals outside social contexts, that we can simply will into existence what we choose, that our motivations are largely self-conscious, or that our lives have the coherence and order of the well-told tale. Rather, I have turned to narrative as a framework to highlight quite other features of human experience, particularly the deeply disturbing relationship between trying to live lives which make sense to us (even narrative sense, I would say) and finding our attempts interrupted by the world around us or, equally disconcerting, finding we need to revise our conceptions of what a good life should or could, realistically, be. *If narrative offers a homology to lived experience, the dominant formal feature which connects the two is not narrative coherence but narrative drama.*

In this final chapter, I examine the notion of narrative drama more closely. There are two key sources to the drama that underlies narrative time in occupational therapy encounters. One is the collision between expectations and unfolding events, especially as precipitated by the action of others. A second is the development of desire. Drama is heightened when what happens really matters. Occupational therapy is routinely a place where desire must be created, giving the therapist a fundamentally dramatic task. These considerations of the drama underlying narrative time pave the way for a last look at the relation between therapeutic plots, healing, and the creation of significant experience.

154

Dramatic collisions

The plot may make a whole out of a sequence, but it is a whole which is always under threat and it is the threat that matters in creating a form peculiarly narrative. What narrative foregrounds is interruption and surprise generated by overturnings of any incipient narrative structures which any particular hero attempts to impose. I have argued that it is not only the teller of the tale who operates from a retrospective vantage point, but paradoxical as it may seem, therapists (and patients) also "see backward" from a future endpoint even while in the midst of action, that is, even when the future remains unknown. And they do so even though past experience teaches them the faultiness of their predictions. This backward orientation from imagined endings is necessary to practical action. For therapists to know what they are doing, they must imagine where they are going. They look over their shoulders from the perspective of a hypothesized ending, or, more accurately, an array of possible endings, what Carr (1986) calls a stance of "as if retrospection" and Olafson describes as the "capacity for self-temporalization" (1979: 102). Therapists see their actions and those of others within a temporal context even as they are acting. They select out of innumerable clinical events only some which they deem relevant for an unfolding story. These, they try to build on or counter. And they describe these events to themselves in a way which shows them to belong to that story. They see a patient's smile as encouraging or as subversive, for instance. In that simple labeling, they are both relying on and elaborating a narrative context, naming the smile as part of a larger, unfolding therapeutic plot. Once a storyline is well formed in their minds, they can then read the meaning of subsequent actions, giving their actions "an orientation in time as blocking or facilitating other possible events or actions" (Olafson 1979: 101).

When therapists lose their way in this projected story shaped by their imagined ending, confusion and frustration are the usual responses. They try, as far as they can, to take the position of the narrator, to predict and control a desirable future as though they could read their present situation from a backwards glance. Carr contends: "we are constantly striving, with more or less success, to occupy the story-teller's position with respect to our own actions" (1986: 66). Carr also adds, we must be able to do this with fair regularity because "for the most part, our negotiation with the future is successful. We are, after all, able to act" (1986: 66). On this last point I take issue. Certainly, for the occupational therapists I have studied, any incipient therapeutic plot serves as an unreliable guide to experience, projecting future shapes which falter and need continual modification as therapists and patients move toward that future. It is true that they can act, but it is far too simple to claim that they simply assume the perspective of a narrator who can shape or accurately predict what will happen next. It is more accurate, and much more narratively interesting, to say that they operate from multiple points of view, sometimes with the backward glance of the confident narrator standing at the story's end, sometimes with the bewilderment or naiveté of the partly informed character or audience. They act holding all these perspectives simultaneously, driven forward by images, goals, and plans as though they could foresee the end, but at the same time, immersed in the contingencies of a present which resists the ending.

Any deterministic view about the relation between narrative and experience is too simple. Experiences themselves do not determine the narratives therapists tell about them. Narratives do not refer in some naively empiricist way to "events out there" or even to "experiences out there." It is too simple to claim that stories govern our lives. What gets neglected in overly simple perspectives is what happens to cultural narratives when actors try to put these into play in particular, concrete situations. Actors have their own pragmatic reasons to improvise on cultural scripts and rules, as Pierre Bourdieu (1977) has taught us. In addition, the idiosyncratic demands of particular situations often require an improvisation upon any narrative script. Presuming that narratives only provide prototypes for action precludes a sufficiently complex account of practical reasoning. Aristotle (1985) argues that the special feature of action is that it is *particular*. From an Aristotelian perspective, practical reasoning, directed toward taking right actions, involves judgments which are unique to the situation. Even if one can plausibly claim that narrative precedes and guides action, the particularity of each action context means that simple imposition is rarely possible. The imported narrative borrowed from prior personal experiences or cultural scripts requires modification to make a better fit to the new situation.

The clinical events occupational therapists try to create are not independent of the narratives they tell. Their narratives help shape their experiences. But cultural or prototypical narratives do not determine their experiences. Narratives are not scripts which therapists simply live out. The relation between narrative and experience is much more subtle, an intricate interplay of actions and stories that might be told about them. Prospective narratives are continually projected, unraveled, and remade in the course of trying to live them out. When narrative is considered a form through which "*an*" experience is created, its deeply social function is most obvious. Therapist and patient will not have the same experience, but when something significant is being created, it requires an interplay between therapist and patient. Neither can impose an experience on the other single-handedly.

An incipient therapeutic plot is projected onto the future as a kind of active wish for what should come to pass. This narrative wishing is utterly vulnerable to the exigencies of fortune, to the wishes of other critical actors, to the vagaries of chance. For a prospective story (which, like any story, is always about a social event requiring that many actors play their parts) is only a guide to an event in the making. While therapists may believe that they are working within a certain kind of narrative, the one in which Mr. Jones recovers sufficiently from his stroke to return home with a collection of adaptive toilet seats and walkers to a loving wife, Mr. Jones may not recover or the wife not be as loving as the therapist hoped. Mr. Jones may be sent off to the nursing home instead. Or, Mr. Jones may return triumphantly home but eschew all the adaptive devices of which therapists are so fond.

The anti-mimetic theorists are right to point out that life-as-lived tends to be thwarted or unexpected except in the most conventional cases where acts are simple or social rules are strict. We may be able to act but often not as we had originally intended. Furthermore, even when we are somehow able to do what we had planned, we often find that we have created unintended consequences, that our very success produced new difficulties we had not foreseen. And even in those lucky times when we can do what we intend and no unpredicted and unwanted consequences follow, the meaning of our actions often looks different in retrospect than when we were busily steering toward that future. Rather than taking this as a sign that a narrative operates from a very different structure than experience, one could argue that this only ties the structure of narrative and experience more closely. After all, encounters with the unexpected are basic to the story. In narrative theory, this unexpectedness allows for that essential element of plot, the reversal. More often than not, the moral of a story concerns things turning out differently than the characters anticipated. The "sense of an ending" which guides the telling of a tale (and its reception) is powerful because it reveals experience as a struggle toward an ending which evades us, or which turns out to hold a different meaning than we had originally guessed. Collision between expectations and experience (what, as it turned out, happened) gives narrative discourse its drama. In narrative terms, I have thought of this as a collision between a prospective story and the story that actually unfolds. If narrative provides a homology to lived experience, it is only because the structure of narrative, like life itself, is built on suspense.

Suspense is intimately tied to another feature of narrative. In a story, all action is interaction. A story may be told by one person but it always concerns events shaped by a multiplicity of actors. This multiplicity is rarely of one mind. Inevitably, there are diverse motives, beliefs, and desires guiding the actions of characters. Action, from a narrative perspective, is deeply and irrevocably social. If therapeutic time takes on a configured unity, a plot, this configuration is fundamentally social. A therapeutic plot emerges in a powerful way only if its various players, with their diverse perspectives and interests, operate with some minimal agreement to contribute to the same, unfolding story. Such agreement requires negotiation. In clinical interactions between therapists and patients, this negotiation is seldom clearly marked. Even when there seems to be a tacit agreement to further the same storyline, this is not an agreement to a script for it is never completely clear just what story will unfold. The ending is always in suspense, and action always requires improvisation. There is never a simple or necessary story which effortlessly develops. In the clinic, therapists find themselves in continued struggles over who will "direct" the story, and it is common for any provisional narrative structure to break down. The social character of action (in narrative and in life), also means that there is little hope for a coherent, pre-planned and freely chosen plot to develop under the guidance of any particular actor. The threat of incoherence and discontinuity is ever present in clinical exchanges, *especially* those most clearly possessing a compelling therapeutic plot. The cases I have offered in earlier chapters reveal the highly improvisational character of much clinical work, situations where the therapist suddenly "sees" a possible story, often presented through the unexpected actions of the patient, and opportunistically builds on this. Competent therapy requires revision of initial plots.

While an initial narrative reading of the client and the situation is necessary – after all, one must start somewhere – it is bound to be sketchy and in some cases, almost completely wrong. The prospective story is a complex portrait built from past particular experiences and generalized stereotypical images which are "matched up" to the new patient who presents himself. Misfit is not caused by therapeutic error but by the need to shape interventions to context, to individualize. For if the client is unique, and if this is important to good therapy, then any rules of thumb or stereotypical pictures (of the usual left-hemi or C6 quad) are necessarily insufficient and must be modified as the therapist becomes better acquainted with the patient. Good practice depends upon recognizing that the new patient in the new situation is not simply a replica of other patients in other situations. Mismatch between a therapist's prospective story and subsequent actions does not necessarily pose any deep threat to the therapist's narrative hopes. Gaps between a plot the therapist wishes to enact and what actually occurs are inevitable. Sometimes, however, therapists are simply unable to find a plot that is tailored to the particular patient but fits the *kind* of therapeutic story they care to create. Initial misfits turn into an impasse with no good narrative in sight. All therapists have a repertoire of tales about times when their initial portrait of a new client and therefore their prospective story was so completely at odds with the situation that they never forgot the case. The dramas may be quiet, almost invisible, and yet haunt therapists for years. Here is a story a therapist told about one such experience. She was working with oncology patients when she met Bob, a 23-year-old working-class Irishman from South Boston with two young children. Bob had discovered he had leukemia when one day he went to the emergency room for what he assumed was an infection in his finger and, to his shock, was quickly diagnosed. He was admitted to the hospital that same day. The therapist's main role on the floor was helping patients with stress management. When the therapist met Bob, he immediately reminded her of another patient, Joe, with whom she'd had great success teaching relaxation and visualization techniques. Like this new patient, Joe had also been young, just 26, working-class Irish with two young children. Joe had been very open in talking about "going stir crazy" trying to handle both the illness and the multiple hospitaliza-tions that it entailed. As he began to trust the therapist he also confessed his difficulties trying to keep his family together and manage things at home while being sick and away at the hospital. Over time their conversation deepened and Joe reflected with her about his fear of death and his inability to be a father and "breadwinner" for his family.

When this therapist initially met Bob, she "had preconceived notions about how [their] relationship would progress" and, as she later saw, she "was very wrong." Bob wanted nothing of her relaxation techniques and he pleasantly but steadfastly refused any help from her. She continued to stop by his room to "chat" with him but he adamantly kept things at a superficial level. She knew he was having great difficulty, was unable to sleep, spent the nights pacing his hospital room, but she never found any way to connect. Her concern to be helpful and her sense of impotence clearly communicated itself to him for one day he "expressed concern about hurting [her] feelings." She "reassured him that wasn't the case" and that her treatment was in no way mandatory. He never talked openly with her, though she continued to stop by periodically. Later he was discharged and soon after, she moved to another unit in the hospital. She never saw him again.

In this example, the therapist uses a set of easily observable cues to identify Bob's and Joe's cases as similar. She then tries to carry out with Bob a therapeutic story similar to one she had been able to create with Joe. It is not merely that Bob reminds her of Joe because certain facts are similar (diagnosis, age, ethnic background, family) but she *sees* these facts in Bob because she is committed to the kind of therapeutic interchange she was able to achieve with Joe. (She was known and respected among colleagues for her ability to move between a psychotherapeutic and occupational therapy role.) Her past experience suggested possibilities for her relationship with Bob and thus she saw the two as similar from a highly committed stance.

When a therapist asks the question, "What story am I in?" she cannot sit back to wait for an answer. The question is posed in the midst of things, at the same moment that action is required. There is no "stop and think," that is associated with reflection (Arendt 1971). For the therapist must have some way to act, some way to make sense, in the first moment of clinical encounter. The notion of the "prospective story" carries with it the familiar recognition that therapists never approach a patient empty-headed, so to speak. Therapists inevitably encounter situations with "pre-understandings" which guide their access to their patients. Prejudice (as pre-judgment) simply describes the anticipatory character of understanding (Gadamer 1975). This anticipatory gaze is inevitably limited for there is no place in which to grasp the whole, to see "in a single glance the totality of effects" (Ricoeur 1981: 74). What therapists are led to expect from a patient is intimately linked with those practical concerns they attend to. Their anticipations are directed by the solutions they have "ready-to-hand." Through prospective stories therapists come to any clinical encounters from what Heidegger (1962) speaks of as a prior position of Care. They are situated in the world, already immersed in projects which organize their sense of what is to be perceived.

Thus their prehensions are not merely cognitive sets of beliefs which tell them what *is*. Most important, these prehensions guide their understanding of what *is possible*, and how to care about what is possible. Their understanding of their patients is not so much a matter of grasping a fact than of apprehending a possibility of being (Ricoeur, in Thompson 1981: 56). Understanding is linked to a fundamental ontological position in the world, a position of "being-thrown" (Heidegger 1962). When the therapist comes to understand "Bob" as someone like "Joe" what she is apprehending is a possibility for action, a story in which she can play some useful part as healer. This Heideggerian concept is not reducible to having a guide for practical action, a treatment plan. Rather, Heidegger's notion of Care speaks to the "sense of an ending" that permeates practical understanding. Self-conscious plans of action emerge from this prior ontological position of connection to the world.

Therapists are often reluctant to speak openly about the preconceptions they carry into their clinical work. They often feel distressed when telling stories about misguided anticipations for these stories reveal truths which violate certain sacred beliefs about therapeutic expertise and the sources of appropriate knowledge about patients. Most difficult, such stories subvert the pretense that the therapist, as a knowing subject, can come to ascertain and measure objective truths about the patient. Therapists have been taught that they must begin their encounters with patients from an open, fact-gathering stance and from this they will be able to formulate an appropriate plan of action. Objective fact-gathering precedes any formulation of possibilities in this idealized and scientistic version of therapeutic expertise. While such fact-gathering is the province of the therapist, the formulation of goals is supposed to be a shared enterprise, even one which follows the lead of the patient. Thus the idea that all this is mixed from the first, that the therapist already "knows" what she sets out to find, and that goals are intertwined with this anticipatory knowing is terribly disconcerting, quite at odds with the standard depiction of clinical reasoning in the modern clinic.

Rather than seeing occupational therapy as an "applied science," it is perhaps better understood as a kind of healing ritual. Certainly the narrative aspects of clinical interactions expose therapy as a performance which has the possibility to fail. Performative break-downs can be triggered by any number of factors, though the most disheartening for therapists are precipitated by collisions or mismatches between them and their patients. Like other healing rituals, therapeutic success depends in part upon an efficacious performance (Tambiah 1985, 1990). But there are other, more subtle connections between therapy time and ritual time. These concern the creation of desire.

Rituals, stories, and plots

In considering stories as something created rather than told, my analysis of therapeutic narrative has a certain kinship with the long anthropological tradition which places primacy on process, event, and performance. There is the assumption, in this anthropological focus, that (at least some) life-as-lived is not an unstructured flow of time but has a definite temporal structure, consists of events which can be set apart from others, which have a marked beginning, middle, and end.

Ritual has been a focus for anthropologists interested in an analysis of social process and event because rituals offer situations marked off as "special time" which can be segregated from ordinary time. Time is special not only in the sense of being different but also because something important is supposed to happen in it. It constitutes the time of "significant experience." Ritual, particularly the sacred ritual, has been an obvious place to analyze social life as event since societies so often partition sacred time from the humdrum of everyday life. This marking is likely to involve the use of special spaces, costumes, language, and a myriad of other highly symbolic and aesthetic media which serve to set this as time apart, as "an experience" which can be distinguished from other times and other experiences (Abrahams 1986).

Ritual studies have also been one place where anthropologists have long attended to the entangled relation between stories told and ritual events enacted. One longstanding tradition treats ritual as the enactment of a culture's core values and beliefs which often take the discursive form of "grand narratives" or myths. Myth is the discourse; ritual the accompanying action. Less frequently, rituals have been examined as performances which do not merely reflect or enact cultural narratives but generate events which precipitate narratives. Ritual performances may create events worth telling stories about. These after-the-fact stories are not social myths well known to the community, but provisional, contested stories told by participants or observers of the ritual event. Any such story offers just one narrative perspective among others and thus is open to the possibility of revision or even renunciation in light of other, more persuasive accounts. V. Turner, for example, sees that some phases of a social drama are likely to initiate a host of such stories. Beyond this plethora of stories, something like a shared story may also begin to emerge which then becomes a collective tale: "as one follows the steps of ritual redress, one becomes aware that a narrative is being slowly constructed from the pieces of behavior scrutinized by diviners and other ritual specialists" (1986a: 38). Myerhoff offers a similar analysis in describing the invention of a ritual – a parade – among a community of elderly immigrant Jews in Venice, California who "watched each other and themselves, bearing witness to their own story" (1986: 269). This event then became the material for later stories.

Analyses such as these which simultaneously address narrative and ritual dramas, thus blurring the boundaries between stories told and events enacted, bear a closer relation to the arguments I have made in this book than any tradition of narrative analysis within medical anthropology. In Myerhoff's explication of a ritual parade, for example, it becomes apparent that the use of the term "story" no longer refers simply to something told but also to something enacted (a drama) and, further, to something already lived which is in danger of being forgotten (a history). Story as discourse, as dramatic event, and as history are intertwined. These three senses of story are similarly intertwined in my analysis of occupational therapists at work. Like the immigrant Jews of Venice, occupational therapists and their patients are also in need of stories – and in all of these senses, as things to be told, as dramas enacted and as references to a more distant past.

Taken in this way, rituals neither simply illustrate prior narratives nor simply generate new ones. Rather they point toward narratives, are stories in the making, have incipient narrative structures. "Thus," Turner pronounces, "in the 'natural unit' of the social drama we have already more than the germ of narrative" (1986a: 38). This notion of ritual time as proto-narrative time also relies upon a distinction between mere experience from an experience. Again from Turner, citing Dilthey. "An experience, like a rock in a Zen sand garden, stands out from the evenness of passing hours and years and forms what Dilthey called a 'structure of experience'" (in Turner 1986b: 35). The Balinese, as described by Geertz, appear to share Dilthey's distinction between mere experience and significant experience as part of their commonsense understanding and "arrangement" of their lives. Geertz declares that they "live in spurts . . . shifting between short periods when 'something' (that is, something significant) is happening, and equally short ones where 'nothing' (that is, nothing much) is – between what they themselves call 'full' and 'empty' time . . ." (1973: 445). Ritual events provide the Balinese with some of their highly distilled moments. Geertz, too, connects ritual time to a kind of story in the making. A ritual such as the cockfight "is a Balinese reading of Balinese experience, a story they tell themselves about themselves" (1973: 448). While therapeutic rituals within the occupational therapy world, unlike many of those classical studies by anthropologists, do not invoke the sacred, therapy sessions often take on qualities associated with ritual time. Above all, they emphasize transformation. In fact, a hallmark of therapeutic work which is highly narratively structured is precisely this emphasis on healing (or rehabilitation) as transformation, not only of the body but of the whole self.

Because therapists treat patients who do not, in general, get well (or, return to a "pre-morbid" state, to use the graphic language of the clinic), what constitutes healing is often more a matter of how the patient comes to see him/herself than any actual physiological changes. Even when therapists emphasize training patients in physical skills where progress can be visibly and quantitatively marked, the deeply embedded belief that justifies this training is that patients ought to be as independent and socially active as possible, contributing members of society. Personal independence in coping with one's body is a value that deeply moves therapists. It is also occasionally one their patients fail to embrace enthusiastically from their perspective. When they complain that patients are not motivated in therapy, they do not simply mean that patients fail to work hard enough to achieve therapeutic goals. Rather, they see this failure as symbolic of a failure to embrace a certain recuperative journey which involves adapting to one's new (disabled) body as well as one might. Much of therapy is directed, through actions more than words, to seducing patients to struggle with failing bodies. Like the religious healing Danforth describes in his depiction of fire-walking among the Anastendria, it is quite accurate to say that a significant goal of occupational therapists is "to reformulate people's interpretation of their own condition," and this may happen even when no cure is possible. "People can be healed even if their disease is not cured or their symptoms alleviated. Healing in this sense is comparable to a conversion experience" (Danforth 1989: 57).

In occupational therapy, transformation and conversion are often metaphorically expressed through the symbol of the journey. Here, too, they share something deep within the structure of many rituals since so many concern a passage of some kind. Even if a ritual voyage brings one full circle, from harmony through breach to harmony again, there is something dramatic and transformative in the movement. Anthropologists have examined healing rituals as "sacred spaces" which allow participants to make crucial transitions. In healing rituals where there is a concern to overcome a crisis brought on by affliction, the metaphor of journey (even of life as journey) appears particularly potent. The body of the afflicted can propel the sufferer into a liminal space, a ghostly zone in which she is neither here nor there, neither who she once was nor some new person. She is between selves. Therapists meet patients in this liminal place. Their therapeutic task, using the language of van Gannep (1960), is to effect a passage. This is a journey to some new phenomenological and social home which, very often, the patient cannot yet envision.

In this sense, therapeutic plots are secular rituals that help patients make the transition from illness reality to new reality and, even, a new self (Csordas 1983, 1994; Danforth 1989; Turner 1992). This passage occurs along many different dimensions all at once. A healing process involves not only the body but social and cultural shifts as well (Danforth 1989: 56). In ritual time, symbolic elements play a powerful role in this multileveled passage. Rituals depend upon and invoke the symbolic and aesthetic qualities of action. Ritual events which are heavily embued with metaphorical meaning may have a seductive power on participants (Turner 1969, 1986; Ortner 1978; Danforth 1989; Jackson 1989). Rituals deploy aesthetic devices that serve, as Tambiah says, to produce "a sense of heightened and intensified and fused communication" (1985: 145).[1] Occupational therapy sessions, like many rituals, are ludically inclined, often combining a casual playfulness with extreme seriousness. In the context of an unfolding therapeutic plot, practical actions also become metaphorically charged.

But therapeutic emplotments, as I describe them, also differ from rituals as classically described. They lack a relationship to any cosmological order, well-delineated boundaries between ritual and non-ritual space and time, formulaic rites, a predictable sequence of events, and a commonly shared cultural view of the meaning of various ritual activities. Anthropologists have attended to the specialness of ritual elements and their differentiation from the everyday. Efficacy often depends upon the strong separation of the ordinary and the practical. It is sometimes argued that ritual actions are taken when practical action comes to its limit (Lienhardt 1961; Ortner 1978). Clearly, this is not the case in occupational therapy. Rather, therapeutic action is an admixture of the symbolic and the technical. The same action "counts" in both domains – it does both symbolic and technical work. And it is occupational therapy's proximity to the everyday which offers interventions their symbolic possibilities.

Occupational therapy is a "ritual of the everyday" played out in the clinical world, the world of the not everyday. It is precisely the mundaneness of the therapeutic tools which give them their symbolic power. In the clinic, patients are caught in a liminal state against their will. It is not only their disabled and stigmatized bodies that have separated them from everyday life. This separation is institutionally marked and increased by the non-ordinary world of the clinic in which they are confined. Here they are divested of their usual surrounds, roles, and occupations. Even their clothes are different. Occupational therapy rooms, by contrast, are full of the ordinary. In addition to the extraordinary devices of the clinical world, splints and wheelchairs and the like, there are kitchens and bathrooms, board games and knitting needles. Many of the activities are ordinary as well, playing checkers, making tea, buttoning one's shirts. Therapists often translate the esoteric language of medicine to the ordinary language of common sense in helping patients understand their condition. This insistence on the ordinary and the "normal" carries the symbolic message that people are capable of making the transition from patient to member of society, assuming in some fashion the roles and cares and community that characterize life without disability.

Perhaps because of this insistence on the mundane, therapeutic plots differ from many rituals in not being well-bounded units which are clearly set apart from other more ordinary moments in time. I cannot speak of clinical time as strictly segregated between time characterized by sequence or some other non-narrative structure and time characterized by plot (which brings it closer to ritual time). I can only speak of clinical time which is "more or less" narrative or where the plot is more or less imbued with sufficient drama and desire to transform it from "mere experience" to "an experience." Therapeutic time also differs from ritual time in depending on a highly improvisational style. Magic may require getting things just right but the efficacious therapeutic plot depends on abandoning any formulaic structure. For this reason, therapists value improvisation as an essential clinical skill. They often talk about the need to learn to change treatment plans midstream when they recognize that what they had anticipated is not transpiring. They smile at novice therapists who are determined to carry out the planned activities no matter how obvious the cues that treatment is not going well. Therapists talk about the need to be "flexible," to "see where the patient is at," to "notice when things aren't going as expected," and the like. In fact, their emphasis on improvisation, which became apparent early in my study of them, helped trigger my interest in describing clinical work not merely in the language of "routines and enduring structures" but in the language of improvisations and dramas. Like the Ilongot Rosaldo describes, their work involves an "interplay of received structures and human activity" (1986: 23). Rosaldo says of these former headhunters, "one of the most deeply held Ilongot values is that their lives unfold more through active human improvisations than in accord with socially given plans . . ." (1986: 23). The same can be said of the occupational therapists.

Plot and the creation of experience

Themes raised in this ethnography intersect more broadly with anthropological concerns about how to investigate action and experience. For my purposes, what is most relevant about the recent attention to experience is not the issue of ethnographic representation and the ethnographer's experience so much as the need to conceptualize "experience" in an anthropologically useful way so that it can be deployed to analyze the life world of one's interlocutors. My use of the term experience is congruent with some anthropologists (Turner 1986b; Abrahams 1986) while others speak in a very different vein of a diffuse "flow of experience" (Jackson 1989; Stoller 1989). Why bring in the construct of experience, with all its unempirical, elusive properties, all its dependence on interpreting "inner states" of individuals? Why not simply speak of ritual structures or performance, read meanings from an interpretation of public culture, and thus avoid the whole psychological morass? In my case, this convenient sidestepping is too costly. It requires leaving out too much of what the therapists and patients attend to, too much of what they think they are up to. One cannot give up completely on the "native's point of view" and these natives are very concerned with their own inner states and other people's as well.

The ritual actions of therapy may sometimes be of the type Austin (1962) calls "illocutionary," thus allowing the anthropologist to arrive at their meaning by reference to a public set of norms and conventions. Tambiah (1985) has demonstrated effectively that a wide range of ritual activities are illocutionary, actions which do not require that particular inner states or emotions accompany them (though public performance of appropriate inner states might be essential). But ritual healing in occupational therapy is mostly not like this. Therapists do not perform actions which hold the sort of semantic and institutional stability of, for example, the minister who marries a couple. For the occupational therapist, efficacy depends upon the capacity to make of therapy a social drama, even a temporary community, where therapist and patient come together to create events which hold transformative potency. Experience has played a central role in my ethnographic study partly because I found that occupational therapists themselves care so much about it. They are forever complaining about patients who are not motivated in therapy, who are "non-compliant" and I soon realized this was not idle irritability or even a mania for control but an expression of deep cultural angst about their own therapeutic effectiveness. Their professional competence, even their ability to see themselves as having healed someone, comes in large part from the way patients receive and creatively build upon their therapeutic interventions. For them, this is about structuring experiences.

It is often presumed that experience is necessarily personal and subjective rather than socially constituted. The role narrative has played in studies of experience has perhaps exacerbated the misapprehension that experience is simply a private matter. When investigating experience primarily by eliciting personal stories, it is possible to miss the fundamentally social and action-oriented nature of both experience and storytelling. Some phenomenologically minded writers presume narrative is a vehicle for visiting personal experience which is somehow not also social and public. Not surprisingly, a common critique leveled at reliance upon first-hand narrative accounts in ethnographies is that these provide purely subjective reports, hence are inappropriate to anthropology as a social science (Aijmer 1992; Sangren 1992; Jarvie 1992).

I have used the term "experience" in a different way, as something which is social, created through interactions, and which, therefore, has some sort of public status. However, whatever is public about experience, as I have used the term, it certainly lacks the stability of the social fact. When therapists believe that "something happened" in therapy, neither they nor I believe the patient will interpret that "something" in the same away. They even recognize that, at times, they believe something is happening and the patient does not. Conversely, they are often surprised later to find out that some small episode in therapy which they had almost forgotten stands out as the single most important therapeutic event from the patient's perspective. Despite this instability of meaning, it is still fair to say that sometimes therapists and patients are able to cultivate a therapeutic time in which "things happen" and "significant experiences" are created and sometimes they are not able to accomplish this.

I have argued that therapists are quite clear that healing cannot be equated with mere increase in skill or capacity to carry out a series of actions. The "something" that counts as good therapy has the (conceptually strange but intuitively sensible) properties of being both a set of public actions and an invisible set of emotions, feelings, judgments, and perceptions. For this "something" to occur in therapy time, therapists are quite clear that a patient's participation must involve more than doing things, or learning skills designed to enhance movement. Patients must be addressed, reached, even changed in some inner way. Therapists generally feel that healing is connected both to a desire for therapy, and beyond that, for a way of life therapy indirectly points to, a life of maximum independence, of "return" to an active, socially responsible life.

The religion might be secular, but most therapists evince an unmistakable evangelical streak. They hope for therapeutic interactions, however apparently mundane, that will penetrate the inner consciousness of patients, like magic (and morally laden) arrows sent to transfigure an inner life (Basso 1984). Another way of saying this is that therapists want patients to experience therapeutic time in a particular sort of way, not as a passing flow (as mere experience) but as "an experience." Used in this special sense, experience takes on a singularity, an object-like status. It is imbued with form, it has duration. It becomes "an experience," as Dilthey says, because "something is held together in consciousness" (1989: 381).

Where is narrative in all this? When Dilthey wants to characterize lived experience as "an experience" he turns, as do those who in various ways follow him (particularly Gadamer 1975; Ricoeur 1984, 1985, 1987), to aesthetic form. I, too, have turned to narrative as a way of understanding the temporal form of significant experience because, more than any other aesthetic medium, stories tell us how we move through time, how impartial time becomes human time (Benjamin 1968). They allow us to contemplate that most elusive of worlds, future time. In clinical time characterized by a plot, therapists and patients are not merely creating a vivid present, they are creating images of a future. "The future," Dilthey tells us, "is a world of possibilities constantly pursuing us like fogbanks when we look down from the Alps. But these possibilities are images connected with the attitude of expectation. The dawning future always influences the changeable consciousness of the present in terms of a mood – great happiness, imminent death . . ." (1989: 382). In clinical work between therapists and patients, this future world may be relentless in its approach, but it is no more clearly formed or easily read than the fogbanks which pursue Dilthey up the Alps. Driven forward toward some goal or image of the future, therapists and patients try to emplot particular actions so that they become part of a narrative which will move them toward that future. They project narrative anticipations onto the present so that the very sounds and sights and smells of the current moment become portents of future meaning and perception itself becomes a narrative act imbued with ghosts of past and future.

Notes

1 FINDING NARRATIVE IN CLINICAL PRACTICE

1 Support for these studies has been provided by federal grants from The U.S. Bureau of Maternal and Child Health, U.S. Department of Education, and the American Occupational Therapy Foundation.
2 The World Bank, a United Nations organization, makes loans to developing countries. It has the complicated task of acting as both a lending bank whose job is to make intelligent loans at low interest rates and a development agency which helps shape a country's development through the process of devising large development projects.
3 In the philosophy of history, philosophers defending narrative history's explanatory power have called this form of explanation "explanation by reason" (Dray 1980; Olafson 1979).
4 However, arguments that narrative is an activity rooted in the human need to "read other minds," offer a compelling case for a universal propensity to narrate (J. Bruner 1986, 1990a, b, 1996; see also Carrithers 1992 for an anthropological treatment of this issue).
5 For example, an analysis of illness narratives among psychotherapy patients (Hyden 1995) draws upon: (1) transcription procedures from sociolinguistic models (Mishler 1986); (2) a life history inspired notion of life as narrative played out in the psychotherapy literature (Schafer 1980, 1981; Gergen and Gergen, 1986) in which chronic illness is interpreted as disruption and healing as reconstruction of a life narrative (and self); (3) ritual theory in which a narrative about psychotherapeutic healing is deconstructed via a process model of ritual healing (Tambiah 1977; Csordas 1983); and (4) cognitive approaches which connect personal narratives to culturally informed scripts, that is master narratives or "story lines" (Linde 1986).

2 THE MIMETIC QUESTION

1 One caveat is needed here. The narrator may not know the ending as well as the author. In postmodern texts we often have unreliable narrators whose inability to play the appropriate authoritative role lends a deep ironic voice to the text.
2 There is an interesting inversion, however. For Lévi-Strauss, the surface structure is the "story" and only at deeper levels, through intertextual

readings of myths with other myths, does the paradigmatic structure of relations become apparent. But in contemporary theory, it is precisely this chronological story which is invisible, hidden beneath discourse.

3 It should be noted that some versions of literary postmodernism, however, particularly feminist traditions, have made a very different case, arguing the necessity of putting the personal, the embodied, the emotional at the very center of things (Suleiman 1994).

3 THE CHECKERS GAME: CLINICAL ACTIONS IN QUEST OF A NARRATIVE

1 Nedra Gillette was instrumental in helping me put together this team. Over the two-year period five occupational therapy graduate students and several occupational therapy professors worked with me. Most significant was Dr. Maureen Fleming, a professor at Tufts who became a partner in this research.

4 THERAPEUTIC PLOTS

1 Madelyn O'Reilly wrote this as part of a graduate seminar Dr. Maureen Fleming and I conducted at Tufts University in 1991. This is a written version of a story she also told orally to us.

5 THE SELF IN NARRATIVE SUSPENSE: THERAPEUTIC PLOTS AND LIFE STORIES

1 There is not complete agreement on this point, however. A countering argument is that Westerners do not have such a sense of their autonomy as it might appear (Spiro 1993). The notion of a Western self as autonomous, cohesive, bounded, is a kind of "foil" to show how selves are very differently conceived in other societies and to argue that this notion of selfhood is but one construction among other (Ewing 1990). Some also argue that the non-Western other is not as "sociocentric" as it might appear. Wikan (1991) discussing the Balinese, Elvin (1985) the ancient Chinese and Ewing (1990) the Pakistani contend that these groups operate with many of the same conceptions of the self as those in Western societies.

2 Geertz declares: "I have been concerned, among other things, with attempting to determine how the people who live there define themselves as persons . . . In each case, I have tried to get at this most intimate of notions not by imagining myself someone else, a rice peasant or a tribal sheikh, and then seeing what I thought, but by searching out and analyzing the symbolic forms – words, images, institutions, behaviors – in terms of which, in each place, people actually represent themselves to themselves, and to one another" (1984: 125–126). Here is a decided rejection of any psychologizing move that would open the door to private language, individual consciousness and the like.

3 The rise of the novel which Bakhtin describes occurred in the West just two centuries ago, a period which marked an acute sense of living in history, of the transience of time, even of the endings of a time. Uncertainties in characters' lives so endemic to the novel are not merely private psychological states but reflect a shifting cultural terrain in which the whole social scene is moving in unknown directions.

The period of the novel begins in the early eighteenth century with the work of Defoe, Richardson, and Fielding. What distinguishes these works from earlier ones is that for the first time they did not rely on traditional cultural plots. Watts refers to this as a growing "aesthetic of particularity" (1957: 19). The view of reality which underlies this innovative form is the position of truth as discoverable through our senses rather than residing in traditional practices. Truth became associated with individual experience and the novel was dedicated to the task of representing experience. The early realist novel, "purported to be an authentic account of the actual experience of individuals" (Watts 1957: 27).

6 SOME MOMENTS ARE MORE NARRATIVE THAN OTHERS

1 This session was observed and videotaped; the therapist was interviewed before and after the session. Portions of the transcribed videotape as well as field notes are offered here.
2 This interviewer was one of the research assistants who helped gather data for the Boston study.

7 THERAPEUTIC PLOTS, HEALING RITUALS, AND THE CREATION OF SIGNIFICANT EXPERIENCE

1 It should be mentioned however, that because rituals are often highly formulaic, their very formalization may disallow or discourage improvised spontaneous actions which would increase emotional involvement among participants. In fact, the very formalization can deaden emotional response, allowing participants to operate at a remove, a "psychic distance" (Tambiah 1985: 133).

References

Abrahams, R. D. 1986, "Ordinary and extraordinary experience," in V. Turner and E. M. Bruner (eds.), *The anthropology of experience* (pp. 45–72), Urbana: University of Illinois Press.

Agar, M. 1980, "Stories, background knowledge and themes: Problems in the analysis of life history narratives," *American Ethnologist* 7: 223–239.

Aijmer, Goran 1992, "Inquiry and debate in the human sciences," *Current Anthropology* 33: 296–297.

Alves, J. 1993, "Transgressions and transformations: Initiation rites among urban Portuguese boys," *American Anthropologist* 95: 894–928.

Anspach, R. R. 1988, "Notes on the sociology of medical discourse: The language of case presentation," *Journal of Health and Social Behavior* 29: 357–375.

Arendt, Hannah 1958, *The human condition*, Chicago: University of Chicago Press.

1971, *The life of the mind*, New York: Harcourt Brace Jovanovich.

Aristotle 1970, *Poetics* (G. Else, trans.), Ann Arbor: University of Michigan Press.

1985, *Nicomachean ethics*, Indianapolis: Hackett Publishing Company.

Atkinson, Paul 1990, *The ethnographic imagination*, New York: Routledge.

Austin, J. 1962, *How to do things with words*, Cambridge, MA: Harvard University Press.

Badone, E. 1991, "Ethnography, fiction, and the meanings of the past in Brittany," *American Ethnologist* 18: 518–545.

Bakhtin, M. M. 1981, *The dialogic imagination*, Austin: University of Texas Press.

Bal, Mieke 1985, *Narratology: Introduction to the theory of narrative*, Toronto: University of Toronto Press.

Barrett, R. and Lucas, R. 1993, "The skulls are cold, the house is hot: Interpreting depths of meaning in Iban therapy," *Man* 28: 573–596.

Barthes, Roland 1974, *S/Z: An essay*, New York: Hill and Wang.

1975a, "An introduction to the structural analysis of narrative," *New Literary History* 6: 237–272.

1975b, *The pleasure of the text*, New York: Hill and Wang.

Basso, Keith H. 1984, " 'Stalking with stories': Names, places, and moral narratives among the Western Apache," in E. Bruner (ed.), *Text, play, and story: The construction and reconstruction of self and society* (pp. 19–55), Prospect, IL: Waveland Press.

Bauman, Richard 1977, *Verbal art as performance*, Prospect Heights, IL: Waveland Press.

1986, *Story, performance, and event*, Cambridge: Cambridge University Press.

Becker, A. L. 1979, "Text building, epistemology, and aesthetics in Japanese shadow theater," in Becker and A. A. Yengoyan (eds.), *Imagination of reality* (pp. 211–243), Norwood, NJ: Ablex Publishing Co.

Becker, Gay 1994, "Metaphors in disrupted lives: Infertility and cultural constructions of continuity," *Medical Anthropology Quarterly* 8: 383–410.

Becker, Gay and Kaufman, Sharon R. 1995, "Managing an uncertain illness trajectory in old age: Patients' and physicians' view of stroke," *Medical Anthropology Quarterly* 9: 165–187.

Benjamin, Walter 1968, *Illuminations*, New York: Schocken Books.

Benner, Patricia 1984, *From novice to expert: Excellence and power in clinical nursing practice*, Reading, MA: Addison-Wesley.

Bettelheim, Bruno 1977, *The uses of enchantment: The meaning and importance of fairy tales*, New York: Vintage Books.

Bilu, Y. and Witzum, E. 1993, "Working with Jewish ultra-orthodox patients: Guidelines for a culturally sensitive therapy," *Culture, Medicine, and Psychiatry* 17: 197–233.

Bing, Robert 1981, "Occupational therapy revisited: A paraphrasic journey," *American Journal of Occupational Therapy* 35: 499–518.

Booth, Wayne 1974, *A rhetoric of irony*, Chicago: University of Chicago Press.

Bourdieu, Pierre 1977, *Outline of a theory of practice*, Cambridge: Cambridge University Press.

Brody, Howard 1987, *Stories of sickness*, New Haven: Yale University Press.

Brooks, Peter 1984, *Reading for the plot: Design and intention in narrative*, New York: Alfred Knopf.

Broyard, Anatole 1992, *Intoxicated by my illness*, New York: Potter.

Bruner, Edward 1984, "Introduction: The opening up of anthropology," in Bruner (ed.), *Text, play, and story* (pp. 1–16), Prospect, IL: Waveland Press.

1986, "Ethnography as narrative," in Turner and Bruner (eds.), *The anthropology of experience*, Chicago: University of Illinois Press.

Bruner, Edward and Gorfain, P. 1984, "Dialogic narration and the paradoxes of Masada," in Bruner (ed.), *Text, play, and story* (pp. 56–79), Prospect, IL: Waveland Press.

Bruner, Jerome 1986, *Actual minds, possible worlds*, Cambridge, MA: Harvard University Press.

1990a, *Acts of meaning*, Cambridge, MA: Harvard University Press.

1990b, "Culture and human development: A new look," *Human Development* 33: 344–355.

1991, "The narrative construction of reality," *Critical Inquiry* 18: 1–21.

1996, *The culture of education*, Cambridge, MA: Harvard University Press.

Burke, Kenneth 1931, *Counter statement*, Berkeley: University of California Press.

1945, *A grammar of motives*, Berkeley: University of California Press.

1966, *Language as symbolic action: Essays on life, literature, and method*, Berkeley: University of California Press.

1969, *A rhetoric of motives*, Berkeley: University of California Press.

Burrell, David and Hauerwas, Stanley 1977, "From system to story: An alternative pattern for rationality in ethics," in H. T. Engelhardt Jr. and D. Callahan (eds.), *Knowledge, value and belief*, New York: The Hastings Center.

Cain, Carole 1991, "Personal stories: Identity acquisition and self-understanding in alcoholics anonymous," *Ethos* 19: 210–253.

Carr, David 1986, *Time, narrative, and history*, Bloomington: Indiana University Press.

Carrithers, Michael 1985, "An alternative social history of the self," in M. Carrithers, S. Collins and S. Lukes (eds.), *The category of the person*, Cambridge: Cambridge University Press.

1992, *Why humans have cultures: Explaining anthropology and social diversity*, Oxford: Oxford University Press.

Casper, M. and Koenig, Barbara 1996, "Reconfinguring nature and culture: Intersections of medical anthropology and technoscience studies," *Medical Anthropology Quarterly* 10: 523– 536.

Chambers, Ross 1984, *Story and situation: Narrative seduction and the power of fiction*, Minneapolis: University of Minnesota Press.

Chatman, Seymour 1978, *Story and discourse: Narrative structure in fiction and film*, Ithaca: Cornell University Press.

Cicourel, A. 1983, "Language and the structure of belief in medical communication," in S. Rischer and A. Todd (eds.), *The social organization of doctor–patient communication* (pp. 221–240), Washington, DC: Center for Applied Linguistics.

Clark, Florence 1993, "Occupation embedded in a real life: Interweaving occupational science and occupational therapy," *American Journal of Occupational Therapy* 47: 1067–1078.

Clifford, J. 1983, "On ethnographic authority," *Representations* 1: 118–1??.

1986, "Partial truths," in Clifford and Marcus (eds.), *Writing culture: The poetics and politics of ethnography*, Berkeley: University of California Press.

Clifford, J. and Marcus, G. E. 1986, *Writing culture: The poetics and politics of ethnography*, Berkeley: University of California Press.

Coles, R. 1989, *Stories and theories: The call of stories*, Boston: Houghton Mifflin.

Collingwood, R. G. 1946, *The idea of history*, Oxford: Clarendon.

Collins, S. 1985, "Categories, concepts or predicaments? Remarks on Mauss' use of philosophical terminology," in M. Carrithers, S. Collins, and S. Lukes (eds.), *The category of the person*, Cambridge: Cambridge University Press.

Crain, M. M. 1991, "Poetics and politics in the Ecuadorean Andes: Women's narratives of death and devil possession," *American Ethnologist* 18: 67–89.

Crapanzano, Vincent 1977a, "The life history in anthropological fieldwork," *Anthropology and Humanism Quarterly* 2: 3–7.

1977b, "On the writing of ethnography," *Dialectical Anthropology*, 2: 69–73.

1980, *Tuhami: Portrait of a Moroccan*, Chicago: University of Chicago Press.

1984, "Life histories," *American Anthropologist* 86: 953–960.

1986, "Hermes' dilemma: The masking of subversion in ethnographic description," in J. Clifford and G. E. Marcus (eds.), *Writing culture* (pp. 51–76), Berkeley: University of California Press.

1990, "On self characterization," in J. W. Stigler, R. A. Shweder, and

G. Herdt (eds.) *Cultural psychology: Essays on comparative human development* (pp. 401–423), Cambridge: Cambridge University Press.

1991a, *Hermes' dilemma and Hamlet's desire: On the epistemology of interpretation*, Cambridge, MA: Harvard University Press.

1991b, "The postmodern crisis: Discourse, parody and memory," *Cultural Anthropology* 6: 431–446.

Csikszentmihalyi, Mihalyi 1975, "Play and intrinsic rewards," *Journal of Humanistic Psychology* 15: 41–63.

Csordas, Thomas 1983, "The rhetoric of transformation in ritual healing," *Culture, Medicine, and Psychiatry* 7: 333–375.

1985, "Medical and sacred realities: Between comparative religion and transcultural psychiatry," *Culture, Medicine, and Psychiatry* 9: 103–116.

1994, *Embodiment and experience: The existential ground of culture and self*, Cambridge: Cambridge University Press.

Culler, Jonathon 1979, "Structuralism and grammatology," *Boundary 2*, 8: 75–85.

1981, *The pursuit of signs: Semiotics, literature, deconstruction*, Ithaca: Cornell University Press.

Danforth, Loring 1989, *Firewalking and religious healing: The Ana Stenari of Greece and the American firewalking movement*, Princeton: Princeton University Press.

Dennett, Daniel C. 1991, *Consciousness explained*, Boston: Little, Brown & Co.

1993, *Content and consciousness* (2nd ed.), London: Routledge.

de Saussure, Ferdinand 1959, *Course in general linguistics*, New York: McGraw-Hill.

Dilthey, William 1989, *Selected works*, vol. I., R. A. Makkreel and F. Rodi (eds.), Princeton: Princeton University Press.

Douglas, Mary 1966, *Purity and danger: An analysis of concepts of pollution and taboo*, London: Routledge and Kegan Paul.

Dray, William 1954, "Explanatory narrative in history," *Philosophical Quarterly* 15–27.

1957, *Laws and explanations in history*, London: Oxford University Press.

1980, *Perspectives on history*, London: Routledge and Kegan Paul.

Dwyer, K. 1977, "Dialogue of fieldwork," *Dialectical Anthropology* 2: 143–151.

1979, "Dialogue of ethnology." *Dialectical Anthropology* 4: 205–224.

Early, E. A. 1982, "The logic of well being: Therapeutic narratives in Cairo, Egypt," *Social Science and Medicine* 16: 1491–1497.

1985, "Catharsis and creation: The everyday narratives of Baladi women of Cairo," *Anthropological Quarterly* 58: 172–181.

1988, "The Baladi curative system of Cairo, Egypt," *Culture, Medicine, and Psychiatry* 12: 65–83.

Eco, Umberto 1979, *The role of the reader: Explorations in the semiotics of texts*, Bloomington: Indiana University Press.

Eisenberg, Leon 1977, "Disease and illness: Distinctions between professional and popular ideas of sickness," *Culture, Medicine, and Psychiatry* 1: 9–23.

Elstein, Arthur 1976, "Clinical judgment: Psychological research and medical practice," *Science* 194: 696–700.

Elvin, Mark 1985, "Between the earth and heaven: Conceptions of the self in China," in *The Category of the Person*, Michael Carrithers, Steven Collins, and Steven Lukes (eds.), pp. 156–189. Cambridge: Cambridge University Press.

Engelhardt, Thomas 1977, "Defining occupational therapy: The meaning of therapy and the virtues of occupation," *American Journal of Occupational Therapy* 31: 666–672.

Ewing, K. 1990, "The illusion of wholeness: Culture, self, and the experience of inconsistency," *Ethos* 18: 251–278.

1991, "Can psychoanalytic theories explain the Pakistani woman? Intra-psychic autonomy and interpersonal engagement in the extended family," *Ethos* 19: 131–160.

Farmer, Paul 1994, "AIDS: Talk and the constitution of cultural models," *Social Science & Medicine* 38: 801–810.

Fernandez, W. 1985, "Exploded worlds: Text as metaphor for ethnography (and vice versa)," *Dialectical Anthropology* 10: 15–26.

Fischer, Michael 1986, "Ethnicity and the post-modern arts of memory," in G. Marcus and M. Fischer (eds.), *Anthropology as cultural critique: An experimental moment in the human sciences*, Chicago: University of Chicago Press.

Fisher, Sue and Alexandra Todd 1983, *The Social Organization of Doctor–Patient Communication*, Washington, DC: The Center for Applied Linguistics.

Fleming, Maureen 1994, "A common sense practice in an uncommon world," in C. Mattingly and M. Fleming (eds.), *Clinical reasoning: Forms of inquiry in therapeutic practice*, Philadelphia: F. A. Davis.

Forster, E. M. 1927, *Aspects of the novel*, New York: Harcourt Brace Jovanovich.

Foucault, Michel 1973, *The birth of the clinic: An archeology of medical perception*, New York: Pantheon Books.

1979, *Discipline and punish: The birth of the prison*, New York: Vintage Books.

Frank, Arthur 1995, *The wounded storyteller: Body, illness, and ethics*, Chicago: University of Chicago Press.

Frank, Gelya 1984, "Life history model of adaptation to disability: The case of a 'congenital amputee'," *Social Science and Medicine* 19: 639–645.

1986, "On embodiment: A case study of congenital limb deficiency in American culture," *Culture, Medicine, and Psychiatry* 10: 189–219.

1996, "Life history," in A. Levinson and M. Ember (eds.), *Human relations area files at Yale University*, vol. II, New York: Henry, Holt & Company.

Frankenberg, R. 1986, "Sickness as cultural performance: Drama, trajectory, and pilgrimage root metaphors and the making social of disease," *International Journal of Health Services* 16: 603–626.

Freccero, J. 1986, "Autobiography and narrative," in T. C. Heller, M. Sasna, and D. E. Wellbery (eds.), *Reconstructing individualism: Autonomy, individuality, and the self in western thought* (pp. 16–29), Palo Alto: Stanford University Press.

Frye, Northrop 1957, *Anatomy of criticism: Four essays*, Princeton: Princeton University Press.

1976, *The secular scripture: A study of the structure of romance*, Cambridge, MA: Harvard University Press.

Gadamer, Hans-Georg 1975, *Truth and method*, New York: Seabury Press.

1979, "The problem of historical consciousness," in P. Rabinow and W. M. Sullivan (eds.), *Interpretive social science: A reader*, Berkeley: University of California Press.

Gallie, W. B. 1964, *Philosophy and the historical understanding*, New York: Schocken Books.

Garro, Linda 1992, "Chronic illness and the construction of narratives," in M. J. DelVecchio Good, et al. (eds.), *Pain as human experience* (pp. 100–137), Berkeley: University of California Press.

1994, "Narrative representations of chronic illness experience: Cultural models of illness, mind, and body in stories concerning the temporomandibular joint (TMJ)," *Social Science and Medicine* 38: 775–788.

Geertz, C. 1973, *The interpretation of cultures*, New York: Basic Books.

1980, "Blurred genres: The refiguration of social thought," *American Scholar* 80: 165–179.

1983, *Local knowledge: Further essays in interpretive anthropology*, New York: Basic Books.

1984, "From the native's point of view: On the nature of anthropological understanding," in R. A. Shweder and R. A. LeVine (eds.) *Culture theory: Essays on mind, self, and emotion* (pp. 123–136), Cambridge: Cambridge University Press.

1988, *Works and lives*, Stanford, CA: Stanford University Press.

Gennette, Gerard 1980, *Narrative discourse: An essay in method*, Ithaca: Cornell University Press.

1982, *Figures of literary discourse*, New York: Columbia University Press.

Gergen, K. and Gergen, M. M. 1986, "Narrative form and the construction of psychological science," in T. R. Sarbin (ed.), *Narrative Psychology*, New York: Praeger.

Gilbert, M. 1989, "The cracked pot and the missing sheep," *American Ethnologist* 16: 213–229.

1994, "Aesthetic strategies: The politics of a royal ritual," *Africa* 64: 99–123.

Ginsburg, F. 1987, "Procreation stories," *American Ethnologist* 14: 623–636.

Goffman, Erving 1963, *Stigma: Notes on the management of spoiled identity*, New York: Simon & Schuster.

1974, *Frame analysis: An essay on the organization of experience*, Cambridge, MA: Harvard University Press.

Good, Byron J. 1977, "The heart of what's the matter: The semantics of illness in Iran," *Culture, Medicine and Psychiatry* 1: 25–28.

1994, *Medicine, rationality, and experience: An anthropological perspective*, Cambridge: Cambridge University Press.

Good, Byron J. and Good, Mary-Jo DelVecchio 1981, "The semantics of medical discourse," in Mendelsohn (ed.), *Yearbook in the sociology of the sciences: Anthropological perspectives in the sciences.*

1980, "The meaning of symptoms: A cultural hermeneutic model for clinical practice," in L. Eisenberg and A. Kleinman (eds.), *The relevance of social science for medicine*, Norwell, MA: D. Reidel Publishing Company.

1994, "In the subjunctive mode: Epilepsy narratives in Turkey," *Social Science and Medicine* 38: 835–842.

Good, Mary-Jo DelVecchio 1990, "The practice of biomedicine and the discourse on hope: A preliminary investigation into the culture of American oncology," in A. Pfleiderer and A. Bibeau (eds.), *Anthropologies of medicine: A colloquium on West European and North American Perspectives*, Heidelberg: Vieweg.

1995, *American medicine: The quest for competence*, Berkeley: University of California Press.

Good, M. J. DelVecchio, Good, B. J., Schaffer, C. and Lind, S. 1990, "American oncology and the discourse on hope," *Culture, Medicine and Psychiatry* 14: 59–79.

Good, M. J. DelVecchio, Good, B. J., Munakato, T., Kobayashi, Y., and Mattingly, C. 1994, "Oncology and narrative time," *Social Science and Medicine* 38: 855–862.

Gordon, Deborah 1988, "Tenacious assumptions in western medicine," in M. Locke and D. Gordon (eds.), *Biomedicine Examined*, vol. V, pp. 11–56.

Hazen, H. 1995, "The ethnographer's textual presence: On three forms of anthropological authorship," *Cultural Anthropology* 10: 395–406.

Heidegger, M. 1962, *Being and time* (E. Robinson and J. Macquarrie, trans.), New York: Harper and Row.

Helfrich, C., Kielhofner, Gary, and Mattingly, Cheryl 1994, "Volition as narrative: Understanding motivation in chronic illness," *American Journal of Occupational Therapy* 38: 311–317.

Hepburn, R. W. and Murdock, I. 1956, "Vision and choice in morality," *Aristotelian Society* 30, London: Harrison and Sons.

Herrnstein-Smith, B. 1978, *On the margins of discourse*, Chicago: University of Chicago Press.

1980, "Narrative versions, narrative theories," *Critical Inquiry* 7: 209–239.

Herzfeld, M. 1986, "Closure as cure: Tropes in the exploration of bodily and social disorder," *Current Anthropology* 27: 107–120.

Holland, Dorothy and Kipnis, A. 1994, "Metaphors for embarrassment and stories of exposure: The not-so-egocentric self in American culture," *Ethos* 22: 316–342.

Holland, Dorothy and Quinn, Naomi (eds.) 1987, *Cultural models in language and thought*, New York: Cambridge University Press.

Hollis, Martin O. 1985, "Of masks and men," in M. Carrithers, S. Collins, and S. Lukes (eds.), *The category of the person*, Cambridge: Cambridge University Press.

Hopkins, Helen L. and Smith, H. D. (eds.) 1990, *Willard & Spackman's occupational therapy* (7th ed.), Philadelphia: J. B. Lippincott.

Hunt, Linda 1994, "Practicing oncology in provincial Mexico: A narrative analysis," *Social Science and Medicine* 38: 843–853.

Hunter, Kathryn 1991, *Doctor's stories: The narrative structure of medical knowledge*, Princeton: Princeton University Press.

Hyden, L. C. 1995, "The rhetoric of recovery and change," *Culture, Medicine and Psychiatry* 19: 73–90.

Hymes, D. 1972, *Reinventing anthropology*, New York: Pantheon Books.

Ingarden, Roman 1967, "Aesthetic experience and aesthetic object," in N. Lawrence and D. O'Connor (eds.), *Readings in existential phenomenology*, New York: Prentice Hall.

Iser, Wolfgang 1974, *The implied reader: Patterns of communication in prose fiction from Bunyan to Beckett*, Baltimore: Johns Hopkins University Press.
   1978, *The act of reading: A theory of aesthetic response*, Baltimore: Johns Hopkins University Press.

Jackson, J. 1994, "The Roshomon approach to dealing with chronic pain," *Social Science and Medicine* 38: 823–833.

Jackson, Michael 1989, *Paths toward a clearing: Radical empiricism and ethnographic inquiry*, Bloomington: Indiana University Press.

Jakobson, Roman 1960, "Closing statement: Linguistics and poetics," in T. Sebeok (ed.), *Style in language*, Cambridge, MA: MIT Press.

Jameson, F. 1991, *Postmodernism, or, the cultural logic of late capitalism*, Durham: Duke University Press.

Jarvie, Jan 1992, "Inquiry and debate in the human sciences," *Current Anthropology* 23: 299–301.

Kapferer, B. 1983, *A celebration of demons: Exorcism & the aesthetics of healing in Sri Lanka*, Bloomington: Indiana University Press.

Kassirer, J. P., Kuipers, B. J. and Gorry, G. A. 1982, "Toward a theory of clinical expertise," *American Journal of Medicine* 73: 251–259.

Kaufman, Sharon 1988, "Illness, biography and the interpretation of self following a stroke," *Journal of Aging Studies* 2: 217–227.

Kearney, R. 1988, *The wake of imagination: Toward a postmodern culture*, Minneapolis: University of Minnesota Press.

Kendall, L. 1996, "Initiating performance: The story of Chini, a Korean shaman," in C. Laderman and M. Roseman (eds.), *The performance of healing* (pp. 17–58), New York: Routledge.

Kermode, Frank 1966, *The sense of an ending: Studies in the theory of fiction*, London: Oxford University Press.

Kielhofner, Gary 1983, *Health through occupation*, Philadelphia: F. A. Davis.

Kielhofner, Gary and Burke, Janice 1977, "Occupational therapy after 60 years: An account of changing identity and knowledge," *American Journal of Occupational Therapy* 31: 675–689.

Kirmayer, Laurence J. 1988, "Mind and body as metaphors: Hidden values in biomedicine," in M. Lock and D. Gordon (eds.), *Biomedicine Examined*, Dordrecht: Kluwer.
   1992, "The body's insistence on meaning: Metaphor as presentation and representation in illness experience," *Medical Anthropology Quarterly* 6: 323–346.
   1993, "Healing and the invention of metaphor: The effectiveness of symbols revisited," *Culture, Medicine, and Psychiatry* 17: 161–195.

Kleinman, Arthur 1980, *Patients and healers in the context of culture: An exploration of the borderline between anthropology, medicine, and psychiatry*, Los Angeles: University of California Press.

1988, *The illness narratives: Suffering, healing, and the human condition*, New York: Basic Books.

1991, "Pain and resistance," in M. J. DelVecchio Good, et al. (eds.), *Pain as human experience: Anthropological perspectives*, Berkeley: University of California Press.

Kleinman, Arthur and Kleinman, Joan 1991, "Suffering and its professional transformation: Toward an ethnography of interpersonal experience," *Culture, Medicine and Psychiatry* 15: 275.

1994, "How bodies remember: Social memory and bodily experience of criticism, resistance, and delegitimation following China's cultural revolution," *New Literary History* 25: 707–723.

1996, "The appeal of experience; the dismay of images: Cultural appropriations of suffering in our times," *Daedalus* 125: 1–24.

Kleinman, Arthur, Eisenberg, Leon, and Good, Byron J. 1978, "Culture, illness and care: Clinical lessons from anthropologic and cross-cultural research," *Annals of Internal Medicine* 88: 251–258.

Kondo, D. 1990, *Crafting selves: Power, gender, and discourses of identity in a Japanese workplace*, Chicago: University of Chicago Press.

Koselleck, Reinhart 1985, *Futures past: On the semantics of historical time*, Cambridge, MA: MIT Press.

Kundera, Milan 1993, *Testaments betrayed: An essay in nine parts*, New York: HarperPerennial.

Labov, W. 1972, "The transformation of experience in narrative syntax," in Labov (ed.), *Language in the inner city* (pp. 354–396), Philadelphia: University of Pennsylvania Press.

1981, "Speech actions and reactions in personal narrative," in D. Tannen (ed.), *Analyzing discourse: Text and talk* (pp. 219–247), Washington: Georgetown Press.

Labov, W. and Fanshel, D. 1977, *Therapeutic discourse: Psychotherapy as conversation*, New York: Academic Press.

Labov, W. and Waletzky, J. 1967, "Narrative analysis: Oral versions of personal experience," in J. Helm (ed.), *Essays in the verbal and visual arts* (pp. 12–44), Seattle: University of Washington Press for the American Ethnological Society.

Lacan, Jacques 1977, *Ecrits: A selection* (S. Sheridan, trans.), New York: W. W. Norton.

Laderman, C. and Roseman, M. 1996, "Introduction," in Laderman and Roseman (eds.), *The performance of healing* (pp. 1–16), New York: Routledge.

Langer, Susanne 1953, *Feeling and form: A theory of art*, New York: Scribner.

Langness, L. and Frank, G. 1981, *Lives*, Novato, CA: Chandler and Sharp.

Lau, J., Kassirer, J. P., and Pauker, S. G. 1983, "Decision maker 3.0: Improved decision analysis by personal computer," *Medical Decision Making* 3: 39–43.

Lawlor, Mary 1994, *The UIC therapeutic partnership project final report*, Chicago: The University of Illinois at Chicago.

Leach, Edmund 1965, *Political systems of highland Burma: A study of Kashin social structure*, Boston: Beacon Press.

1976, *Culture and communication: The logic by which symbols are connected*, Cambridge: Cambridge University Press.

182   References

Leder, Drew 1984, "Medicine and paradigms of embodiment," *Journal of Medicine & Philosophy* 9: 29–44.
Lévi-Strauss, Claude 1962, *The savage mind,* Chicago: University of Chicago Press.
    1963, *Structural anthropology,* New York: Basic Books.
    1969, *The raw and the cooked,* New York: Harper & Row.
Levine, Ruth 1987, "The influence of the arts and crafts movement on the professional status of occupational therapy," *American Journal of Occupational Therapy* 41: 248–254.
Lienhardt, G. 1961, *Divinity and experience: The religion of the Dinka,* Oxford: Clarendon.
Linde, C. 1986, "Private stories and public discourse," *Poetics* 15: 183, 196–202.
    1987, "Explanatory systems in oral life stories," in D. Holland and N. Quinn (eds.), *Cultural models in language and thought* (pp. 343–366), New York: Cambridge University Press.
    1993, *Life stories: The creation of coherence,* Oxford: Oxford University Press.
Luria A. R. 1972, *The man with a shattered world: The history of a brain wound,* Cambridge: Harvard University Press.
Lyotard, J. 1984, *The postmodern condition: A report on knowledge,* Minneapolis: University of Minnesota Press.
MacIntyre, Alisdair 1980, "Epistemological crises, dramatic narrative, and the philosophy of science," in G. Gutting (ed.), *Paradigms and revolutions,* South Bend: University of Notre Dame Press.
    1981, *After virtue: A study in moral theory,* South Bend: University of Notre Dame Press.
Malinowski, Bronisliaw 1935, *Coral Gardens and their magic,* London: G. Allen and Unwin.
Mallinson, T., Kielhofner, Gary, and Mattingly, Cheryl 1996, "Metaphor and meaning in a clinical interview," *American Journal of Occupational Therapy* 50: 338–346.
Marcus, G. E. and Cushman, D. 1982, "Ethnographies as texts," *Annual Review of Anthropology* 11: 25–69.
Marcus, George and Fischer, Michael 1986, *Anthropology as cultural critique: An experimental moment in the human sciences,* Chicago: University of Chicago Press.
Matthews, H., Lannin, D. R., and Mitchell, J. P. 1994, "Coming to terms with advanced breast cancer: Black women's narratives from eastern North Carolina," *Social Science and Medicine* 38: 789–800.
Mattingly, Cheryl 1989, *Thinking with stories: Story and experience in a clinical practice,* Ph.D. Thesis, Massachusetts Institute of Technology.
    1991a, "Narrative reflections on practical actions: Two learning experiments in reflective storytelling," in D. Schön (ed.), *The reflective turn: Case studies in and on educational practice* (pp. 235–257), New York: Teachers College Press.
    1991b, "The narrative nature of clinical reasoning," *American Journal of Occupational Therapy* 45: 998–1005.
    1991c, "What is clinical reasoning?," *American Journal of Occupational Therapy* 45: 979–998.

1994, "The concept of therapeutic emplotment," *Social Science and Medicine* 38: 811–822.

In Press, "What is 'the good' for this patient? Narrative reasoning in clinical practice," *Medical Anthropology Quarterly.*

Mattingly, Cheryl and Fleming, Maureen 1994, *Clinical reasoning: Forms of inquiry in a therapeutic practice*, Philadelphia: F. A. Davis.

Mattingly, Cheryl and Gillette, Nedra 1991, "Anthropology, occupational therapy and action research," *American Journal of Occupational Therapy* 45: 972–978.

Mattingly, Cheryl, Fleming, Maureen, and Gillette, Nedra 1997, "Narrative explorations in the tacit dimension: Bringing language to clinical practice," *Journal for Critical Social Science.*

Mattingly, Cheryl and Lawlor, Mary 1997, "The disability experience from a family perspective," in E. Crepeau and M. Neistadt (eds.), *Willard & Spackman's occupational therapy*, Philadelphia: J. B. Lippincott.

McCreery, J. 1979, "Potential and effective meaning in therapeutic ritual," *Culture, Medicine, and Psychiatry* 3: 53–72.

Merleau-Ponte, Maurice 1962, *Phenomenology of perception*, London: Routledge and Kegan Paul.

Meyer, Adolph 1977, "The philosophy of occupational therapy," *American Journal of Occupational Therapy* 31: 639–642.

Mink, Louis 1965, "The autonomy of historical understanding," *History and Theory* 5: 24–47.

1970, "History as mode of comprehension," *New Literary History* 1: 541–558.

1987, *Historical understanding*, Ithaca: Cornell University Press.

Mishler, Elliot 1984, *The discourse of medicine: Dialectics of medical interviews*, Norwood, NJ: Ablex Publishing Co.

1986, *Research interviewing: Concept and narrative*, Cambridge, MA: Harvard University Press.

Monks, J. and Frankenberg, R. 1995, "Being ill and being me: Self, body, and time in multiple sclerosis narratives," in B. Ingstad and S. R. Whyte (eds.), *Disability and culture* (pp. 107–134), Berkeley: University of California Press.

Morgan, L. 1987, "Dependency therapy in the political economy of health: An anthropological critique," *Medical Anthropology Quarterly* : 131–154.

Murdoch, I. 1972, *The sovereignty of the good*, New York: Schocken Books.

Murphy, Robert 1987, *The body silent*, New York: Henry Holt and Company.

Myerhoff, Barbara 1986, "Life not death in Venice: Its second life," in V. Turner and E. M. Bruner (eds.), *The anthropology of experience*, Chicago: University of Illinois Press.

1987, *Number our days*, New York: Simon & Schuster.

Nussbaum, M. 1990, *Love's knowledge*, New York: Oxford University Press.

Obeyesekare, G. 1981, *Medusa's hair: An essay on personal symbols and religious experience*, Chicago: University of Chicago Press.

Olafson, Frederick (1971), "Narrative history and the concept of action," *History and Theory* 9: 265–289.

1979, *The dialectic of action: Philosophical interpretation of history and the humanities*, Chicago: University of Chicago Press.

Olson, Stein 1978, *The structure of literary understanding*, New York: Cambridge University Press.

Ortiz, K. 1985, "Mental health consequences of life history method: Implications from a refugee case," *Ethos* 13: 99–120.

Ortner, S. B. (1978). *Sherpas through their rituals*, Cambridge: Cambridge University Press.

Paget, M. A. 1988, *The unity of mistakes: A phenomenological interpretation of medical work*, Philadelphia: Temple University Press.

Parham, Diane 1987, "Toward professionalism: The reflective therapist," *American Journal of Occupational Therapy* 41: 555–561.

Peacock, J. and Holland, D. C. 1993, "The narrative self: Life stories in process," *Ethos* 21: 367–383.

Perry, W. 1979, *Forms of intellectual and ethical development in the college years*, New York: Holt, Rinehart & Winston.

Pierce, C. S. 1931–35, *Collected papers of Charles Sanders Pierce*, vols. I–VI, C. Hartshorne and D. Weiss (eds.), Cambridge, MA: Harvard University Press.

Polanyi, M. 1966, *The tacit dimension*, Garden City, NY: Doubleday.

Polkinghorne, Donald E. 1991, "Narrative and self-concept," *Journal of Narrative and Life History* 1: 135–153.

Pratt, Mary 1986, "Fieldwork in common places," in J. Clifford and G. E. Marcus (eds.), *Writing culture: The poetics and politics of ethnography*, Berkeley: University of California Press.

Price, L. 1987, "Ecuadorian illness stories: Cultural knowledge in natural discourse," in D. Holland and N. Quinn (eds.), *Cultural models in language and thought* (pp. 313–342), Cambridge: Cambridge University Press.

Propp, Vladimir 1968, *Morphology of the folk tale* (L. Scott, trans.), Austin: University of Texas Press.

Quinn, Naomi and Holland, Dorothy 1987, "Cultural cognition in cultural models," in Holland and Quinn (eds.), *Cultural models in language and thought*, Cambridge: Cambridge University Press.

Radin, P. 1983 [1926], *Crashing thunder: The autobiography of an American Indian*, Lincoln: University of Nebraska Press (originally published by Appleston).

Reddy, William 1992, "Postmodernism and the public sphere: implication for an historical ethnography," *Cultural Anthropology* 7: 135–168.

Ricoeur, Paul 1976, *Interpretation theory: Discourse and the surplus of meaning*, Fort Worth: The Texas Christian University Press.

  1978 *The philosophy of Paul Ricoeur: An anthology of his work*, C. E. Reagan and D. Stewart (eds.), Boston: Beacon Press.

  1980, "Narrative time," in W. J. T. Mitchell (ed.), *On narrative*, Chicago: University of Chicago Press.

  1981, "The narrative function," in J. Thompson (ed.), *Hermeneutics and the human sciences: Essays on language, action, and interpretation.* Cambridge: Cambridge University Press.

  1984, 1985, and 1987, *Time and narrative* (3 vols.), (vols. I and II, K. McLaughlin and D. Pellauer, trans., vol. III K. Blamey and D. Pellauer), Chicago: University of Chicago Press.

  1992, *Oneself as another*, Chicago: University of Chicago Press.

Riessman, Catherine K. 1990, "Strategic uses of narrative in the presentation of self and illness: A research note," *Social Science and Medicine* 30: 1195–1200.

1993, "Narrative analysis," *Qualitative Research Methods*, vol. 30. Newbury Park, CA: Sage Publications.

Rittenberg, W. and Simons, R. C. 1985, "Gentle interrogation: Inquiry and interaction in brief initial psychiatric evaluations," in R. Hahn and A. Gaines (eds.), *Physicians of Western Medicine* (pp. 177–191), Dordrecht, Holland: D. Reidel Publishing Co.

Rogers, Joan 1982a, "Educating the inquisitive practitioner," *Occupational Therapy Journal of Research* 2: 3–11.

1982b, "The spirit of independence: The evolution of a philosophy," *American Journal of Occupational Therapy* 36: 709–715.

1983, "Clinical reasoning: The ethics, science, & art," *American Journal of Occupational Therapy* 37: 601–616.

Rogers, J. C. and Holm, M. B. 1991, "Occupational therapy diagnostic reasoning: A component of clinical reasoning," *American Journal of Occupational Therapy* 45: 1045–1053.

Rogers, J. C. and Kielhofner, Gary 1985, "Treatment planning," in Kielhofner (ed.), *A model of human occupation: Theory and application* (pp. 136–146), Baltimore: Williams & Wilkins.

Rogers, J. C. and Masagatani, G. 1982, "Clinical reasoning of occupational therapists during the initial assessment of physically disabled patients," *Occupational Therapy Journal of Research* 2: 195–219.

Rosaldo, Renato 1980, *Ilongot headhunting, 1883–1974: A study in society and history*, Palo Alto: Stanford University Press.

1986, "Ilongot hunting as story and experience," in Bruner and Turner (eds.), *The anthropology of experience*, Chicago: University of Illinois Press.

1989, *Culture and truth: The remaking of social analysis*, Boston: Beacon Press.

Roseman, M. 1988, "The pragmatics of aesthetics: The performance of healing among Senoi Temiar," *Social Science and Medicine* 27: 811–818.

1990a, "Head, heart, odor, and shadow: The structure of the self, the emotional world, and ritual performance among Senoi Temiar," *Ethos* 18: 227–250.

1990b, *Healing sounds from the Malaysian rain forest: Temiar music and medicine*, Berkeley: University of California Press.

1996, "Pure products go crazy: Rainforest healing in a nation state," in C. Laderman and M. Roseman (eds.), *The performance of healing*, New York: Routledge.

Roseman, S. 1991, "A documentary fiction and ethnographic production: An analysis of Sherman's March," *Cultural Anthropology* 6: 505–524.

Rosenwald, George and Richard Ockberg (eds.) 1992, *Storied Lives: The Cultural Politics of Self-Understanding*, New Haven: Yale University Press.

Sacks, Oliver 1972, "Foreword," in A. R. Luria, *The man with a shattered world*, Cambridge: Harvard University Press.

1984, *A leg to stand on*, New York: Summit Books.

1987, *The man who mistook his wife for a hat and other clinical tales*, New York: Perennial Library.

1995, *An anthropologist on Mars*, New York: Alfred Knopf.

Sahlins, Marshall 1985, *Islands of History*, Chicago: University of Chicago Press.

Sangren, Steven 1992, "Rhetoric and the authority of ethnography," *Current Anthropology* 33: 277–296.

Sarbin, T. (ed.) 1986, *Narrative psychology: The storied nature of human conduct*, New York: Praeger.

Schafer, R. 1980, "Narration in the psychoanalytic dialogue," *Critical Inquiry* 7: 29–53.

   1981, *Narrative actions in psychoanalysis*, Worcester: Clark University Press.

Scheper-Hughes, N., and Lock, M. 1987, "The mindful body: A prolegomenon to future work in medical anthropology," *Medical Anthropology Quarterly* 1: 6–41.

Schieffelin, Edward 1996, "On failure and performance: Throwing the medium out of the science," in C. Laderman and M. Roseman (eds.), *The performance of healing* (pp. 59–90), New York: Routledge.

Scholes, Robert and Kellogg, R. 1966, "The nature of narrative," in Laderman and Roseman (eds.), *The performance of healing*, New York: Routledge.

Schon, D. 1983, *The reflective practitioner: How professionals think in action*, New York: Basic Books.

   1987, *Educating the reflective practitioner*, San Francisco: Jossey-Bass.

Schutz, A. 1975, *On phenomenology and social relations*, Chicago: University of Chicago Press.

Shostak, M. 1981, *Nisa: The life and words of Kung woman*, New York: Vintage Books.

Shweder, R. A. and Bourne, E. J. 1984, "Does the concept of the person vary cross-culturally?," in Sweder and R. LeVine (eds.), *Cultural theory: Essays on mind, self, and emotion* (pp. 158–199), Cambridge: Cambridge University Press.

Sontag, S. 1988, *Illness as metaphor*, New York: Farrar, Strauss & Giroux.

Spence, D. 1982, *Narrative truth and historical truth*, New York: W.W. Norton.

Spiro, Melford 1993, "Is the Western conception of the self 'peculiar' within the context of the World Cultures?" *Ethos* 21: 107–153.

Starr, Paul 1982, *The social transformation of American medicine*, New York: Basic Books.

Stein, H. F. 1990, "The story behind the clinical story: An inquiry into biomedical narrative," *Family Systems Medicine* 8: 213–227.

Stoller, Paul 1989, *The taste of ethnographic things: The senses of anthropology*, Philadelphia: University of Pennsylvania Press.

Suleiman, Susan 1994, *Risking who one is: Encounters with contemporary art and literature*, Cambridge, MA: Harvard University Press.

Suleiman, Susan and Crossman, Inge 1980, *The reader in the text*, Princeton: Princeton University Press.

Tambiah, Stanley 1977, "The cosmological and performative significance of a Thai cult of healing through mediation," *Culture, Medicine, and Psychiatry* 1: 97–132.

   1985, *Culture, thought, and social action: An anthropological perspective*, Cambridge: Cambridge University Press.

1990 *Magic, science, religion, and the scope of rationality*, Cambridge: Cambridge University Press.

Taussig, Michael 1993, *Mimesis and alterity: A particular history of the senses*, London: Routledge.

Taylor, Charles 1979, "Interpretation and the sciences of man," in P. Rabinow and W. M. Sullivan (eds.), *Interpretive social science: A reader*, Berkeley: University of California Press.

Taylor, L. J. 1989, "The uses of death in Europe," *Anthropological Quarterly* 62: 149– 154.

Tedlock, D. 1983, "The analogical tradition and the emergence of a dialogical anthropology," in *The spoken word and the work of interpretation* (pp. 321–338), Philadelphia: University of Pennsylvania Press.

Thompson, J. 1981, *Critical hermeneutics: A study in the thought of Paul Ricoeur and Jurgen Habermas*, Cambridge: Cambridge University Press.

Todorov, Tzvetan 1977a, *The poetics of prose*, Ithaca: Cornell University Press.

1977b, *Theories of the symbol*, Ithaca: Cornell University Press.

1980, "The categories of literary narrative," *Papers on Language and Literature* 16: 3–36.

Turner, E. 1992, *Experiencing ritual: A new interpretation of African healing*, Philadelphia: University of Pennsylvania Press.

Turner, Victor 1969, *The ritual process: Structure and anti-structure*, Chicago: Aldine.

1986a, *The anthropology of performance*, New York: PAJ Publications.

1986b, "Dewey, Dilthey, and drama: An essay in the anthropology of experience," in V. Turner and E. M. Bruner (eds.), *The anthropology of experience*, Chicago: University of Illinois Press.

Turner, Victor and Bruner, Edward M. (eds.), 1986, *The anthropology of experience*, Urbana: University of Illinois Press.

Tyler, S. A. 1987, *The unspeakable: Discourse, dialogue, and rhetoric in the postmodern world*, Madison, WI: University of Wisconsin Press.

van Gannep, A. 1960, *The rites of passage* (M. B. Vizedam and G. L. Caffee, trans.), Chicago: University of Chicago Press (originally published as *Les rites de passage*, 1909).

Watts, Ian 1957, *The rise of the novel: Studies in Defoe, Richardson, and Fielding*, Berkeley: University of California Press.

White, Hayden 1972, "The structure of historical narrative," *Clio* 1: 5–19.

1973, *Metahistory: The historical imagination in nineteenth-century Europe*, Baltimore: Johns Hopkins University Press.

1980. "The value of narrativity in the representation of reality," in N. W. J. T. Mitchell (ed.), *On narrative*, Chicago: University of Chicago Press.

1987, *The content of form: Narrative discourse and historical representation*, Baltimore: Johns Hopkins University Press.

Wikan, Unni 1980, *Life among the poor in Cairo* (Ann Henning, trans.), London: Tavistock Publications.

1990, *Managing turbulent hearts: A Balinese formula for living*, Chicago: University of Chicago Press.

1991, "Toward an experience-near anthropology," *Cultural Anthropology* 6: 285–305.

188   References

1995, "The self in a world of urgency and necessity," *Ethos* 23: 259–285.
Williams, Bernard 1981, *Moral luck: Philosophical papers 1973–1980*, Cambridge: Cambridge University Press.
Wyatt, F. 1986, "The narrative in psychoanalysis: Psychoanalytic notes of storytelling, listening, and interpreting," in T. Sarbin (ed.), *Narrative Psychology* (pp. 193–210), New York: Praeger.
Zemke, Ruth and Clark, Florence 1996, *Occupational science: The evolving discipline*, Philadelphia: F. A. Davis.
Zimmerman J. and Dickerson, V. 1994, "Using a narrative metaphor: Implication for theory and clinical practice," *Family Process* 33.

Index

189